The Origins
of the
Football League

The Origins of the Football League

The First Season
1888/89

Mark Metcalf

AMBERLEY

Front cover: The Preston North End 'Invincibles', 1888/89. Back row (non-players)
R. W. Hanbury MP, Sir W. E. M. Tomlinson MP, W. Sudell (secretary manager). Back row
(players): Drummond, Howarth, Russell, Holmes, Graham, Dr Mills-Roberts. Front row:
Gordon, Ross, Goodall, Dewhurst, Thomson. (Image courtesy of the PNE historian)

First published 2013

Amberley Publishing
The Hill, Stroud
Gloucestershire, GL5 4EP

www.amberley-books.com

British Library Cataloguing in Publication Data.
A catalogue record for this book is available from the British Library.

ISBN 978 1 4456 1881 4 (print)
ISBN 978 1 4456 1860 9 (ebook)

Typeset in 10pt on 12pt Sabon.
Typesetting and Origination by Amberley Publishing.
Printed in the UK.

Contents

Introduction

On Saturday 8 September 1888, League football kicked off. Twelve clubs had combined to play regular fixtures and the result was to revolutionise not only English football but virtually every nation and sport since then.

Here, for the first time, the history of the Football League season 1888/89 is told in great depth, with reports on every match and profiles of all those who played – amateur and professional – during this thrilling, historic season in which Preston were 'invincible' and set the standard for other great teams to follow. Key players and their skills are highlighted. Doubts about who scored the first-ever League goal are ended. The standard of football, equipment used and the tactics adopted to win matches is analysed.

Controversial incidents that paved the way for the introduction of the goal net and penalty kick are brought back to life. The clubs, their pitches and grounds (and the fans that filled them) are explored within the economic circumstances and developments of the day. The difficulties faced by reporters in ensuring accuracy as they reported the on-field events of the inaugural League season are aired.

Illustrated with contemporary photographs and newspaper cuttings, this is the story of the 1888/89 Football League season, when Preston North End were 'invincible'.

Disclaimer: 125 years is a long time

The reader will find some inconsistencies in this book – for example, in some cases I have reported a scorer as taken from a paper or papers of the day that is at odds with the official club records compiled, in some cases, many decades later. As always, I have done my best to be objective with the 'facts', but accept that some errors may be present.

Mark Metcalf

Organising the League

It was a Scot, William McGregor, who was responsible for first organising League football in England. In 1887, professionalism as a legal entity was only two years old and the Aston Villa committee man recognised that clubs needed a guaranteed source of income if they were to have the funds to pay players.

High-profile friendly matches and cup competitions were one thing, but on many occasions a growing band of fans was being forced to make do with one-sided contests, or left frustrated at not knowing in advance who their side might be playing at the weekend. Football might have been – in fact, still is – a distraction from the cares of everyday life for fans, but that doesn't mean they were content to watch uncompetitive matches.

With support from his fellow Villa committee members, McGregor set out to see which other clubs might join the Birmingham club in turning his new idea into reality. By early March the following year, he was confident enough to send a formal letter to five clubs: Blackburn Rovers, Bolton Wanderers, Preston North End, West Bromwich Albion and his own club, Aston Villa.

In this, he suggested that clubs might overcome their current problems by ensuring that 'ten or twelve of the most prominent clubs in England combine to arrange home and away fixtures each season'. A conference was proposed to discuss the matter more fully and the five already invited to get involved were asked to suggest the names of other clubs who should be approached to join them. Bolton's secretary, John Bentley, put forward eight more names although, in the event, two (Mitchell St George's from Birmingham and the amateur team Old Carthusians) never made it to the big kick-off in September 1888.

On the eve of the 1888 FA Cup final, held at the Oval between Preston North End and West Bromwich Albion, representatives of Aston Villa, Notts County, Blackburn Rovers, Wolverhampton Wanderers, Burnley,

Stoke and West Bromwich Albion held a successful meeting and invited Preston North End, Everton, Accrington, Bolton Wanderers and Derby County to join them in formalising affairs, and arranging fixtures for the 1888/89 season, at the Royal Hotel, Manchester, on Tuesday 17 April 1888.

It is this meeting that marks the birth of competitive League football, though its historic nature didn't stop club representatives disagreeing among themselves! Even the name proved a problem, with McGregor's suggestion of Football Union being overruled in favour of William Sudell of Preston North End's preferred title of Football League.

McGregor had wanted clubs to divide gate money but delegates who felt that a guaranteed sum of £15 for visiting clubs was a better option rejected that idea. Egalitarianism had been quickly snuffed out in pursuit of profits. If McGregor was upset he didn't show it, and was duly elected as chairman of the new organisation, with Sudell taking on the role of treasurer and Harry Lockett that of honorary secretary.

Meanwhile, Sheffield Wednesday, Nottingham Forest and Halliwell, who claimed they were the second-best team in Lancashire, were all left disappointed when their applications to join the new League were rejected on grounds that it was impossible to find sufficient dates for any additional fixtures.

So while the merits of some of the clubs were queried – Everton[1] for example, were considered inferior to local rivals Bootle, Accrington's playing record was mixed and gates poor, Notts County had just experienced their worst season, and even three-time FA Cup winners Blackburn Rovers' supremacy in the East Lancashire cotton town was coming under threat – those who had met on 17 April were happy to become a select band of pioneers. To their credit, they clearly knew what they were doing because eleven of them – Accrington being the exception – are all still playing in the Football League today.

The clubs were also clearly open to change as they adopted rules that required the bottom four clubs to reapply for their place in the League in a re-election battle with non-League clubs who wished to join. With each League club allowed to cast four votes, Stoke became the first to lose out when they were replaced by Sunderland for the start of the 1890/91 season.

The Cricket and Football Field of 21 April 1888 reported developments thus:

A dozen Association clubs, who style themselves the pick of the talent, have joined hands for their own mutual benefit, apparently without a care for those unhappily shut out in the cold.

The first public intimation of the hatching of the plan came on the eve of the FA Cup final, where clubs met at Anderton's Hotel and sent forth a circular.

They stressed they weren't against FA or the provincial associations and said there was nothing to stop other clubs forming a second League and they pointed to the Baseball Leagues in the USA where they have a dozen different leagues.

They would work amicably with the second League and the four best in that would play the four worst in the Football League.

The twelve clubs who competed for the first League championship were:

Accrington	Founded in 1876. Played at Thorneyholme Road. Not to be confused with Accrington Stanley.
Aston Villa	Founded in 1874. Played at Wellington Road. FA Cup winners in 1887.
Blackburn Rovers	Founded 1874. Played at Leamington Road. FA Cup winners in 1884, 1885 and 1886.
Bolton Wanderers	Founded 1874. Played at Pikes Lane.
Burnley	Founded in 1881. Played at Turf Moor.
Derby County	Founded 1884. Played at Racecourse Ground.
Everton	Founded in 1878. Played at Anfield.
Notts County	Founded 1862. Played at Trent Bridge Cricket Ground.
Preston North End	Founded 1881. Played at Deepdale.
Stoke City	Founded 1863. Played at the Victoria Ground.
West Bromwich Albion	Founded 1879. Played at Stoney Lane. FA Cup winners in 1888.
Wolverhampton Wanderers	Founded 1877. Played at Dudley Road.

Fixtures Arranged

The fixtures for the new season were drawn up at a meeting on 1 May 1888 in Birmingham. This was also the day on which the 'registration of professional footballers [was] fixed for all clubs, so that every club will have equal chances in the kidnapping business', as reported in the *Accrington Times*.

Wins to Decide League Positions

It wasn't until 21 November 1888 that two points for a win, a point for a draw and no points for losing became the format by which positions in the League was to be determined, with teams tied on points to be separated by goal average, in which goals scored were divided by those conceded.

Football in 1888

While a form of football has probably existed for as long as men have had feet with which to kick things, the game as we know it today was under 100 years old in 1888.

Various forms of football had come into being in the major public schools during the second or third decade of the nineteenth century. Attempts to merge the different strands and establish a unified system of rules were given a big boost when the Cambridge (University) Rules were drawn up in 1848.

These were revised over the following decade. In November 1862, a match at Cambridge took place between Cambridge Old Etonians and Cambridge Old Harrovians on a level playing field under a set of rules that remained recognisable 150 years later. Happily, the rules, which included eleven players on each side, worked and the revised Cambridge Rules of 1863 became the basis for the first laws of the Football Association (FA) that was formed on 26 October 1863.

Within eight years, on 11 November 1871, the first-ever matches in the longest-running competitive football competition in the world took place when eight sides lined up in the FA Cup. Its success and that of the subsequent first international matches provided the grounding for the establishment of the Football League in 1888.

Over this period, the tactics of football had altered significantly. So while some sides continued to rely on the individual approach – in which each forward ran or dribbled with the ball as far as he could before either losing it to a defender or having it taken from him by a frustrated colleague – more and more, particularly professional teams were combining (or in more modern terms passing the ball from player to player) to create openings for an effort at goal.

And while Scottish side Queens Park are recognised as being the first side to master the art of 'letting the ball do the work', it was Preston North End who had by 1888 started to 'scientifically' refine it. The changes in approach meant it was out with the policy of just a couple of defenders, one half-back and seven forwards (with two centre-forwards) and in with team formations that began to combine both attack and defence with a 2-3-5 line-up of two full-backs, three half-backs and five forwards.

The centre-half did not, however, simply mark the opposing centre-forward, and had much greater freedom to assist other defending players while principally supporting his forwards. Over time it was usual for most sides to play their most creative player in this important position, until rule changes in 1925 meant that players could now be onside if there were only two players between themselves and their opponents' goal rather than three.

The two full-backs rarely advanced up the field in 1888 and were selected for their ability to overpower the attacking forwards and for clearing the danger by kicking the ball well upfield, preferably accurately to the wings. With heavy pitches, this was not easy, and those who achieved the task were often warmly applauded.

At right- and left-half, players were required to provide passes to the forwards and help out in defence. As such, like the inside-forwards, they required great stamina, tackling ability, a never-say-die attitude and skills in finding their forwards with an accurate pass. Some of the better ones could also be expected to chip in with a goal or two.

Wingers (of which every side would have two) were required to build partnerships with their respective inside-forwards, beat opponents either through pace or dribbling beyond them, and then create opportunities for the focal part of the attack, the centre-forward – the man who scored the goals. How the latter did so wasn't important and some were much better in the air, while others relied on pace over a few yards, anticipating a ball over the full-backs or worrying the life out of a 'keeper.

The names of those who managed to put the leather through the posts was cherished in the memories of all fans and there were always more good forwards than good defenders, as the delight of shooting a goal far exceeds the pleasure of saving one. History does not tell of the men who save goals or even those who work well towards making one.

In 1888, new rules had restricted goalkeepers' use of their hands to their own half, the aim being to prevent them from joining in the attacks. What didn't change was that the men between the sticks could still be shoulder charged, with or without the ball, and there were some very rough challenges on them in 1888/89. Choosing whether to punch or catch a cross, or even a shot, often required a 'keeper to decide if he could subsequently get rid of the ball fast enough before an approaching forward clattered him.

If he didn't and was left injured, there were no such things as substitute 'keepers on the bench to replace him. In fact, there were no such things as substitutes until 1965. So if a player did get injured he was usually required, if possible, to limp out the match on the left wing. There was also no such thing as advertising on strips, and numbering on the shirts in 1888 was a good fifty years away.

Meanwhile, the match ball could become a very heavy, misshapen object when it became wet. Players' boots were largely adapted workmen's boots, and designed for strength with a permanent indestructible block toe and studs hammered into the soles. Given the equipment, some of the play exhibited by the early giants of League football was extraordinary.

The pitches, which in 1888 had very few markings and lacked adequate drainage systems, bore no similarity to the fabulous billiard table-like surfaces of the Football League today and had little grass on them, especially in the winter. Heavy rain brought puddles for the players to overcome, and on particularly rainy days the middle of the pitch would soon resemble a mud bath. This made it essential for teams to get the ball out to their wingers to attack the full-backs.

Deciding if any challenges in a game were, in fact, fouls was complex. It required a player to appeal for one, and then two umpires, one from each side, would decide whether to award a free-kick. Only if the umpires disagreed was the referee called upon to make the final decision.

The end of the 1890/91 season was to bring radical changes in the system, with the referee being given full control of the game and the umpires being moved to the touchlines to become linesmen.

Match Reports in 1888/89

Early reporters faced a difficult job in reporting accurately on the games. The location from which they reported was not always conducive to following the play, and with no numbers on the jerseys of the players in an era when most had a 'short back and sides' haircut, it was never easy to be certain who had made a last ditch tackle or scored a goal. This was especially so in the latter case, as many goals were scored during fierce close-to-the-goal tussles (or scrimmages as they were then reported) among defenders and forwards.

Given that many reporters were relatively new to the game of football – and most only covered matches as part of their weekly work – they also suffered from unfamiliarity with the players, particularly those playing for the opposition. It is hardly surprising, then, that mistakes were made, with papers often reporting different scorers or simply the wrong ones.

There was also no way of gaining access to the players afterwards to confirm facts and figures, especially for reporters working on Saturday night sports editions. For all of these reasons, the reader may find some inconsistencies in this book, for example in some cases I have reported a scorer as taken from a paper or papers of the day that is at odds with the official club records compiled, in some cases, many decades later. As always, I have done my best to be objective with the 'facts', but accept that errors may be present; none of which should take away from the fine job that these early match reporters did in bringing to life the first League games in English and world football. To them and the early players we are all indebted. Not that we always agree with their content, of course; in March 1891, Derby and Sunderland objected to a report of their match which appeared in *Athletic News*. FA Committee member John Bentley promised to take matters up as only he could, since he was the newspaper's assistant editor.

Fans unable to go to the games in 1888/89 relied on the written word to learn about on-field events, as there was no television coverage or action replays, radio commentary or after-match interviews with the club committees or managers responsible for team selection. The reports had a certain symmetry to them, in that it was usual for them to start with news of who had won the toss, the winners generally preferring to take advantage of any wind or slope on the pitch in the first half – the aim being to build up a significant lead by half-time.

There was also usually something on the weather conditions. This would indicate to the reader the pitch conditions as, with no such thing as specialist groundsmen or drainage systems then, heavy rain would inevitably mean it was muddy, while ice would make it a problem for players to keep their feet. Accrington's ground was probably the best pitch in 1888/89, a factor no doubt influenced by it also serving as a first-class cricket ground.

In 1889, specialist photographic equipment capable of capturing moving images had not yet been invented. On major occasions, such as FA Cup semi-finals or key League matches, some papers might bring the action alive by employing an artist to draw the winning goal or a section of the ground and crowd. Such was the case for a number of Preston's games in 1888 and 1889.

Some 'Facts'

The first football paper is believed to have been *The Goal*, printed in November 1878. The *Athletic News* was first printed in 1880, and by the mid-1880s a number of towns and cities had their own Saturday night 'football specials'. The author's personal favourite is Bolton's 'Buff' that was officially called *Cricket and Football Field* and which could be bought across many parts of Lancashire by 7.30 p.m. on Saturday evenings.

The first time reporters could telephone in their reports to their papers is believed to have been for the 1886 FA Cup final replay between Blackburn Rovers and West Bromwich Albion played at the Derby Racecourse.

Professionalism

All of the clubs that formed the Football League in 1888 contained a majority of professional paid players. In the quarter of a century since the FA had been formed, football had changed from being a game once played for keen enjoyment and keeping fit. No longer were teams composed of representatives of the best players in a team or a district. In order to find funds to pay a groundsman and for rent of a ground, clubs had placed fences and constructed stands and terraces in order to charge for entry to matches.

Increased crowds, particularly for FA Cup games, had brought surplus funds into clubs. These could be used to pay the better local players for not working, thus at a stroke removing the advantage many amateurs from better-off backgrounds held by having more time in which to practise their skills and keep fit, as well as offering payment to better players from far and wide.

Not everyone, though, was happy with such arrangements, and it took a struggle to achieve professionalism in the game of football. Darwen are believed to be the first to employ professionals when Jimmy Love and Fergus Suter of Partick Thistle helped the East Lancashire side become the first from the North to reach the last eight of the FA Cup in 1879, where they only lost out after three matches to eventual winners Old Etonians.

By 1883, Blackburn Olympic had won the FA Cup with a side largely composed of players being paid to play and yet, that same year, Accrington were expelled from the FA for paying players. Then, in 1884, Preston North End were disqualified from the FA Cup after admitting they were paying players (including Fergus Suter) in order to compete with Blackburn Rovers, who won the competition for three consecutive seasons starting in 1884.

In response, thirty-seven clubs that were determined to play professionally set up the British Football Association as a rival to the Football Association. This threat of secession did the trick, with the FA agreeing to legalise professionalism on 20 July 1885. All professional players had to register with the FA, had to have been born or lived for two years within a 6-mile radius of the ground (these residential qualifications were removed in May 1889) and those seeking to play for more than one club in a season had to gain the organisation's permission.

Despite the changes, not everyone was happy and for a long time afterwards professionals chosen to represent England at international level could expect to be handed a tight-fitting, often coarse shirt, while in newspaper reports it was usual to give only their surname instead of also including their initials, as was the case for the amateur player.

Professionalism saw all the major clubs seek to induce players from Scotland to join them, football over the border being superior at the time due to a greater willingness to combine teamwork rather than rely on individuality.

By the time the Football League started, the FA Cup had been won for seven consecutive seasons by clubs with professional players in them. The days of the amateur were coming to an end, although for a number of seasons afterwards they continued to make up the bulk of the England international side selected by the FA committee.

While players were often referred to as labourers, they did not receive protection under the Employers Liability Act 1880 and it was not to be until 1907 when the Football League established the Football Mutual Insurance Federation. Even then, the matter was left to the club and it took another five years for it to become compulsory for clubs to insure their players. Clubs, meanwhile, also attempted to extend their authority over the personal lives of their players – especially when it came to drink.

Despite the better wages, a footballer's life was close to the unskilled masses because of his constant insecurity. Injury could halt a promising career at any point, while contracts were subject to yearly renewal for all but a select few.

Captaincy

The role of captain in football is an important one. This was especially so in 1888/89, as most teams were selected by a club committee (later known as directors) rather than a single manager. In addition, with no such thing as dugouts – the first being at Pittrodrie, Aberdeen, during the 1920s – those responsible for team selection would generally be seated in the main stand and, as such, some distance away from the pitch.

There was also only a five-minute interval, which on occasion was not even taken if the weather was poor and there was a chance of it becoming dark before the intended end of the match.

All this increased the captain's role, and a good one would look to change players' positions during the match if he felt it would help his side. James Brown was one of the best-known captains of the 1880s and he held aloft the FA Cup for Blackburn Rovers three times, in 1884, 1885 and 1886.

Weeks Leading Up to the First League Season

On 11 August 1888, the *Cricket and Football Field* reported that 'the public are getting a little anxious to spend their Saturday afternoons on the football field'. Fans' appetites had been whetted by the prospect of regular matches, and they had seen League teams boost their playing squads by bringing in new players, mainly from Scotland. The higher wages paid to them quite naturally had the more established members of the various teams keen to be better paid and the paper also reported that FA Cup winner 'Bayliss [of WBA] was seeking more money'.

Not that all the players were, as yet, ready for action, as the following Saturday the same paper noted: 'The Everton men are all on the big side and it will take all their time to get it off for the shouting in September.' This view was echoed by the *Stoke Sentinel* who, after Stoke beat

Northwich 2-1 in a friendly held on 1 September, reported that 'the match was of a very uninteresting character ... the players – the majority of them – were sadly out of condition ... if a little training is not indulged in, Stoke will come off second best in some of their early matches'.

There was also action off the pitch, Everton reporting that they were hoping to 'be in a position of launching forth into the expenditure of a grand structure at the Anfield Road end similar to that at the opposite end of the ground. The object is to provide real accommodation for 12,000 spectators, not sturdy but a facility for obtaining a good view of the play.' Further south it was reported that over 1,000 fans had bought season tickets for Derby County's inaugural League season.

With the big kick-off date only a week away, there were some competitive friendly matches on 1 September as Wolves beat Notts Rangers 7-0, while Aston Villa thrashed Ayr United 10-0 and West Brom beat Wednesday 3-1. However, travelling north Blackburn Rovers were beaten 4-3 by Sunderland. And they weren't the only League side to suffer at the hands of non-League opposition, as in the previous week Bootle had beaten both Accrington (3-1) and Burnley (3-0).

Thrills and Spills

Although the Preston 'Invincibles' dominated the first season of League football, there was still plenty to keep fans of the other eleven clubs entertained.

The regional character of the League, with all twelve clubs drawn from the Midlands or the North West, meant the fixtures threw up many local Derby matches that were fierce, no-holds-barred encounters. In this regard, special mention should be made of the Blackburn *v.* Burnley game on 4 February 1889 and West Brom *v.* Villa a few weeks earlier.

There were also harsh and controversial refereeing decisions, constant complaints about whether the ball had gone over or under the bar that led to goal nets being developed, and incidents of cheating close to goal, paving the way for the penalty kick to be introduced.

Irate fans were also a problem and there were pitch invasions on quite a number of occasions as players were assaulted and the police called on for assistance. Fortunately, there appear to have been no incidents of rival fans fighting even when both sides were well represented. Fans were willing to applaud good play from either side while heaping abuse on sides that were felt to have overstepped the mark with rough challenges.

Every side had its share of characters, and great players were widely admired throughout the land. For some, such as Goodall and Ross from Preston, Hodgetts from Villa and Bassett from WBA, it was their pace, combined with skills on the ball. For others it was their courage – Accrington 'keeper Johnny Horne, for example, played much of the season after breaking his rib in the first match, while on 29 December 1888, Burnley's Bill McKay was knocked out and, after being revived by a bucket of water, he returned to play out the final few minutes of a vital win against Notts County.

There were many players with a never-say-die attitude that has always drawn a crowd's approval, full-backs with fierce tackles and hefty clearances, half-backs who knitted teams together, wingers with pace and an accurate cross and, of course, the heroes, like today, of most sides – those who regularly put the ball into the net, such as Blackburn's John Southworth.

Goals there were aplenty with 585 in all, an average of 4.4 per match. Some were brilliant, such as Sam Thomson's for Preston against Burnley on 15 December, while others were netted from close-in, one or two were knocked past their own 'keeper and then there were the occasions when the 'keeper should have done better.

Few of the goals were scored by half-backs, and rarely was one knocked home by a full-back. No goalkeeper scored. Kicking the ball to the halfway line was difficult enough – booting it more than 100 yards was impossible.

And while, on occasion, a late-running train delayed the kick-off or a side arrived missing a couple of players, this was all part of a learning experience that ultimately paved the way for the Football League of today that remains totally unique in world football by its depth of talent and competitive quality.

Why Saturday Afternoon?

The inaugural Football League season got underway on Saturday 8 September 1888, with a kick-off time of mid-afternoon.

The day of the week, starting time and period of the year were all-important. The importance of religion in everyday life at the time was underlined in rule 25 of the Football Association. This stated that 'matches shall not be played on Sundays within the jurisdiction of the Association'. Unable to utilise the one day in the week when the vast majority of people would not be at work, the game's authorities had rightly chosen the next-best day – Saturday – where, starting in the 1840s, there had been a significant number of changes in the number of hours worked by many.

Increased wages, in part the result of trade union agitation, especially among industrial workers, meant that in Nottingham many hosiery workers now had regular Saturday half-holidays, while in Lancashire builders stopped at 1.00 p.m.

In addition, many of the more traditional craft trades were less rigid about hours of work and workers could, if they wished, take Saturday afternoon off. Crowds, therefore, tended to be socially mixed, as was never the case for those behind the organisation of football clubs, with a survey of the occupation of 740 men who were directors of professional clubs from 1888 to 1915 showing an overwhelming majority who were middle class.

By starting the season in September, clubs, many of which had started life sharing grounds with the local cricket club (in 1888 Accrington, Derby and Notts County were still doing so), could be assured of a pitch on which to play. It is a tradition that largely still exists to this day. Of course, with no such thing as floodlights, it also proved important to ensure that games, especially in the middle of winter, got started early enough to finish before the darkness engulfed the pitch.

The first Football League season was to record a total attendance of 602,000, making the average gate that season 4,560. As the reports from the games indicate, some of these were away fans, rail companies having quickly realised they could make a profit by providing transport to matches. This not only boosted attendance figures, but helped increase the atmosphere at games and made the English Football League a crucial part of English society and unique in the world of football.

How many of those attending that first season were schoolchildren, it's impossible to say. Probably not too many, but plenty of them were quickly developing an interest in the game as schooling numbers had continued to rise rapidly from the mid-1870s onwards. Just as importantly, the numbers of male staff had leapt from 6,395 in 1870 to pass 21,000 in 1893, and with a belief in team games having gained currency, football, even in 1888, was moving towards replacing cricket as the nation's number one sport.

No wonder, therefore, that the numbers attending matches were to leap considerably over the next few seasons, so that by 1905/06 over 5 million are believed to have attended the matches of the twenty teams in the First Division.

MATCH DAY 1

8 September 1888

Five games were played on the opening day of the season, and Bolton's Kenny Davenport scored the first-ever League goal.

The first day of any new season is always one of the best, as every side starts with the same number of points and, technically, the same chance of winning the League. It must have been particularly exciting in September 1888 because, while no one involved could possibly have known the 'history' they were making, it was clear that a break with the past had been made. Fans now had the chance to regularly watch some of the finest players in a truly competitive environment.

There were to be twenty-three goals in all scored on 8 September 1888, with nine coming in the Bolton match at home to Derby County, where the away side were to come from three down to win a real thriller 6-3. Preston, Everton and West Bromwich Albion were to draw level with the East Midlanders by all winning their opening games, while Wolves and Aston Villa played out the first draw in League history.

To give a flavour of how matches were reported on back then, each of the accounts from 8 September 1888 is taken directly from a newspaper of the day.

PRESTON LOOKS INVINCIBLE
PNE 5 (Gordon, Ross 2, Dewhurst 2) *v.* Burnley 2 (Gallacher, Poland)

A splendid afternoon favoured the opening League match at Deepdale today, when the North End made their first appearance at home to receive Burnley. The latter were late in arriving – shall we say as usual? – And it was not until ten minutes to four that the players faced each other as follows:

North End: Trainer, Holmes and Howarth, Robertson, Graham W., Graham J., Gordon, Ross junior, Goodall, Dewhurst, Drummond.

Burnley: W. S. Smith, goal Berry and Lang, backs Abrams, Friel and Keenan; half-backs, Brady, Tait, Poland, Gallacher and Yates, forwards.

Referee – Mr H. Brownlow.

Fully 5,000 persons were present when Goodall kicked off, Dewhurst dribbling down the hill and shooting just wide for a start. The spectators had soon occasion to grow enthusiastic, for in something like three minutes both Dewhurst and Gordon had scored, the latter with a terrific screw shot. A merry soul behind the goal created a diversion by tolling a loud-mouthed bell as the ball went through in each case.

The powerful sun and the grand passing of the North End bewildered the visitors, who found it difficult to penetrate the Preston half. Smith stopped a host by Dewhurst in good style, and Keenan was impartially cheered for clever tackling, as was Howarth for a plucky exhibition. Gordon almost lowered the Burnley colours a second time, the ball grazing the top of the bar. The goalkeeper showed up well on several occasions, twice saving when the opposing forwards were right on the top of him. Yates and Gallacher now breasted the ball, and after some lively exchanges Gallacher rushed the ball past Trainer, the feat being accompanied by another 'peal' from the bellman.

Gallacher got in with a grand shot; which compelled Trainer to concede a corner, Gordon galloped off to the other end, but screwed in too late, and the ball passed behind. Just now the Burnley forwards were playing up well, and found the Preston backs plenty to do. A senseless claim of offside failed to check Ross, who sent a flyer to Smith, which that gent just turned aside. From a free-kick the ball was kicked hard against the Burnley post. Gordon's runs on the right were done in the best fashion and from one of his centres Dewhurst came near to scoring, Smith throwing away the very instant he was bundled through. Holmes came in for specific notice for neatly robbing Brady at a time when the last-named was threatening serious trouble.

Half-time Preston 2 Burnley 1.

Although the home team had now the rise in the ground and sun against them, the first few minutes after resuming were spent in the Burnley territory, Drummond being seen doing battle on the right wing, leaving Dewhurst to gaze on in apparent amazement. Poland was penalised for tripping Dewhurst, a good deal of feeling being shown as this stage on both sides. Tait, Poland, Ross and Gordon eventually getting on badly. The Burnley forwards now got clean away, but Holmes shot past them magnificently, and returned the ball amid cheers. A sharp pass from Dewhurst enabled Ross to score the third goal, Friel saving another the next instant. A long return by Willy Gordon was headed over by Gordon.

Burnley was not often dangerous, although they were quick on the ball. Tait shot a trifle wide, and then Poland almost beat Trainer. Rushing away again North End got close in, and Ross made the score 4-1 with a marvellous shot off the goal line.

Burnley had another look in, Trainer being called on twice in succession, and then Goodall spoiled a chance by a wild pass. Trainer against saved finely from a shot by Brady. The visitors were hereabouts quite holding their own, the Preston forwards apparently tiring. Dewhurst, however, raised the total to five very smartly, and then Poland shot through at the other end, time being directly called.

(*Cricket and Football Field*)

OPENING MATCH AT PIKES LANE

Bolton Wanderers 3 (Davenport 2, Brogan) *v.* Derby County 6 (Plackett 2, Cooper 2, Bakewell 2)

Summer had come at last, and this afternoon the season was inaugurated at Pike's Lane before about 3,000 spectators. The stand did not present the healthy appearance that one might hope for at the commencement of the season, but possibly supporters are waiting until the Wanderers have revived their name and fame.

Referee Mr T. Helme.

The visitors were late in making an appearance and some impatience was manifested at the delay. At a quarter to four the County kicked off with the sun at their backs, the Wanderers having won the toss but preferring to give their opponents the advantage.

The visiting right made an attack that was cleared by 'Bethell' but the ball was kept in the Wanderers quarter for a minute or so, until Davenport coming away transferred the play to the other end, and in two minutes from the start Kenny had scored a fine goal for the Wanderers. A protest for offside was raised in vain.

Scarcely had the ball been kicked off from centre when the Wanderers again dashed forward, and Weir putting the ball in front Davenport repeated his former success. Shortly afterwards Brogan deserved to improve matters, Marshall making a fine save right on the posts. The home supporters were destined from more fun, as Brogan cane down in fine style and waiting until his opponents obliged by putting him on-side, took a long shot for goal, which Marshall improved upon by putting through his own posts. Three goals in five minutes looked well for Wanderers.

The County in the meantime were not idle, though unlucky, and their efforts were rewarded with goal twelve minutes from the start, Bakewell doing the needful. By really fine play Bakewell carried the leather right down the field, and crossing over in the thick of time, Bakewell once more lowered the home colours, the goal being justly applauded as a grand piece of work.

With the score at three to two, and the game still young, matters looked lively, and there were anticipations that a long record would be piled up. Play continued fast, but remained even for some time. By sheer pressure the County established a lead, and by the end of twenty-five minutes were distinctly pressing, finishing up with an equalising goal, credited to Bakewell, which was secured in grand style.

'Kenny' tried to improve on matters, but his efforts met with ill success and 'red shirt' Cooper [Derby] established a lead for County with a goal cleverly kicked out of a scrimmage. Seven goals in half an hour was calculated to satisfy the greatest glutton, but it must be said that the Wanderers defence was very mediocre, and contrasted badly with the performance of Powell and Co. at Newton Heath last Saturday.

The County obtained hands and claimed, just as Cooper [Derby] put the leather through for the fifth time and the visitors doubtless regretted the claim that cost them a goal. Cooper [Wanderers] dallied miserably with the ball when well up with a fine opportunity for shooting and Marshall saved capitally at the expense of a corner, a stinging shot by Davenport. The visitors maintained their lead to half-time.

Half time Derby County 4 Wanderers 3.

The second half commenced very fast, and the pace and heat combined were evidently telling on some of the players. With the sun at their backs the Wanderers appeared to have an opportunity of retrieving their ill-luck, but they were fated to further disaster, as after the game had been in progress a few minutes Derby County improved their score, Harrison inadvertently kicking the ball through his own goal from a rapid pass on the right.

The game veered from end to end, but the County maintained their own, Bakewell 'the man in white' proving a most dangerous man on several occasions. At length Barbour came down at a rattling pace, and seemed to have the goal at his mercy, but Marshall was once more equal to the occasion, and got out with a corner. Bakewell fairly brought the 'house' down with a flying goal, the shot completely beating Harrison, though he made a good attempt to reach it. With the total standing 6-3 against them, the Wanderers prospects looked black indeed and the cries of 'good lad, white un'; testified to the crowd's appreciation of the County sprinter's prowess. He certainly shone out conspicuously as the pick of the field, and fully merited the applause bestowed. The Wanderers' efforts in front of goal were not very brilliant, although on one occasion Cooper went very near scoring. Play became loose as 'time' approached, Derby occasionally resorting to a kick-out, while the Wanderers were feeble in both attack and defence.

Finally the result stood – Derby County 6 Wanderers 3.

(Report from *Cricket and Football Field* – Saturday 8 September 1888)

ANFIELD ROAD
Everton 2 (Fleming 2) *v.* Accrington 1 (Holden)

A crowd of close on 12,000 turned up at Anfield-Road ground on Saturday, to witness the above encounter, which was the first of the series of fixtures arranged by the League. The Accrington team was the strongest they could put on the field, while the home club substituted R. Jones at half-back instead of Warmby, and W.Lewis (Bangor) in Costley's place at centre forward, Smalley again taking his position between the posts. The weather was fine, with a strong sun and very little wind, and the field ground in good order.

The visitors who turned up twenty minutes late, won the toss, and Lewis sent the ball rolling against the sun. Waugh was the first to be conspicuous by passing nicely to Fleming who sent it to Farmer and the latter put in a scorching shot. Horne clearing at the expense of a corner, which was badly taken.

A goal-kick to the visitors enabled Joe Lofthouse to get within shooting distance, but Dobson cleared nicely and gave Lewis a chance. Stevenson robbing him, however, while in the act of testing Horne, from a throw in Chadwick had a corner conceded him, which Farmer put to the side.

Aided by Dobson and Holt, the home right got away and Waugh sent in a low swift shot which Pemberton negotiated following by Chippendale being eased by Holt, who returned the leather well down, but Lewis found the defence impenetrable.

An exciting bit of play now ensued. Howarth, in clearing a shot headed into Horne, who threw out in nice style, and Waugh rushing down, kicking on to the crossbar, the ball falling over.

Dobson having had a trail for goal the visiting forwards rushed up in a body, only to find Dick ready to meet them by planting to his right wing pair, and Waugh was loudly cheered for making a passage through the visitors and troubling Horne.

Stevenson off disaster, but Lewis eventually got cleverly away, and gave a long pass to Fleming, who could not get down, in time, and the ball rolled out. By means of a goal-kick.

Holden and Chippendale dribbled up, but the latter had his shot spoiled by Ross. Holt now got his hands in the way, and from the penalty Howarth sent the ball spinning over Smalley's charge for the first time. R. Jones, who appeared to be lame, managed to beat Kirkham and then the home left worked down, Farmer's attempt going wide, arousing themselves to the call of their captain to 'play up Reds' Chippendale and Bonar each had shies, but Ross and Holt relieved and play was taken to the 'Reds' end, where Lewis, Dobson and Chadwick had shots in rapid succession. Horne however, defended well, and managed to avert a downfall.

Dobson, who had to keep watching Lofthouse, enabled Joe to get freedom, that player giving Smalley his first handful with a stunner. Everton than had a couple of free-kicks, from one of which Lewis had hard luck in heading over the crossbar. Coming again, the home forward's swarmed around Horne, and Stevenson managed to spoil Waugh in a tricky run. Hands to the visitors in the home quarters gave the home teams a chance, and Fleming, from a pass by Chadwick, was pushed off the ball by Horne while in the act of shooting it through half-time arriving with a clean sheet.

On changing ends, Accrington became busy, but Dobson managed to clear, Ross having intercepted Chippendale who was playing a grand game in his new position, the home club took up the running, and literally swarmed Horne, who was in splendid form.

Pressure was at length eased by Holden running to the other end, where Dick relieved and Dobson had the misfortune to foul Bonar. From the free-kick Ross returned the ball, and Horne's charge was again in danger, the visitors conceding a corner to Holt. The kick was nicely taken with Dobson heading in, and McLallan and Stevenson preventing disaster. Another corner having been got rid of by the visitors.

Lofthouse was stopped in a run by Dobson, who gave the pass to Waugh, who in turn gave it to Farmer, and that player enabled Fleming to head the first goal.

Striving hard to equalise, Bonar and Lofthouse was held, in check by Holt, but the visitors still kept in the home quarters, and Dick was the hero of the finest bit of back play seen on Everton ground for some considerable time, keeping his lines clear in grand style.

Taking the play up the hill, Chadwick and Lewis looked dangerous, and the former sent in a low shot, when Horne, in clearing, fractured a rib, necessitating a stoppage of play. McLennan went in goal, and Howarth back. Resuming, Everton again became aggressive, and Fleming soon registered a second goal from a pass by Farmer.

Accrington next had the best of the play, and after Holden had headed on the bar and Kirkham had hard lines, a free-kick was conceded them, from which Holden beat Smalley. Everton then had another try to score after which Holden severely tested the home custodian, but without effect, a strongly contested game thus ending with the result Everton two goals; Accrington one.

Teams; Everton: Smalley, goal, Dick and Ross (captain), backs, Holt. Jones (r), and Dobson, half-backs, Fleming, Waugh, Lewis (w), Chadwick, and Farmer forwards. Umpire Berry (e), Accrington:- Horne, goal, Stewart, and McLennan backs Haworth, Wilkinson, and Pemberton, half-backs, Lofthouse, Bonar, Kirkham (e) Holden and Chippendale forwards, Umpire Oldham (o), referee J. J. Bentley.

(*The Liverpool Mercury*, Monday 10 September 1888)

STOKE
Stoke City 0 *v.* WBA 2 (Wilson, Woodhall)
Attendance 4,524.

The first really important match of the Stoke club was the one of Saturday last when the West Bromwich Albion were once more encountered. In addition to the ordinary interest that always attaches to a fixture with the English Cup holders, there was the fact that this was the first League match between these clubs, and a good game was anticipated and fully realised. The weather was beautifully fine, and the attendance of spectators was very great, it being estimated that over 4,000 people were present, who were rewarded by witnessing a grand exposition of Association football.

Before dealing with the actual game itself, I may say that the difference in the play for that and the Saturday previous was very marked. Not only was the Stoke team strengthened, but also the players were in much better condition, and as natural consequence play were greatly improved. It had been given out that we were to see two more Scotchmen in the team in addition to Kilmarnock player – McSkimming and I believe arrangements were made with two noted Scotch players to put in an appearance for the Stoke club, and it was not until last Saturday morning that it was known they would not be available.

This caused some disappointment to Mr Lockett, but with plenty of good players at command, there was no difficulty in getting a good eleven, and it was evidently a matter of pleasure to the spectators to see Sayer again in the team, he coming in for an ovation. The other alternation in the team was Staton, who replaced Whitehurst as centre-forward, a very desirable change truly.

The Albion team contained the names of many well-known players who have frequently been seen at Stoke, and the really only changes in the eleven from last year was Hendry, who was the centre forward, and J. Horton who took the place of Albert Aldridge at back. It was true there were alterations in the positions of the team, the most noticeable one being that of Bayliss, who played half-back instead of forward as formerly, and right well did he acquit himself in the new place.

Coming now to the game itself, I may at once say it was a grandly contested one and the play all through was a treat to witness. It was very fast from start to finish, and a most scientific display of football was seen. The game never flagged, and what is more it was of a fairly even character, and at one stage in the second half it looked as if Stoke would win their first League fixture, but as is generally the case when these teams meet Stoke succumbed to the Albion.

In the first half the latter played with a wind in their favour, and, if anything held a slight lead, the Stoke defence having more to do than did the Albion defence, the visitors having three corners conceded to them; while Stoke failed to obtain one. This, however, was the only advantage gained by the Throstles, as at half-time no goals had been scored.

On crossing over Stoke, of course, had the advantage of the wind; and it was no small advantage either; and with this in their favour the home team had as much of the play as their opponents. The game in the second half was just as fast as in the first part, and it continued to be fought in a most determined manner, both sides putting in all they knew to achieve victory.

Both goals were alternately besieged, but the back play and the goalkeeping of both teams was grand and very effective. Time went on, and at six minutes to the call of the time no goal had been scored, and it appeared to be any odds that the game would end a draw. The Stoke partisans were jubilant with this anticipated result, but within the last few minutes a complete change came over the game, Wilson scoring a goal for the visitors. This disaster completely upset the home team, and just before the conclusion of the game a second goal was scored, and a splendidly contested game terminated in a victory for the English Cup holders by two goals to none.

It would be invidious to single out any individual player for special praise, when all the eleven of each team played such an admirable game, and showed such extremely good combination play. I question very much whether a better game than that of Saturday will be witnessed during the present season at Stoke.

(Report from *Stoke Sentinel*, Wednesday 12 September 1888)

THE FIRST LEAGUE GOAL?
Wolverhampton Wanderers 1 (Cox, own goal) *v.* Aston Villa 1 (Green)

These clubs met at the Wanderers' ground, Wolverhampton, in fine weather, and before about 3,000 spectators. The game was a fast one all through, and very even, the result being in doubt up to the call of time.

Playing down the hill in the first half, and with the sun at their backs, though the wind was against them, the home team forced the play for the first few minutes, and Warner had soon to fist the ball out from a combined rush. The Villa were kept after this on the defensive, till at length Brown and Green getting the ball away the latter had a feeble try at the Wanderers goal, which Baynton easily averted.

The next point worthy of note was a fine run down the centre by Anderson, who gave the ball to Cannon, and the latter but for the timely intervention of Cox would have scored a certain goal. Anderson, a few minutes later returned to the charge, and caused Warner to fist the ball out. The Wanderers at this point were having the best of the play, and a shot from Anderson's foot caused the ball to strike the goal post and rebound out of play. The Villa now wakened up, and for a while the Wanderers could not get beyond midfield, the Birmingham backs checking their advances.

Garvey dribbled the ball right through the Wanderers' back up to the goal, and Baynton, by a brilliant display of goalkeeping, cleared his position; Brown, who returned to the charge, sending the ball over the goal. Dawson next tried two long shots – the first good, the second wild. A minute after Hodgetts centred the ball right in front of the goal, but again Baynton was ready for it and got it away.

It was now the Wanderers turn at offensive play, and Cooper shot over the Villa lines with a good opening, while Cox met a well-meant shot by White and sent the ball to the right wing. Cooper pounced on it, and centred right across the Villa goal, White headed it into goal, and in the loose scrimmage that followed it struck Cox's body and went through the goal, making the first point for the Wanderers half an hour from the start.

This success seemed to enliven the home team, and they pressed the Villa desperately, but Cox and Coulton kept them out. As half-time drew near Brown, Garvey and Green broke away and Garvey, again dribbling well into goal, shot. Green was in the way, but the ball came out to Brown, who passed it into the centre, and Green getting it on the side of his foot sent it against the goal post and it glided through the Wanderers' goal, making the score equal.

In the second half the play on both sides lost much of its vigour, though at the beginning the Villa had the best of it till the Wanderers' was reached, when the forwards fell away. Later on Cooper had a couple of splendid long shots which Warner saved well, and a minute from time the Wanderers all but scored, the ball glancing past just the wrong side of the post. Time was then called, with the score one goal each.

(*Stoke Sentinel*, 15 September 1888)

First League Scorer

It has generally been accepted that Aston Villa full-back Gershom Cox scored the first League goal when he put through his own goal after thirty minutes of the match at Wolves Dudley Road ground.

This would appear to be based on the belief that, unlike the other games that were advertised to start at 3.30 p.m., the Wolves *v.* Villa game kicked off at 3.00 p.m. This is what a number of respected authors and historians told the author of this book.

Newspapers in Birmingham and the West Midlands were rigorously checked, all to no avail. The newspapers *Athletic News* and *Cricket and Football Field* also proved unfruitful. Fortunately, Robert Boyling, a Millwall fan and a librarian at the Colindale newspaper library, was prepared to help out. In his dinner hours he trawled through every paper before finally finding what was needed, an advert for the kick-off time for the Wolves *v.* Aston Villa game. This is taken from *The Midland Evening News* of 7 September 1888 (see following page). The advert showed 3.30 p.m., meaning that by scoring an own goal on thirty minutes Cox had scored at 4.00 p.m. on 8 September 1888.

We know that no goals were scored before half-time in the Everton *v.* Accrington and Stoke *v.* WBA games; this meant that if anyone had scored before Cox, it had to be in the other two matches. For this we are indebted to the reporters of the *Cricket and Football Field*, who reported on the kick-off times at Pikes Lane, Bolton and Deepdale. As a result, we know the match at Bolton kicked off 3.45 p.m. and that at Preston at 3.50 p.m.

This is what happened at the Bolton match that was played at the Wanderers Pikes Lane Ground:

The visitors were late in making an appearance and some impatience was manifested at the delay. At a quarter to four the County kicked off with the sun at their backs, the Wanderers having won the toss but preferring to give their opponents the advantage.

The visiting right made an attack that was cleared by 'Bethell' but the ball was kept in the Wanderers quarter for a minute or so, until Davenport coming away transferred the play to the other end, and in two minutes from the start Kenny had scored a fine goal for the Wanderers. A protest for offside was raised in vain.

Davenport repeated his feat within a minute and a third goal was added by James (Jimmy) Brogan before the Preston match had even got underway, with Fred Dewhurst scoring early on for Preston.

Kenny Davenport thus holds the record of being the scorer of the first League goal in English and, as such, world history.

FOOTBALL LEAGUE.
FIRST MATCH OF THE SERIES.
ASTON VILLA
VERSUS
WANDERERS,
ON THE DUDLEY-ROAD GROUND,
TO-MORROW. SEPT. 8TH.
KICK-OFF 3.30 PROMPT,
ADMISSION 6D., RESERVE 6D.
PAVILION 6D EXTRA.
Vehicles: 2 wheelers .. 1s ; 4 wheelers .. 2s. 6d.
WANDERERS' TEAM :—Goal, Baynton ; Backs, Mason, Baugh;
Half Backs, Fletcher, Allen, Lowder ; Forwards, Hunter,
Cooper, Anderson, White, Wykes.
SATURDAY NEXT, SEPT. 15TH,
PRESTON NORTH END.

The newspaper advert for the Wolverhampton Wanderers *v.* Aston Villa game. Note the kick-off time of 3.30 p.m., rather than 3.00 p.m. as previously supposed.

Admission Prices

As the adverts for the Wolves–Aston Villa match on 8 September and Blackburn Rovers–Accrington on 15 September reveal, the cost of standing at Dudley Road was 6*d* (2.5p today) and at Leamington Road 4*d* (1.5p today). An extra 6*d* was charged for entry to the seats, referred to as Pavilion and Stand respectively, thus raising entry prices to 1*s* (5p) and 10*d* (4.5p) at the two grounds.

In 1888, England, after a long period in which wages had remained stagnant, was enjoying something of an economic boom that would last until the mid-1890s. Average wages rose and the half a million cotton workers of the time earned around 20*s* 10*d* (£1.04) a week (males) and 19*s* 11*d* (99p) (females). A coal miner could expect a wage of £1 a week.

In 1888, the article 'Life on a Guinea a Week' (£1.05 – the price of a 1888/89 Bolton season ticket) revealed that around a quarter of weekly expenditure would go on rent, a fifth on meat, an eighth on butter and fruit, with approximately 6.5p spent on coal to keep a house warm. A person on an average wage would have been unlikely to have a shilling to spend each week and entry costs of either 4*d* or 6*d* to stand at the match would have cut into their weekly income by around 1/60th to 1/40th (i.e. 1.66 per cent to 2.5 per cent of their weekly income). As a comparison with today, this is considerably less than the cost of modern-day football.

15 September 1888

GAME OF TWO HALVES

Aston Villa 5 (Dixon, Brown, Green, Hunter, Allen) *v.* Stoke 1 (Staton)

This was very much a game of two halves. Playing in claret-and-blue quartered shirts, white shorts and claret socks, Villa recovered from a terrible first forty-five minutes, in which they were a goal down, to win with ease. For Stoke, defeat might have been even greater if not for the fine play of Tom Clare at the back and 'keeper Billy Rowley.

Stoke's lead and their first goal in League football was reported in many papers as coming through Billy Tunnicliffe (but has in recent times been credited to Staton) and they were unlucky not to have a second when Bob McSkimming's shot beat James Warner in the Villa goal, only for the ball to whistle inches outside the post.

After the break, it was Villa who pushed forward. Debutant Arthur Dixon scored 'with a splendid shot' (*Birmingham Daily Post*) thus becoming the first half-back to score in League football.

Then 'Green made a fine run, and centred well, and Brown, rushing in, placed the Villa in the majority (lead)' bringing the score to 2-1.

It was 'the Old Warhorse' Archie Hunter who made it 3-1, before Tom Green created a goal for Albert Allen and then got the goal his play deserved when he timed his run perfectly to head home an accurate cross from Dennis Hodgetts, making it 5-1 after ninety minutes.

Match Played at Wellington Road

Villa moved from their first pitch in Aston Park to Wellington Road in Perry Barr two years after their formation in 1874. Shifting a haystack from the middle of the pitch was necessary before any match kicked off and, with a hump near one end and a line of trees down one touchline, facilities were not ideal, especially as Birmingham's first steam tram depot and bus garage was just yards away. The ground was to host two FA Cup semi-finals in 1890 and in 1896 when 35,000 packed it out to witness Wolverhampton Wanderers beat Derby County 2-1. One year later, Villa played their final game there before moving to Villa Park.

In 1888 Birmingham, with a population of 470,000, was easily big enough to accommodate a Football League side. The 'city of a thousand trades' had numerous workshops and factories. From one of these, toolmaker Joseph Hudson's, came the referee's whistle. This replaced the original handkerchief used to indicate that the man in charge wished to signal a decision. It is believed that the whistle was first used in a match between Nottingham Forest and Sheffield Norfolk. Hudson's is today still active in the form of Acme Whistles and estimates to have manufactured over 160 million.

Archie Hunter wrote a book in 1890, *Triumphs of the Football Field*. After moving from Ayr to Birmingham, he was persuaded to join Aston Villa in 1876 because a 'brother Scot', Mr George Ramsay, was the captain of the side. According to Graham McColl in *Aston Villa: 1874–1998*, 'The influence of Ramsay, then Hunter, led Villa to develop an intricate passing game, a revolutionary move for an English club in the late 1870s. It was a style of play pioneered by Queen's Park in Scotland. This type of sophisticated teamwork had rarely been employed in England.' Ramsay held the position of club secretary at Villa from 1884 to 1926.

Hunter's book is a fascinating read and includes tips on training, attitude, teamwork, diet and pre-match routines, as well as reports on some of the great games he played in.

GREAT DERBY MATCH

Blackburn Rovers 5 (Jack Southworth, Beresford, Townley 2, Fecitt) *v.* Accrington 5 (Kirkham 2, Holden, Chippendale, own goal)

These two local rivals had drawn 3-3 in the East Lancashire Charity Cup final in June and were meeting for the fifth time in 1888 for a match that kicked off the home side's Football League history.

Playing in light blue-and-white halved shirts, white shorts and dark blue socks, Rovers were behind on five minutes, England international John Arthur in goal making the elementary mistake of misjudging a Lofthouse cross. He found himself and the ball bundled over the line by Kirkham to the cheers of those supporting Accrington, who were playing in red shirts and socks with white shorts.

Within two minutes 'the Reds' had lost the lead when a fine pass by Harry Fecitt saw John Southworth create space to beat Horne, playing bravely after his injury the previous weekend at Anfield, and record his and Rovers' first League goal.

Southworth, who was to finish as League top scorer in 1890/91 and in 1893/94, almost made it two before another effort of his was well saved by the Accrington 'keeper. Horne, though, was then left helpless when William Townley squared the rebound for James Beresford to put his side ahead.

Holden drew the sides level when he swept home a Lofthouse cross, and by half-time the away eleven had hit home two more through Chippendale and Kirkham, whose link up with Holden was one of the features of the game. It might have been even worse for Rovers, but Arthur more than made up for his initial mistake with a number of important saves before Townley beat Horne with a hard hit shot. At the interval Accrington led 4-3.

After fifteen minutes of the second period, Blackburn were level when, following a goalmouth tussle, Townley scored his second goal and then the home side looked to have taken the lead, only for Horne to deny James Forrest with a superb save.

If his brother, John, had scored Rovers' first League goal, James Southworth became the first to score their first own goal when, in a desperate attempt to clear, he bashed the ball past Arthur to make it 4-5 on seventy-seven minutes.

There were only a couple of minutes remaining when Horne made a fine save from a Beresford shot and, when the ball ran loose Fecitt, with support from his forward colleagues, helped push it over the line and ensure a ten-goal thriller ended all square. As a result, both sides now had their first League point.

Match Played at Leamington Road

Formed in 1875, Blackburn moved to Leamington Road six years later, club officials recognising that if Rovers were to become one of the game's leading clubs, they needed a ground where football was the primary sport, rather than at Alexandra Meadows where they shared with the local cricket club.

Around 6,000 fans packed out the ground for the opening fixture against local rivals Blackburn Olympic on 15 October 1881, including around 700 spectators seated in a new grandstand, erected at a cost of £500.

Three years later, Rovers recorded their biggest victory by beating Rossendale FC 11-0 at Leamington Road, setting the side up for the second of three consecutive FA Cup successes. Three England internationals were played at the ground before a hefty rent increase saw Rovers seek pastures new and a move to current home Ewood Park, where the first League game was played on 13 September 1890.

FIRST LEAGUE HAT-TRICK

Bolton 3 (Brogan, Davenport, Cooper) *v.* Burnley 4 (Taint 3, Poland)

Just like the previous weekend, Bolton, wearing white shirts, dark-blue shorts and socks, were to race into a three-goal lead before ultimately losing a thrilling encounter. Barbour set Wanderers rolling with a first-minute effort that flashed just wide. Tyrer then shot just over and on five minutes some lovely play by Roberts set up Brogan for the opening goal.

The scorer shortly after barged Bill Smith over the line as he collected a high cross, but had done so from an offside position and Burnley, wearing striped blue-and-white shirts, dark-blue shorts and socks, escaped. It was Davenport who 'registered the second point', arriving 'like a steam train' to hit 'a splendid shot', reported the *Accrington Times*.

When Burnley did escape their own half, Harrison and full-back Parkinson combined to keep Bolton's goal intact and, on twenty-five minutes, the home side made it three when Couper dashed past Daniel Friel to finish from 10 yards out.

With the interval beckoning, Burnley got back into the match when, from a long Pat Gallacher free-kick, Bill Tait drove home to make it 3-1.

When the game restarted, Smith kept his side's deficit to two goals with a brilliant save, and shortly afterwards Friel went close to halving it with a long shot that passed narrowly wide.

On fifty-four minutes, Fred Poland made it 3-2 and it should have been 3-3 soon after but Tait missed from just a few yards out on fifty-six minutes. The Burnley inside-right, though, didn't have to wait too long for his second of the match, lashing the ball home from a scrimmage in front of goal.

With fifteen minutes to go, Burnley took the lead for the first time when, following some fine passing, Tait ran through to finish and complete a hat-trick, the first ever by any player in the Football League. A clearly deflated Bolton side tried hard to push forward in search of an equaliser but, with full-backs Bill Bury and Billy McFetteridge in a determined mood, Wanderers rarely looked like scoring a fourth. At the end Burnley had won for the first time in the Football League.

Pikes Lane

In 1888, Bolton's home games were played at Pikes Lane. Bolton had moved there in 1881 after wandering around seeking a permanent pitch since being formed seven years earlier. This was a notoriously muddy ground situated at the foot of a hill. Then a cotton-manufacturing town, the population of Bolton was just over 90,000, making it big enough to support a successful Football League team.

The first season of League football saw dressing rooms installed at Pikes Lane, which was last used at the end of the 1894/95 season.

The ground hosted the first Inter-League game on 11 April 1892 when Football League drew 2-2 with Scottish League. Pikes Lane is now covered by housing (see p. 118).

WEST BROM MAINTAIN WINNING START
Derby 1 (Plackett) *v.* West Bromwich Albion 2 (Bassett, Pearson)

The FA Cup holders won their second consecutive away League game after they withstood a determined second-half challenge from the home side. Derby had been grateful for some fine play from full-backs Arthur Latham and Archie Fergusson in the first half. Often outnumbered, they did well to contain West Brom's five-man front line, although there was little they could do to prevent first Billy Bassett and then Tom Pearson scoring as half-time approached.

The goal that gave Derby, playing in white shirts, black shorts and socks, a chance was a very fine one, George Bakewell and Lewis Cooper creating space for Henry Plackett, showing good control in heavy boots to hit a well-placed shot beyond Bob Roberts. The 'keeper, the first player from Albion to play for England, was rarely troubled after that as victory went to the Baggies. As to why Albion are called the Baggies, no one seems able to give a definitive answer.

Racecourse Ground
Cricketing offshoots Derby were formed just four years before the Football League started and played at the Racecourse Ground. This was opened in 1871 and still remains the home of Derbyshire County Cricket Club today. The ground was chosen for the first FA Cup final replay, when in April 1886 the first final ever to be held outside London drew a crowd of 12,000 to witness Blackburn Rovers beat West Bromwich Albion 2-0.

In 1895, disappointment at the continuing failure of the ground's owners, Derby Recreation Company, to prioritise football rather than cricket and horse-racing saw Derby move 1½ miles to the Baseball Ground.

This also moved the club closer to a growing industrial conurbation at the centre of which was the railway industry, the town of Derby doubling in size from 45,000 in 1851 to over 90,000 in 1888.

TOUGH TUSSLE
Everton 2 (Chadwick, Ross) *v.* Notts County 1 (Moore)

This, the first match of the Notts club's League fixtures, was played at Everton on Saturday, before 6,000 people.

The early play was somewhat in favour of Notts, and Ted Harker was near to scoring from a miskick by one of the Everton backs. Then

Dick made a long, well-judged kick, nicely placing the ball in goal, and Chadwick scored from the partial return of John Holland. The Everton forwards showed improved play, and the game was in their favour, though Billy Hodder made several good spins on the left and forced Nick Ross to concede corners. When half-time arrived, Everton were leading by one goal to none.

On resuming, Smalley had a difficult shot to stop early on, and then from a free-kick for a foul Ross kicked a second goal. This was the first League goal scored by a full-back.

Play continued to be exciting, and Fleming was cheered for a good run and centre, Lewis kicking over. Albert Moore eventually did the same at the other end.

Even play followed, Ross and McKinnon nicely stopping combined runs by the Notts forwards. By good play Notts won a corner, but 'hands' against them staved off danger. After even play, Notts scored a nice goal. Bobby Jardine, in the centre, passed neatly and well for Notts, who showed very promising form. They could not score again, however, and retired beaten after an excellent game by two goals to one.

LARGE CROWD SEE PRESTON AT THEIR BEST
Wolves 0 *v.* PNE 4 (Gordon, Ross, J. Goodall, A. Goodall)

Today it is the visit of Manchester United, Chelsea, Arsenal or Manchester City that draw the crowds when they are the visitors. Back in 1888 it was Preston North End, the best team of the era. As such there were twice as many at Dudley Road for the visit of PNE than had attended Wolves inaugural League match against Aston Villa.

Within seven minutes Preston were ahead, Johnny Goodall firing home. This produced a determined response by the home side, but Jimmy Ross looked like he had made it 2-0 only to be denied for offside. With both sides having a number of good opportunities it was something a surprise that at half-time only one goal had been recorded.

Only desperate defending yards from their own line helped keep Preston ahead but with Wolves pushing forward in search of an equaliser John Gordon showed fine pace with a run into the home half before finding Sam Thomson who made it 2-0. If that was bad enough for the home side within another four minutes the Preston lead was doubled when first Archie Goodall and Ross added to their sides lead. Ross's constant movement in search of a goal had the Wolves defence in a state of panic.

As full-time approached Tom Hunter should have reduced Preston's lead but it would simply have been a consolation goal anyway.

(Report from the *Nottingham Daily Express*, Monday 17 September 1888)

Dudley Road Ground

Wolves moved to Dudley Road in 1881 and, by the time the Football League started, the ground's capacity had increased from around 2,500 to over 10,000. Wolves quit the ground at the end of the first season and, with the support of the Northampton Brewery Company, moved to Molineux, where they continue to this day to play their home matches.

22 September 1888

VIOLENT ENCOUNTER
Aston Villa 2 (Hodgetts 2) *v.* Everton 1 (Watson)

No sides have faced each other on more occasions in the Football League than Aston Villa and Everton. The first was one of the roughest.

With Warner injured, Walter Ashmore came in for what proved to be his only League game in goal for the home side, whose supporters were to be condemned after the match for their constant hissing and booing of the visitors. No one knows at what exact point they started doing this, with a letter in the *Cricket and Football Field* the following weekend even suggesting the Everton side were booed onto the pitch.

What certainly did upset the Villa fans was the rough play they witnessed, although reading the reports it appears that both sides were guilty and in the aftermath a player from each side – the first in Football League history – was to suffer a suspension by the Football Association.

The Merseysiders hardly had time to settle before they fell behind to a smart Hodgetts goal on four minutes. The Villa man was a master with the ball at his feet, using the outside of his right foot to race away from defenders, and he showed good pace before hitting a powerful shot for his first League goal.

In response, Chadwick for Everton was unlucky not to equalise when his shot shaved the upright before Hodgetts struck his second with a header from what some match reporters felt might have been an offside position. As this was long before television was invented, we shall never know!

Changing over and with the sun behind them, it was Everton who pressed, but when the ball was cleared long, only a great save from Smalley prevented Hodgetts grabbing his hat-trick.

The game then became a very rough affair, with Brown for Villa and Higgins for Everton conducting a personal duel. Hodgetts and Dick were also in battling mood and, according to the *Stoke Sentinel* match report, things reached a climax when:

Dick (not N. J. Ross as extensively reported), the Everton right-back, kicked Dennis Hodgetts fully and violently in the stomach, and receiving without delay a violent blow in the mouth for his trouble. Both men, in my opinion, should have been ordered off the ground, and reported to the association, but the referee thought otherwise.

When the ball was in play, Waugh tested Ashmore and Watson was then tripped up as he was in the act of shooting from close in, with Everton's players clearly angered at being denied a possible goal (see Penalty Kicks, below).

Continuing to pile on the pressure Everton, playing in light-blue and white halved shirts, blue shorts and socks, hemmed Villa back towards their goal and, after many repeated attempts to score, Watson beat Ashmore with a scorcher that was met with deadly silence.

Only desperate defending maintained Villa's lead, but just on the final whistle it seemed that Everton had grabbed the point their play had deserved. There was, therefore, real disappointment when, after lashing home his shot, Waugh realised that the referee had sounded his whistle at the very moment he had struck the ball, to leave Villa 2-1 winners.

Penalty Kicks

Penalty kicks were introduced to prevent teams profiting from deliberate fouls or handballs close to their own goal. When the idea was originally suggested it had been rejected as implying that some players were ungentlemanly. This was a view totally at odds with the Victorian idea of an amateur gentleman sportsman. After all, surely no one would stoop so low as to cheat their opponents out of a goal by handling the ball when close to their own goal or even tripping their opponents!

Wealthy Irishman and keen sportsman William McCrum was a man with some clout and, as a member of the Irish Football Association, he submitted a proposal to the June 1890 meeting of the International Football Association Board for penalty kicks to be legalised.

The 'Irishman's motion' or 'death penalty' was roundly condemned, but public opinion swung in favour after an indirect free-kick was awarded for a deliberate handball on the goal line in the FA Cup quarter-final between Stoke City and Notts County on 14 February 1891. Stoke, having earlier beaten Preston North End and Aston Villa, had high hopes of a first trophy.

With County leading 1-0 in the final minute of the game, their full-back Jack Hendry punched a shot off the line when his 'keeper George Toone was beaten. Stoke were given a free-kick on the goal line but Toone smothered it easily. County won 1-0 and went on to reach the final.

The rules were quickly changed, and on 2 June 1891 the penalty kick rule was adopted in the Laws of the Game. The first side to score from one was Rotherham Town, Albert Rodgers doing the business on 5 September 1891 in a game at Darlington St Augustine's.

In 1998, Gary Lineker made a BBC documentary on McCrum and the penalty kick.

ENTERTAINING GAME
Blackburn 6 (Townley, Walton 2, Southworth, Fecitt 2) *v.* WBA 2 (Pearson, Bayliss)

If this was to be the standard of League football, there was every prospect it would be a success as, despite a four-goal winning margin, both sides played impressively. There was no doubt that Rovers deserved their success, but in goal Arthur had played splendidly.

It took the home side thirty minutes to score the opening goal, Townley hitting a beautiful shot, only for Pearson to equalise almost immediately. Then a fierce scrimmage in front of the posts saw Nat Walton beat Roberts and the Baggies 'keeper was to be beaten again before half-time when John Southworth made it 3-1.

The Rovers centre should have added to the total when the game restarted but, for once, his touch in front of goal seemed to desert him as he missed a number of opportunities. In a dash down the middle, Walton did, however, make it 4-1, before Townley repeated his first-half exploit to make it 5-1. Despite 'Jem' Bayliss reducing the arrears, Fecitt restored the four-goal gap as Rovers won a magnificent game 6-2.

FAIR RESULT
Derby 1 (Higgins) *v.* Accrington 1 (Brand)

Poaching another side's better players with an offer of greater rewards has a long tradition. The Accrington side that played at Derby in September 1888 had been strengthened midweek by the arrival of two new players.

The *Cricket and Football Field* reported on how their move had upset fans of Queen of the South Wanderers, left without two key players:

Scots fans in protest after Accrington poach best players
When news got round that Bob Brand and Billy Barbour were leaving Queen of the South Wanderers without telling their teammates a large crowd turned out at the station to wave them on their way after finding out an hour before their departure.

Brand was abused, not because the crowd rated him highly as a player but because it was believed he had persuaded Barbour to join him after previously refusing three good offers from English clubs and but for Brand would never have deserted his team.

Brand was to make an immediate impact by scoring on his debut. He had to wait to do so, as while kick-off times in 1888/89 were often delayed because of the late arrival of the away side, it was this time the home XI who were fifteen minutes late in arriving.

Missing Bakewell through illness, Derby were behind after just five minutes when Brand knocked home a Howarth free-kick. The score remained at 0-1 until the thirty-fifth minute when, following a series of passes by the Plackett brothers, Lawrence and Henry, Sandy Higgins equalised.

The scorer was unlucky just after half-time when his shot flew narrowly wide. L. Plackett continued thereafter to put in some well-placed centres, but his fellow forwards were in poor form and rarely looked like scoring the winner.

'The Derby club is still without an efficient centre half-back and until they get this position satisfactorily filled up they will be severely handicapped in their League matches', reported the *Cricket and Football Field* on 22 September 1988.

HARD-FOUGHT BATTLE
PNE 3 (Gordon 2, Drummond) *v.* Bolton 1 (Weir)

Bolton Wanderers: Trainer, Holmes, Howarth, Robertson, Russell, Graham J., Gordon, Ross junior, Thomson, Dewhurst, Drummond.

Preston North End: Harrison, Jones, Robinson, Roberts, Weir, Bullough, Tyrer, Milne, Barbour, Davenport, Brogan.

Mr Jas Cooper of Blackburn was the referee.

With Bolton having lost both their opening League games, Preston were big favourites to record their third successive victory. The Wanderers side had been refashioned, with Bullough replacing Davenport at half-back, the latter going forward in place of Coupar. There was a League debut for David Russell on the Preston side.

Kicking off up the hill, Preston was under pressure when Barbour hit a low drive that whistled just wide. Brogan was unfortunate to find Trainer in fine form, but the 'keeper was grateful when Weir missed a glorious chance. Bolton fans in the crowd were encouraged by their side's start and Barbour was, once again, narrowly wide before Preston finally exerted some pressure on the Bolton goal with George Drummond's shot hitting the upright. Gordon shot the ball past Harrison but he was well offside, though at half-time it was a relieved Preston side that left the field drawing 0-0.

The second half commenced amid great excitement among the crowd, and as usual the presence of away fans gave the game a greater atmosphere. On fifty-four minutes, Preston opened the scoring when Drummond scored, and three minutes later the home side showed their passing ability when Ross and Fred Dewhurst combined superbly to set up Gordon for a second.

Bolton were determined though to make a game of it and first Milne had a fine shot just wide before James Trainer was forced to make a fine save from Brogan. Tyrer headed over when he should have reduced the arrears, and finally Weir sent in a shot that went in the goal after deflecting off Holmes. At 2-1 down, Bolton must have fancied their chances of grabbing their very first League point but Preston were made of stern stuff and, after forcing the pace in the final quarter of an hour, scored when Gordon followed up a Ross shot to give Preston a rather flattering 3-1 victory.

When the referee blew the final whistle he ended one of the best encounters ever seen at Deepdale. Every man in the Wanderers' team played splendidly and they had quite as much as if not more of the play than their opponents.

(The Cricket and Football Field)

FIRST VICTORY FOR POTTERS
Stoke 3 (Tunnicliffe 2, McSkimming) *v.* Notts County 0

Stoke won for the first time in League football by overcoming a determined Notts County side that didn't deserve to lose by three goals. County's forwards had played energetically, but some stout defending and good goalkeeping ('Rowley was impregnable' reported the *Stoke Sentinel,* also making a case for the 'keeper to be capped by England) had denied them and there was also praise for 'the much better condition the Stoke men are now in following a heavy [fitness] programme'.

Unusually warm weather was enjoyed by a large crowd, including a number who had journeyed from Nottingham to see if their side could grab a first victory.

County started off the game as the better side, but dangerous crosses towards goal were all fisted away with great power by Rowley, and when Jardine was on the ball he found himself quickly harassed by Clare and Underwood. Secure at the back, Stoke, wearing thin red-and-white striped shirts, white shorts and black socks, was to go in at half-time with a 2-0 lead, Tunnicliffe scoring both. In the second half, the home side were much more in control and McSkimming added to Stoke's advantage before Holland in the County goal kept the score down with a series of good saves.

Programmes
The programme for this match was sold at auction for £8,760 in February 2009. Owner Andy Clayton inherited it from his cousin Margaret Staton,

a relative of Frank Staton, who played for Stoke against Notts County in 1888.

The programme was sold on the day for 1*d* (½p). The arrival of organised League football heralded the football programme era. There had been a programme for the 1888 FA Cup final that consisted of a single sheet, bearing the date, team names and player positions. Fans of Everton are fortunate in that, due to the David France Collection, there are copies of all programmes from the Anfield home games in 1888/89. In comparison, Burnley did not publish a programme in 1888 and it was not until 1912/13 that the Turf Moor club did so.

WOLVES VICTORY
Wolves 4 (Hunter, Knight, White 2) *v.* Burnley 1 (Brady)

Put through by a fine ball from Hunter, Walter White quickly put his side ahead before Tom Knight doubled the home side's advantage with a fast run and shot. From 2-0 up, the home side sought a third, and would have got it had the Burnley 'keeper and backs not played so well. Alex Brady gave the away side some hope with an early second-half goal, but after that it was all Wolves and it was no surprise when White and then Knight scored to ensure a first-ever victory in the Football League.

Table (Based on the System in Place at the Time of Only Counting Victories)

Team	Games	Victories
PNE	3	3
Aston Villa	3	2
Everton	3	2
WBA	3	2
Accrington	3	1
Blackburn	2	1
Derby	3	1
Burnley	3	1
Wolves	3	1
Stoke	2	1
Bolton	3	0
Notts County	3	0

29 September 1888

MAGNIFICENT VILLA

Aston Villa 9 (Allen 3, Hunter 2, Green 2, Hodgetts, own goal) *v.* Notts County 1 (own goal)

These two teams met at Perry Barr to play off a League fixture. About 4,000 people were attracted to the ground by the probability of witnessing a close and exciting game. In this hope they were disappointed, for the game from the kick-off to the finish was most one-sided, the visitors being outplayed by the home team.

In the first half, Villa scored four times and in the second half scored five, the County only making a single point, obtained through a miss kick by Coulton.

Archie Hunter kicked off, and the Villa at once attacked, but were kept at bay by Tom McLean. They returned to the assault, and Hunter made a fine shot, which Holland, the goalkeeper, partially saved, but Allen, rushing in, drove the ball through the post five minutes after the start.

For some minutes, the County waged equal war with the home side, whose goal was attacked, but kept safe by Warner. The Villa then forced their opponents back, and had much the best of the play, making three more goals before half-time. Allen scored two of them and Hunter one.[2]

After the changeover the Villa at once resumed the pressing, and McLean and Frank Gutteridge were busily employed in checking assaults. Time was occupied by even play and then the County roused themselves and played a fine dashing game. England cricket international Bill Gunn [the Rory Delap of his day – see Gazetteer of Players] in particular made some splendid runs, and had he been better supported the County might have scored several times.

After a time, Harry Daft made a fine attempt to score, but the ball struck the crossbar and rebounded into play. Gunn pounced upon it and centred, Frank Coulton tried to kick the ball out, but it twisted through the goal.

The Villa now played with great determination and the County were powerless against them. Hodgetts headed a fifth goal from a corner-kick by Brown. This was followed in rapid succession by a sixth, scored by the last named player, a seventh and eighth, by Green, and a ninth scored by Hunter. The whistle was then blown and Villa was left victorious at 9 goals to 1.

(Report taken from *Birmingham Daily Post*, 1 October 1888)

TOFFEE FANS HOPES DOWSED

Bolton 6 (Davenport 2, Tyrer 2, Milne 2) *v.* Everton 2 (Lewis, Watson)

A large travelling following of around 800 fans hoped to see Everton win for the first time away in League football. Even today, going to away games remains extra-special, so it must have been a great thrill for every one of the 800 as they departed from Liverpool Lime Street station for the 150-minute journey to Bolton. In an age when most people had never visited places such as London, the chance to enjoy a day out to previously unvisited locations must have been a real occasion. And as there was no doubt you could have a drink or two on the way (and maybe a chance to meet a fair lady) then even if your team let you down with a poor performance it would still have been worth the trip.

Of course the arrival at grounds of away fans also added to the occasion for followers of the home team, who could be expected to raise their own voices in support of their favourites. As the best-supported home team in 1888/89, Everton fans also travelled to large numbers of away games and no doubt their arrival was warmly welcomed by all those who appreciate the unique atmosphere of an English game in which both sides are backed by their followers. On this particular occasion, the away fans were to see their side beaten long before the end on a sodden pitch not conducive to good football.

Having won the toss, Everton elected to play with the wind at their backs, but were behind within sixty seconds when Davenport, left unmarked, swept home a long Weir free-kick. Within another minute it was 2-0 when Tyrer ran unmolested from 35 yards to beat Smalley and double Bolton's advantage, with the referee overruling Everton protests that the 'keeper had prevented the ball from going into the goal.

When Everton did press, they found Harrison in fine form, the 'keeper keeping out a succession of shots before the home defence cleared three quick corners. Lewis got the Toffees back into the match when his swift run down the middle saw him break clear before beating Harrison with a powerful shot. This fine effort was the scorer's only League goal for Everton.

Some superb passing by Everton was then rewarded when Watson, amid great excitement in the travelling support, made it 2-2 with 'a scorcher'.

Having done the hard work, the away side then gifted Bolton a third goal, Tyrer dashing clear to again put the ball between the posts and make it 3-2. As half-time approached, only a fine tackle by Brogan on Lewis prevented the equaliser.

When the game restarted, Bolton used the wind behind them to fine effect. Weir missed when well placed, before Milne doubled his side's advantage and Bolton could have added to Everton's misery, were it not for Brogan's miss from close in. With some of the away side appearing to be suffering from a number of injuries, and with no substitutes to replace them, the final quarter of the match was one-way traffic. It was no surprise when Davenport made it 5-2 from a scrimmage close in and then Milne beat Smalley to give his side a 6-2 victory. It was a result that flattered the home team, but Bolton had deserved their first League success.

SOUTHWORTH SUPERB
Wolves 2 (Cooper, Wykes) *v.* Blackburn 2 (Southworth 2)

Wolves were unfortunate not to take an early lead but, after a fine run, White's shot was just wide of the post. Arthur, in the Rovers goal, made some fine punches but was beaten on twenty-five minutes when, following a dribbling run, Jeremiah Cooper hit the ball beyond the 'keeper. It was Jack Southworth who got his side back on level terms when, after earlier seeing Jack Baynton prevent him with a fine save, the lethal goalscorer used great ball control to beat two defenders before striking home to make it 1-1 at half-time.

On the resumption, with Wolves continuing to press, Arthur again kept his side in the game before Southworth grabbed his second on fifty-five minutes. Any hopes of Rovers' first away victory in the League were dashed shortly afterwards when former Walsall man David Wykes forced home the equalising goal after a tussle for the ball in the penalty area, after which both sides had chances to win in a match described by the *Birmingham Daily Post* as 'exciting right up to the finish'.

PRESTON SHOW MENTAL STRENGTH
Derby 2 (Plackett, Wright) *v.* PNE 3 (Robertson, Ross 2)
Played at the County Ground.

Derby County: Marshall, Latham, Ferguson, Williamson, Wright, Rowlston, H. Plackett, Cooper, Higgins, Bakewell, L. Plackett.

PNE: Trainer, Holmes, Howarth, Robertson, W. Graham, J. Graham, Gordon, Ross, Goodall, Dewhurst, Drummond.

The match was less than a minute old when Derby opened the scoring, Bakewell finding H. Plackett with a fine pass that he finished in style. Ross should have equalised, but missed when well placed, and when the away side rushed forward Latham intervened to kick clear.

Preston's undefeated start to their League campaign was in big danger when, after Trainer had saved marvellously, Levi Wright pounced on the loose ball and amid great cheers fired home what proved to be the County cricketer's only League goal.

Preston were rocked and it wasn't until just before half-time when they got back in the game, courtesy of a mistake by the Derby 'keeper, Joe Marshall, who missed a long-range Sandy Robertson effort. Almost immediately from the kick-off, Preston drew level when Ross fastened onto a long ball to make it 2-2 at the break. On the balance of play this was harsh on Derby, who had been the better side.

The home side might have thought it wasn't to be their day when on the restart they hit the bar, and when Ross hammered an unstoppable shot to make it 3-2 Derby must have feared the worst. They poured forward and when Gordon committed a late foul he was to earn the disapproval of the crowd, who booed him from then on. Yet Preston were by now the superior side and could have increased their lead on a number of occasions, but with Marshall making a number of good saves, the match ended with Preston winning by a single goal at 3-2.

ACCRINGTON EASE HOME

Stoke 2 (Staton, McSkimming) *v.* Accrington 4 (Brand 2, Barbour, Holden)

Having beaten Notts County 3-0 the previous weekend, Stoke were unchanged but fell behind after five minutes when Brand's low shot flew past Rowley. Buoyed by this success, the visitors continued to press and after a goalmouth scramble Brand scored his and Accrington's second. Good play down the Stoke right by Jimmy Sayer and McSkimming opened up the away defence, but when Frank Staton was injured the home side were reduced to ten men just before half-time. Soon after the restart, Barbour put his side 3-0 ahead, and it might even have been four if the same player had not had a fine effort disallowed as offside.

It was McSkimming who reduced the arrears with a 'clever goal', reported the *Birmingham Evening Post*. Tunnicliffe then thought he had reduced the arrears even further but had his effort disallowed as offside before Holden made it 4-1. Finally, right at the end of the game Staton, who had returned on sixty minutes, scored to cut Accrington's winning advantage.

Victoria Ground

It was in September 1878 that the Victoria Ground, sited next to the River Trent, became the home of Stoke FC, when the club amalgamated with Stoke Victoria Club and moved to a new athletic ground that was originally oval-shaped to accommodate a running track. Both sides were open banking, with just one small wooden stand on the East Side, on Boothen Road. These facilities were considered good enough to allow Stoke to host the 1888 FA Cup semi-final between West Bromwich Albion and Derby Junction on 18 February 1888, which the latter won 3-0 before a crowd of 5,996. The final game played at the Victoria Ground was at the end of the 1996/97 season and, appropriately enough, it was against Stoke's first opponents in the Football League, West Bromwich Albion.

In 1888 Stoke, which later became a city in 1925, was at the heart of a thriving pottery industry. Formed in 1863, Stoke City are the second-oldest club in the Football League.

LAST-MINUTE WINNER CONTESTED
WBA 4 (Perry, Bassett, Hendry, Shaw) *v.* Burnley (Tait, Gallocher 2)

Forced to kick uphill, it was Burnley who started the stronger, and on ten minutes Tait scored with a 'beautiful shot'. Some fine passing between Tait and centre-forward Poland then opened up the Throstle's defence only for Gallocher to miss from close in. The Burnley inside-forward didn't wait long to make amends, hammering a great shot past Roberts to put his side two goals ahead. The ball burst as it entered the goal, and a second one was needed.

Initially, the home side found it difficult to make any impact on the Burnley defence, but on forty minutes Walter Perry was up smartly to head home, and within a couple of minutes Bassett, playing a fine game throughout, made it 2-2. Disappointed Burnley may have been, but they were still to go into the interval leading when Gallocher scored.

Albion resumed on the attack and Bobby Kay did well to tip Pearson's effort over the bar, and when the Albion left-winger then got beyond the away defence, only a great last-ditch tackle by Alex Lang prevented the equaliser.

Undeterred, Albion drew level through Billy Hendry 'amid loud cheers' and then pushed forward in search of the winning goal. The Burnley half-back line – John Keenan, Friel and John Adams – worked tirelessly to preserve their side's point. They appeared to have succeeded, but in the last minute the referee, Mr Jope, agreed with Albion's claims that a shot from Charlie Shaw, in his only League game for the Baggies, had gone under the bar before being fisted away by Kay, a decision 'hotly contested by the visitors'. Albion had won 4-3, but both sides had provided great entertainment for the crowd.

West Bromwich Albion at Stoney Lane
Albion had moved into Stoney Lane in the summer of 1885 and were to stay fifteen seasons before moving to their current ground, the Hawthorns.

Converting the ground into a suitable home saw the field returfed and a wooden grandstand, affectionately known as the Noah's Ark Stand, built with covering for 600 spectators in the middle and space for a further 1,500 at the ends.

On the opposite side, the ground was covered in ash, which eventually was raised back to give everyone a good view. The first season tickets at Stoney Lane cost 5*s* (25p), the usual admission charge being 6*d* (2.5p).

The first game played there was against the Third Lanark Rifle Volunteers from Glasgow on 5 September 1885. Albion won 4-1, with the first goal coming after five minutes from Tom Green. Albion's record victory, a 12-0 defeat of Darwen, was recorded at Stoney Lane in 1892, and the ground saw the most successful period in the club's history.

6 October 1888

EXCITING MATCH
Accrington 4 (Barbour 2, Holden, Brand) *v.* Wolves 4 (Knight, Wood, Fletcher, Stevenson own goal)

As a further sign of the emerging popularity of the game of football, as well as the need for politicians to be seen supporting it, the match was watched by local MP Robert Trotter Hermon-Hodge. He was to witness a very exciting match that saw Knight open the scoring on twelve minutes when he seized on a miscued L. Hunter shot. Harry Wood then added to Wanderers' advantage, only for the home side to hit back quickly. First, Barbour hit a fine free-kick, before Holden scored from close in. Wolves, though, were ahead soon after and led 3-2 at the interval.

However, on fifty minutes Brand hit a powerful shot from distance to level the scores, and when Lofthouse then made a determined run, his cross was only inches away from being turned home by Brand as the game continued to thrill the 4,000-strong crowd at Thorneyholme Road.

Barbour then headed his side ahead from a lovely Haworth cross, before Wolves pushed forward in search of an equaliser. Harry Allen was narrowly wide, and just when the Accrington defence (in which McLennan was outstanding) looked like holding on, Wolves struck to ensure a deserved draw in a very fine game.

BOLTON WELL-BEATEN
Burnley 4 (Poland 2, Brady, Tait) *v.* Bolton 1 (Roberts)

Having lost the toss, the away side were forced to kick against a strong wind with the sun in their eyes. They were quickly behind with Poland scoring from a free-kick. This was the start of a series of attacks on the Bolton goal and Poland might have done better when left unmarked just 6 yards out.

Harrison showed good form in Bolton's goal but was powerless to stop Tait's shot on twenty-five minutes, the ball emerging at pace from a fierce scrimmage in front of the posts.

Wanderers, though, were unlucky not to reduce the arrears when Davenport made a run the whole length of the pitch before finishing 'up with a rattling shot, which Kay saved'. However, this was only a temporary reprieve, as by half-time Poland had added Burnley's third and the same player would be only inches away from making it four on the restart following the half-time interval.

Nonetheless, Tait did manage to make it 4-0 when he scored from a free-kick amid loud applause. Towards the end, Bolton were able to reduce the arrears when Roberts scored from a corner, but the away side left the field a well-beaten outfit, having succumbed to Burnley for the second time in three weeks.

Burnley at Turf Moor

On 17 February 1883 Burnley, just nine months old, played their first match opposite the Wellington Hotel, which is still standing today, at Turf Moor against Rawtenstall. As it sounds, it was a piece of turf surrounded by moors, and it didn't take long for the club's pioneers to make it splendid enough to accommodate a crowd of 12,000 for the match with local rivals Padiham in March 1884 – 800 being seated in a grandstand, with an uncovered stand along two sides of the field for 5,000 more and the rest being able to watch the football on natural earth banks.

The facilities were good enough for a prince, and in October 1886 Queen Victoria's son Albert turned up with 9,000 others to take in the action in the local derby match with Bolton. This would appear to be the first time a football ground was visited by a member of the Royal Family. The patronage of Britain's most important family was important to a game still cautiously making its way into the world. The Royal Family had long enjoyed horse-racing, and its members were known to enjoy playing golf and tennis, but football less so. Their ancestors had, of course, banned the unorganised games of centuries past, with more than twenty laws between 1314 and 1667 outlawing a game believed at times to be taking people's attentions away from practising archery skills needed to deter potential invaders.

Times, though, were a-changing, as was demonstrated on 13 October 1888 when the Prince of Wales (the later Edward VII) attended the Kennington Oval to watch the London Swifts take on a Canadian touring side in a 2-2 draw. By 1914, the popularity of football was such that King George V was the first reigning monarch to attend the FA Cup final, where he saw Burnley beat Liverpool 1-0. And, of course, with the Royals attending football matches other notable members of society also attended so that once the FA Cup final was moved permanently to Wembley in 1923 it then became both a major sporting and social occasion.

Burnley continue to play their League games at Turf Moor, only Preston at Deepdale having been in longer continuous residence at their ground.

In 1888, the loom town of Burnley and nearby Nelson had a population of close to 100,000 people.

EVERTON GAIN REVENGE
Everton 2 (Farmer, Waugh) *v.* Aston Villa 0

Villa was boosted by the return of Warner in goal and included Fred Dawson at half-back in place of the injured Dixon.

Having suffered consecutive away defeats, Everton was boosted by the return of Frank Sugg, Johnny Holt and McKinnon at the expense of J. Keys, Harry Warmby and Higgins. The home squad had been put through their paces in the previous week with special training sessions organised by trainer Fred Willis, and the *Liverpool Mercury* reported they 'entered the enclosure strong and in good trim'.

After events at Villa Park, and in an attempt to calm the atmosphere before kick-off, there was a handshake between Hodgetts and Dick. The *Liverpool Mercury* reported that 'Hodgetts openly apologised to Dick for the treatment that player was subjected to at Birmingham, and said he was sorry for what he had done'.

It was the home side who were first into their stride and Ross soon tested Warner with a fine shot that was well-saved. Dick, showing attacking abilities not normally associated with full-backs of the period, then combined with Waugh, but when the latter pulled the ball back Sugg was unable to stretch out far enough to push the ball home.

Continuing to force the pace, Everton were twice denied when first Watson and then Chadwick brought fine saves from Warner. The 'keeper then made a brilliant save to deny Sugg from close in but, just as it seemed Villa might go into half-time level, they conceded a goal when Waugh converted Watson's pass.

On the restart, Warner was loudly cheered for his first-half performance, although the 'keeper then enjoyed some good fortune when Waugh and Watson both beat him with shots that narrowly missed. With Waugh and Brown both injuring themselves, each side was then reduced to ten players before George Farmer doubled the home side's lead, after which Everton held out fairly comfortably to earn the cheers of the large crowd at the conclusion of the match.

A SHARE OF THE POINTS

Notts County 3 (Daft, Jardine, Moore) *v.* Blackburn 3 (Fecitt, Townley, Walton)

The match was played immediately after the Notts County reserves match with Eckington had been completed, the reserves winning 4-0 to progress to the second qualifying round of the FA Cup.

Exerting early pressure, Daft put the ball just over before the game moved quickly from end to end without either side seriously troubling the 'keepers. As such, it wasn't until thirty-five minutes that the first goal arrived, when Daft shot home amid great applause.

Rovers were level within a minute, Fecitt scoring with what the *Nottingham Daily Express* on the following Monday reported was a 'beautiful overhead kick'. Charlie Shelton almost immediately restored the home side's lead but Arthur made a fine save. With County, playing in dark-brown shirts, white shorts and socks, ending the half on top, Daft and Jardine both shot narrowly wide.

On the resumption, Holland in the County goal was forced to make two quick saves, and Rovers continued to apply the pressure for a good quarter of an hour, but without success.

County restored their lead when Allin and Hodder linked up to find Jardine, who shot home. 'Play up Notts' was now the cry and Rovers were fortunate to have such a fine 'keeper as Arthur as he kept his side in the contest with a series of polished saves. This was to provide a platform for the East Lancs side to draw level when Townley made it 2-2, and after the 'keeper had made another two fine saves, they took the lead when Walton scored following Charlie Shelton's mistake.

Defeat would have been harsh on a County side that had played well and, following some fine attacking play, Moore notched the equaliser to conclude the match at 3-3. Considering that the pitch had hardly proved conducive to good play, the players had provided fine entertainment for the paying spectator.

These sides were to play a much more important game three seasons later, when they clashed in the 1891 FA Cup final, with cup-holders Blackburn winning 3-1. Only two of the County players who played in October 1888 (Daft and Alf Shelton) were in the side that represented the club at the cup final, whereas the Rovers side contained Barton, Forrest, Walton, Southworth and Townley.

Notts County at Trent Bridge Cricket Ground

Older even than the Football Association itself, Notts County was formed in 1862 for 'gentlemen only'. Having hired Trent Bridge on a number of occasions for important matches, a host for County and Test cricket since

1838, County moved there when Nottingham Forest left for a new ground in Lenton in 1883.

Three years later, the architecture of the ground was to start changing considerably, and within another three years a new pavilion, which even today remains the ground's most distinctive feature, had been constructed to take in the action on the large field that was roped off to prevent spectators entering the field of play. It was the continuing prioritisation of cricket at the start and end of the season, forcing County to play elsewhere, that eventually persuaded County to move to Meadow Lane in 1910, where they have remained since.

In 1888, Nottingham, with over 150,000 residents, many employed in the textile industry, could easily sustain a League club.

It was the captain of Nottingham Forest, Sam Weller Widdowson, playing for the club for twenty years, who invented shin-guards (pads) in 1874. Worn over the socks, they restricted mobility but provided protection in an era when the metal toe-cap was popular with many players as it was believed to assist power in kicking the ball.

STOKE THRASHED

PNE 7 (Ross 4, Whittle, Goodall, Dewhurst) *v.* Stoke 0

Preston North End: Trainer, Holmes, Whittle, Robertson, Russell, Graham, Gordon, Ross, Goodall, Dewhurst, Drummond.

Stoke: Rowley, Clare, Underwood, Smith, Shutt, Ramsey, Tunnicliffe, Dempsey, Smalley, Slater, McSkimming.

Referee – Mr Evans of Liverpool.

When the away side arrived with only nine players, it was agreed that the home side would assist them by providing two players, in Alf Dempsey and Bill Smalley, from the North End reserves. With Bob Howarth out injured, Dick Whittle came in for his League debut.

Preston, playing in white shirts, blue shorts and socks, began the match kicking down the hill but against the wind. Ross and Drummond were quickly into their stride but there was disappointment when the former, who had already earned the nickname of 'the little demon', fired over the Stoke bar. Preston maintained the pressure and Robertson had two shots before Drummond and Ross both drove shots narrowly wide. Full-back Arthur Underwood was in impressive form for Stoke and, along with Eli Smith and George Shutt, worked tirelessly to try and prevent their side going behind.

Preston was awarded a free-kick just 10 yards out following a handling of the ball but Ross put the ball past the post. On nineteen minutes, the incessant home pressure finally brought its rewards when Ross, showing good close control, dribbled his way past the Stoke defence before beating Rowley. The same player then made it 2-0 eleven minutes later with a long shot that might have been saved, and he then scored the third soon after to ensure he went into the record books as the first Preston man to record a hat-trick in League football.

There was more to come, however, from the inimitable Ross, when he became the first Preston man – and the first ever to score four in a Football League match – by drilling home on the stroke of half-time to make it PNE 4, Stoke 0.

Preston continued their assault on the Stoke goal once the game restarted, but despite knowing they had no chance of earning even a point the Stoke side continued to work hard and showed they would fight to the bitter end by even forcing a couple of corners, although neither threatened Trainer in the home goal.

On sixty-three minutes, Dewhurst made it 5-0. Rowley then prevented Ross scoring his fifth with a smart save, but the 'keeper was beaten soon after when Whittle advanced to hit a powerful shot from 30 yards that surprised the Stoke man to make it 6-0. Nevertheless, as *The Cricket and Football Field* reported, 'Rowley continued to play well in goal and had a tremendous lot of work, the game now being very one-sided.'

On the stroke of full-time, Goodall wrapped up the Preston victory by making it 7-0 to maintain the Deepdale side's fine start to the season. Many record books – even up to the 1980s – had Jimmy Ross recorded as having scored a record seven goals in this game.

Preston at Deepdale

Deepdale had already been used for football three years before Preston North End was formed in 1881. PNE quickly established themselves as one of football's leading lights with a series of high-profile friendly games against first-class Scottish opposition and the likes of Old Carthusians.

By 1883, a large stand holding 600 had been erected on the west side of the ground, and this was followed later by a smaller one with a press box in between. League football, and the subsequent success it brought, saw the club advance adventurous plans for a new stadium next door, but these were to wait until the start of the twentieth century, by which time bigger, more ambitious rivals had overtaken Preston, both on and off the field.

Deepdale witnessed English football's highest victory, when on 15 October 1887 Preston beat Hyde FC 26-0 in the first round of the FA Cup. Four players scored hat-tricks, including Jimmy Ross who struck eight times.

With Preston still at Deepdale, the ground is the oldest continually used site for League football in the world.

In 1888/89, the pitch at Deepdale was not particularly conducive to good play, often being heavy in the middle with the ball sticking in the mud on wet days. Nevertheless, Preston still played some fine football there.

BAGGIES BAG FIVE

WBA 5 (Pearson 2, Perry, Bassett, Henry) *v.* Derby 0

Kicking uphill and against the wind in the first period, it was nevertheless the home side that attacked from the start. Marshall in the Derby goal made several fine saves but Pearson, Joe Wilson and W. Perry all should have scored from easy chances. The first goal saw Wilson make space out on the left wing before delivering a fine cross that Perry pushed home. Bassett then found Pearson and it was 2-0. By half-time West Brom, playing in blue-and-white striped shirts, white shorts and blue socks, had strengthened their hold on the game with a third.

Despite being three goals down, Derby rallied in the second half and, for a time, the game was evenly contested with both sides missing some decent chances before Pearson accurately headed home a Jack Horton. Derby's problems were then compounded when Cooper collided with George Timmins and had to retire from the action with a broken collarbone. Just before the final whistle the home side completed the rout with a fifth goal.

13 October 1888

BRAND GRABS THREE

Accrington 6 (Brand 3, Kirkham 2, Barbour) *v.* Derby 2 (Higgins, Plackett)

Kicking off with the sun behind them, the away side were denied a quick goal when Chippendale cleared before Barbour shot just over for Accrington. On five minutes, a cross from England international Lofthouse was forced home by Brand and when Walter Roulstone then miskicked Kirkham made it 2-0.

A further goal from Barbour and a flying shot from Kirkham had Accrington 4-0 up at the interval and although Higgins reduced the arrears, Brand restored the four-goal lead when he finished off a fine Lofthouse pass. Brand then became the first player to score a League hat-trick for the East Lancashire side and might have added another only for his header to hit the post. In the final minute, Derby Plackett half-volleyed Bakewell's cross beyond Horne to reduce the goal difference.

GOODALL IMPRESSES ON DEBUT

Aston Villa 6 (Hunter, Green, Goodall, Brown, Allen 2) *v.* Blackburn Rovers 1 (Walton)

Aston Villa maintained their impressive home form with a fourth consecutive home success. In doing so they ensured Blackburn lost for the first time in the League after three draws and a victory. There was also an impressive debut for Archie Goodall, 'brother of the famous centre forward in the North End', who scored once and had a hand in at least two of the other goals.

Goodall had become the first man to be transferred between clubs in the League when North End allowed him to join Villa. No fee was involved and if Sir Frederick Wall (FA Secretary at the time) is correct, none was ever paid until Manchester City paid Preston North End £450 for right-back John McMahon in late 1902. By February 1905, Middlesbrough had caused consternation by paying Sunderland £1,000 for Alf Common. On New Year's Day 1908, the FA acted to limit maximum fees to £350, a policy abandoned four months later after it became clear it was unworkable.

With little to choose between the sides in the first half, the final result was a surprise, and Villa might even have equalled their 9-1 scoreline in the previous home game if James Southworth hadn't played so well for Rovers at the back.

The opening goal arrived on thirty-five minutes, when Green headed a Hodgetts corner home, and within a minute a great drive by Goodall beat Arthur to make the score 2-0, which is how it remained at half-time. On forty-six minutes, a Brown header made it 3-0 and Allen soon afterwards made it 4-0 before Walton scored to reduce the arrears. Any hopes of a late Rovers flourish were quickly extinguished as Villa pushed the ball around and it was no surprise when Allen and Hunter added further goals to make it 6-1 at the end.

LAST-MINUTE OWN GOAL DENIES POTTERS
Bolton 2 (Milne, own goal) *v.* Stoke City 1 (Slater)

Having won the toss, Stoke kicked with the sun on their backs, but were fortunate to remain on level terms when two Davenport efforts flew narrowly wide. Tom Moore then missed when well-placed for the away side before Bullough found Couper, his clever pass finding inside-left Milne who finished in style to put Bolton ahead. Despite continuing to press forward, the home side were unable to add to their advantage before half-time and when Brogan passed up a good opportunity, Stoke equalised with ten minutes remaining through George Slater.

However, with less than a minute to go, a fierce goalmouth scramble was ended when one of the Stoke players scored an own goal to give the home side a narrow victory.

WAS IT A GOAL?
Burnley 0 *v.* Wolves 4 (Wood 2, Knight, Hunter)

Burnley opened the match brightly and Friel was unlucky with a shot that flashed past the post. There was then a moment of controversy when a Wolves shot that, according to the *Birmingham Daily Post*, 'appeared to go over the bar was given as a goal' (see Goal Nets, next page) and there was further disappointment for Burnley fans when referee Mr Fitzroy Norris disallowed what many felt was a goal. Two further goals meant that at half-time Wolves led 3-0. Any hopes of Burnley getting back into the match were ended when the referee ruled out a strong claim that a free-kick had gone over the line. Wood then made it 4-0 in the second period, which is how the game ended.

Cricket and Football Field reported on 20 October 1888 that, 'The first goal against the Wanderers at Burnley ought not to have been a goal at all.'

Goal Nets

Goal nets were another invention introduced to football to resolve 'we wuz robbed' disputes, the aim being to resolve arguments over whether the ball had gone between the posts.

The impetus for nets came with the introduction of the Football League. The first season saw a number of disputes, including West Brom's winner in September against Burnley – the Wolves' goal described directly above and Blackburn's first against Notts County on 15 December. There was also the decision of the referee not to award a goal for West Brom in their defeat at Notts County in January 1889.

Later in 1889, Everton faced Accrington at home. The referee was J. J. Bentley, one of the main men behind the founding of the Football League, who later became its president.

Accrington took an early lead through J. Entwistle but, 'with a goal against them, the home lads played up with more determination and Latta from a position almost parallel with the goal posts kicked the ball splendidly, a great cheer being sent up by the crowd. The referee however ruled that the ball had not gone through and he was promptly and vigorously hooted ... The decisions of Mr. J. J. Bentley at this point roused the fire of the crowd, and there were loud cries of disapprobation, which were certainly not justified.' (*The Liverpool Courier*)

Watching this match was civil engineer John Brodie who, appreciating the referee's difficulties, set out to resolve them. Brodie had taken out a patent for his 'net pocket' and, after resolving a dispute with the FA over royalty fees, these were trialed and then first officially used on Monday 12 January 1891 in the North–South match played at the Forest Ground, Nottingham.

As they were made on Merseyside, it was appropriate that a player from there was the first to put the ball into them – Fred Geary scoring after fifteen minutes.

They were generally agreed a success. *The Cricket and Football Field* reported on 17 January 1891 that, 'Mr Brodie's goal nets are likely to be generally adopted. They are to be used in the Corinthians–Everton match next Saturday.'

By the start of the following season, every major team was using them. However, goal nets were not compulsory and despite being mentioned as a necessity in all competition rules, a game could go ahead without them, as remains the case. The 2008/09 FIFA Laws of the Game state that, 'Nets may be attached to the goals and the ground behind the goal, provided that they are properly supported and do not interfere with the goalkeeper.'

Brodie Avenue in Liverpool is named in John Brodie's honour and an English Heritage blue plaque is positioned at the late Victorian detached villa he occupied in suburban Ullet Road. He died in 1934, aged seventy-six.

FIRST WIN OVERSHADOWED BY TROUBLE ON AND OFF THE PITCH
Notts County 3 (Jardine, Daft, Moore) *v.* Everton 1 (Ross)

The Everton team received a great cheer when they entered the field. Travelling by train to Nottingham had taken three hours and the side had had three hours for rest before the game got underway at 3.00 p.m. prompt.

With the weather unseasonably pleasant, the crowd saw Notts go off at a rush, and a fine shot hit the Everton bar before being cleared. The home side was not going to be denied, and when Daft and Jardine showed good control of the ball, the latter put his side ahead with a firm shot that left Smalley helpless.

The 'keeper was also left nonplussed by a fine effort from Daft that tore past him to make it 2-0, and as the home side kept up the pressure, only a brilliant save by him prevented Hodder making it 3-0. However, after Holt had been roundly jeered for flooring Jardine, the Everton 'keeper made a poor mistake, allowing Moore's shot to fumble out of his hands and over the line to give Notts a deserved 3-0 lead at the break.

With Ross moving to centre-forward for the second half, Everton was a much better outfit. After he had forced a fine save from Holland, the 'new' man wound up a powerful run by scoring a splendid goal.

Maintaining the pressure, Chadwick followed up with a good shot, the ball grazing the bar, and for some time afterwards Everton's passing had their opponents very much on the back foot.

Defending superbly, Guttridge was a constant mischief when any Everton forward did create space to try his luck, and as a result County maintained their advantage in front of a highly partisan home crowd, at least some of whom jumped the ropes to come onto the pitch at the end to mob the away players. Their ire had been raised by what the *Liverpool Mercury* described as Dick having 'resorted to his old doubtful tactics of giving a knee' and having 'indulged in an old weakness of going for his man after the ball had been dispatched clear away'.

Furthermore, alleged some of the Nottingham players, the Everton full-back had 'used industrial language [in the vicinity of the press seats] and

... even in the company of a large number of ladies that were present'. At the same time, it was noted that those who had hooted him towards the end had hardly restrained their own language when doing so, even if the ladies present could clearly hear them.

In the ensuing melee Dick was hit on the head by one of his assailants, who subsequently escaped after being held by one of the crowd before the police had been able to get to the ground after being summoned for help. Dick himself was perhaps fortunate not to have been more badly hurt, as it would appear that his many possible attackers got in each other's way.

Everyone must feel a heartening dispensation for the cowardly crowd that mobbed round the unfortunate player but all Everton supporters must want to see their full-back play a honest manly game.

(*Nottingham Daily Express*, 15 October 1888)

PRESTON GAIN REVENGE
PNE 3 (Dewhurst, Edwards, Ross) *v.* WBA 0

PNE: Trainer, Holmes and Drummond, Graham, Russell and Robertson, Gordon, Ross, Goodall, Dewhurst and Edwards.

WBA: Roberts, Green and Horton, Timmins, Perry, Bayliss, Pearson, Wilson, Hendry, Bassett and Wood.

Referee – Mr Fairhurst of Bolton.

Could Preston exact revenge for their previous season's FA Cup final defeat? This was the main topic of conversation in the Lancashire cotton town in the week leading up to this game – a sure indication that the popularity of football was growing among ordinary folk.

West Brom had surprised all but their most ardent supporters by beating Preston 2-1 in the 1888 FA Cup final. Preston's overconfidence, including asking to be photographed with the trophy before the match, had meant nothing once the game got underway. And although Dewhurst managed to equalise for Preston, George Woodhall hit the winner for West Brom with thirteen minutes remaining. Bayliss had opened the scoring for the Black Country side in the first half.

The match was played at Kennington Oval and, with a crowd of 19,000 in attendance, the gates were closed for the first time at a football game in England. Seven years earlier, the very first game at which the gates were closed saw Queen's Park and Dumbarton attract a crowd of about 15,000 to the Scottish FA Cup final replay at Kinning Park.

All three cup final goalscorers were on display and the game got underway in magnificent October weather at 3.07 p.m. before a very sizeable crowd of 9,000 drawn from all parts of Lancashire. The hard-earned cash they had laid out to see the game would prove to be money well spent.

Dewhurst, hoping to put Preston into an early lead, was denied by Roberts, but it was Trainer who made the first real save by hurling himself acrobatically to deny Bassett. The 'keeper was then floored in a heavy challenge from Bassett but, fortunately for Preston, Holmes was able to get to the loose ball first and clear it to safety.

Nobody could take their eyes off the match, play moving quickly from one end to the other as both sides searched desperately for the opening goal that would be crucial to the outcome of the game. Goodhall shot just wide and Jack Edwards, on his debut, could have done better with a ball at his feet just yards out, but then there was relief for the home crowd when a shot went whizzing just outside Trainer's left-hand post.

Soon after, a keen tussle for the ball in front of the Preston goal was cheered by the crowd before, breaking away, Ross hit the top of the West Brom bar. Despite this, the Preston forwards were finding it hard to break down the West Bromwich defence, in which half-backs Jack Horton, Charlie Perry and Bayliss showed themselves to be at least as quick as their opponents.

There was little they could do, however, when Johnny Graham, coming forward at a corner, rose to power the ball past Roberts but, to his dismay, the ball clipped the top of the bar and flew behind for a goal-kick. Goodall maintained the Preston pressure, but found Roberts in good form, and at half-time the score remained goalless.

Following the five-minute interval, both teams started energetically, but within ninety seconds Preston struck the decisive opening blow when, to the delight of the crowd, Edwards fastened onto a Gordon centre. Trainer then kept the scores level with a dramatic save from Woodhall, and followed this up with another from Hendry as Preston's defence was put under a severe examination. Goodall was denied by a marvellous Roberts save, but with nine minutes remaining Preston broke the West Brom resilience with a second goal, Russell driving a long ball over to Dewhurst to score from 20 yards.

Needing to score quickly in order to retain any chance of avoiding defeat, West Brom attacked and Woodhall was only denied by a last-ditch Bob Holmes tackle. The Throstles' hopes were finally extinguished when, with two minutes remaining, Preston clinched a fine game when Ross drove home.

In the opinion of *Cricket and Football Field*, 'The game all through was one of the best ever played at Deepdale, the defence of both sides being of grandest description, and everybody seemed to agree that never a better game was seen in Preston.'

20 October 1888

HARD-FOUGHT ENCOUNTER
Accrington 0 *v.* Preston 0

This was the first meeting between the sides since Preston had refused to play Accrington in the Lancashire Cup final for 1888. The match was due to be played on 21 April and was certain to be fiercely competitive as the two had clashed twice in April, with Preston winning the matches 2-0 and 2-1. 3,000 fans had travelled from Accrington for the second game where it was reported they 'made far more noise than the home crowd'.

Preston, however, were unwilling to journey to neutral Leamington Road, Blackburn complaining that on the two occasions they had played there during the 1887/88 season they had been the victims of 'unsportsmanlike behaviour from Blackburn fans'. One of these had been a fiercely contested Lancashire Cup tie on 21 January 1888 when, in a game described as the 'battle of the Champions of England', Lancashire Cup holders Preston had beaten FA Cup holders Blackburn Rovers with a late goal in a 4-3 thriller.

The Lancashire FA had its headquarters in Blackburn and was not willing to back down. Everyone knew that Preston had just agreed to participate in a league with Blackburn Rovers the following season and they were instructed to play. When it became clear that they had no intention of doing so, Witton Albion were asked to travel to East Lancashire and, after Accrington had 'won the cup' by kicking off and Howarth had scored 'the winning goal', a friendly match was played.

Incensed by Preston's actions, the Lancashire FA hit back by imposing a suspension on North End until 31 December 1888, a move that would effectively have put the Deepdale side out of business and out of the inaugural Football League season. Even before a ball had been kicked in anger, it had all the hallmarks of pitching League against the FA, before the national Football Association overruled their regional association and rescinded the proposed suspension.

On a sticky pitch, Accrington were the first attackers. Trainer had to run out to save, before, defying the conditions, Goodall drove down the middle and was powerfully charged to the ground. Trainer then had to be alert again as the 'reds' sought to gain the advantage of an early goal.

The first real chances of a score fell to Accrington, Brand just missing a glorious opening after beautiful work by Kirkham and Lofthouse. At half-time neither side had scored.

Brand was busy on the resumption and Trainer stopped a couple of hot shots. Then Lofthouse got away and centred, and when Trainer missed the ball Brand dashed in a second late. Horne kicked out finely again and the game was contested desperately hard right up to the finish. Several times the ball got near the goals, but all danger was averted and the result was a draw, no goals being scored – a fair reflection of the play.

(*Birmingham Daily Post*, 22 October 1888)

TOUGH TUSSLE
Blackburn 2 (Haresnape, unknown) *v.* Wolves 2 (Wood, Brodie)

Starting as the better side, Wolves were awarded a free-kick just 6 yards out when Jon Beverley handled, but the away side were unable to profit from the chance to shoot at goal. Also unfortunate soon after was a nearby householder, who had to deal with the after-effects of a huge clearing kick from one of the Wolves defenders, as the match ball sailed out of Leamington Road and through a nearby front window.

When the game restarted, Wood put his side ahead on ten minutes with a shot that Arthur got his hands to but couldn't stop going into the goal. The 'keeper was then badly at fault with the second goal, rushing out to try and be first to a long clearing kick but missing the ball to leave Jack Brodie, scorer of Wolves' first-ever competitive goal against Long Eaton Rovers in the 1883 FA Cup, with a simple chance to make it 2-0.

The goal that brought Blackburn into the match came just after half-time, one of the home forwards kicking home as attackers and defenders tangled for the ball close in. An equaliser was prevented when Dicky Baugh, covering for his wandering 'keeper Baynton, headed the ball from the line, but when Walton found Bob Haresnape he hit a good shot to earn huge cheers as the ball rocketed home to make it 2-2.

TWICE BEHIND VILLA RECOVER TO TAKE BOTH POINTS

Bolton 2 (Weir, Barbour) *v.* Aston Villa 3 (Hodgetts, Allen, Hunter)

A crowd of 7,000 saw a fierce opening half; both sides trying hard to take the lead, and Bolton would have done so if Warner in the Villa goal hadn't played so superbly. It was Weir who put his side ahead, taking advantage of a loose ball to beat the 'keeper, but even before the cheers of the crowd had died down, Hodgetts had equalised. Barbour then made it 2-1, only for Hunter to again bring the scores level. Amid great excitement, Allen then drove the Villains into the lead and despite chances and near misses at both ends the game ended in a narrow victory for the 1887 FA Cup winners. 'Villa won a most interesting game,' commented the *Birmingham Daily Post* (20 October 1888).

FIRST AWAY VICTORY

Derby 2 (Chatterton, Bakewell) *v.* Everton 4 (Costley 2, Chadwick, McKinnon)

Despite missing three of their regular first teamers in Smalley, Dick and Waugh, Everton were too strong for a poor Derby side, who quickly found themselves behind when James Costley scored. The Liverpool man is an important part of football's history, as in 1883 he scored the winning goal in the FA Cup final at Blackburn Olympic by beating the Old Etonians, cutting forever the stranglehold Southern Amateur sides had on the competition, and heralded in the era of professional football. Olympic, with a side containing a plumber, spinner, metal worker and two weavers, had out-passed their illustrious gentleman opponents, who had stuck steadfastly to the traditional method of play for the period, dribbling.

The former cotton spinner was always a useful man to have around, having also scored in the 1883 FA Cup semi-final when much-fancied Old Carthusians were walloped 4-0. And just to prove he hadn't lost his scoring touch, he put Everton 2-0 into the lead against Derby in 1888 with a well-placed shot. The home side did, however, manage to reduce the arrears when on thirty minutes Bill Chatterton, with what proved to be his only League goal, headed home to make it 2-1 at half-time.

There would have been an early second-half equalizer, but Joliffe made a fine save from L Plackett before McKinnon doubled Everton's advantage. Chadwick then made it 4-1 before, close to the final whistle, Bakewell reduced the home side's arrears in a match that marked Everton's first League away victory.

LATE WINNER
Stoke 4 (Sloane, Tunnicliffe 2, Lawton) *v.* Burnley 3 (Poland, own goal, unknown)

For Stoke, with Moore having returned to Arbroath, there was a first appearance for Jimmy Sloane, signed from Rangers. Out on the left wing, Alf Edge had been preferred to Slater and, on a surprisingly warm October day, the new-look home side were quickly into their stride and the new boy put his side ahead on twenty minutes. With both sides showing great attacking enthusiasm, the crowd was thoroughly entertained and it was no surprise when a further goal arrived, Tunnicliffe putting his side 2-0 ahead with a fine header. His second, another header, made it 3-0 as the half-time whistle sounded.

Burnley gave themselves a lifeline on fifty minutes when Poland pulled a goal back, and although the name of the East Lancs side's second is not recorded, the newspaper reports of the time largely blame Rowley for falling to catch a long shot. On eighty-five minutes the away side equalised – again, there is no record of who did the damage – but any hopes of a draw were to be extinguished when George Lawton atoned for some earlier misses by putting his side ahead two minutes later.

PEARSON THE POACHER
WBA 4 (Pearson 2, Wilson, Woodhall) *v.* Notts County 2 (Allin 2)

The home side were quickly ahead when the alert Pearson swept Wilson's pass home. Allin equalised on twenty minutes, after which the away side were pinned back around their goal. It was no surprise when Wilson put his side back into the lead, his shot rebounding off the post and into the goal. The advantage was quickly added to with first Pearson, with his second goal of the game, and Woodhall making it 4-1. With less than a minute of the first half remaining, County reduced the arrears with another goal from Allin. Try as he might, in the second half the Nottingham side were unable to score the goal that may have established a platform to snatch a draw and at the end the home side had deservedly won 4-2.

27 October 1888

GOODALL THE GREAT

PNE 5 (Gordon, Ross, Goodall 3) *v.* Wolves 2 (Brodie, Wykes)

PNE: Trainer, Howarth, Holmes, Robertson, Russell, Graham, Thomson, Edwards, Goodall, Ross, Gordon.

Wolves: Baynton, Braugh, Mason, Lowder, Allen, Fletcher, Hunter, Cooper, Brodie, Wood, Wykes.

Referee – Mr McIntyre from Manchester.

Wolves arrived at Deepdale seeking to reverse their only defeat from their first seven League games. With George Drummond missing, back in Scotland after his wife became seriously ill, and Fred Dewhurst out with a leg injury, there were chances for John Edwards and Sam Thomson in the home forward line. Wolves had kept to the same side that had drawn at Blackburn Rovers the previous weekend.

The match got underway with Preston kicking up the hill against the wind. They were under pressure at the start, but Robertson and Russell were prominent in blocking the forward runs of Wolves and on five minutes the home side struck. The goal came from a good exchange of passes between Gordon and Ross, and when the latter crossed, Goodall finished the move off in style, bringing a great cheer from the 5,000 spectators. Preston could have doubled their lead, but Baynton made a good save from Thomson, before Hunter and Cooper seemed to have fashioned an equaliser, only for Trainer to scurry out and boot the ball to safety.

The crowd were clearly delighted to be watching such a good game. Both pairs of half-backs were in fine form and some sturdy challenges were met with a roar of applause from the spectators. Brodie could perhaps have done better with a shot from 20 yards, but with Preston pushing the Wolves' defence back, Gordon sent in a long, fast drive that Baynton could only watch hit the post and enter the goal to make the score 2-0.

Wolves were certainly not out of the game, however, and twice Trainer had to be alert to fist the ball away before the onrushing Wykes was blocked by a Holmes clearance. On the stroke of half-time the away side got their reward when Brodie scored from a corner, and at half-time the League leaders led 2-1.

When play restarted, it looked like Wolves were going to be right back in the game and only some desperate defending kept the ball out of Trainer's goal. Edwards and Gordon then broke away with the ball to find Goodall, who made it 3-1.

Yet again, Wolves were not downhearted and within minutes Wykes, from a Hunter pass, headed his side's second goal to make it 3-2 to PNE. Were Preston going to lose their first home point in their short League history? The response was no: Ross and Gordon combined to set up Goodall for his third to make it 4-2, and make him the second Preston player to record a hat-trick in League football, following Ross's four in the earlier match against Stoke City. And it was Ross who scored the fifth to make it PNE 5-Wolves 2 at the end of what the *Cricket and Football Field* newspaper reported as 'an excellent game'.

One of the First Players to Write a Book

In 1898, John Goodall became one of the first players to write a book on football. Entitled *Association Football* and costing 1s (5p) it provides a fascinating and unique insight into the game at the time. It was dedicated to Corinthians forward G. O. Smith, who Goodall rated as 'the best centre-forward in my time'.

In the book, Goodall offers advice to players, impressions of the game and hints for positions. He describes football as an art that can only be mastered by practice and enthusiasm. He bemoans the professional player who fails to constantly try and improve his game. Although sturdiness is essential to be a goalkeeper, Goodall knocks any idea that there is an ideal size for a footballer and writes, 'It is purely a question of skill in the best class, in which there is less rough play than in the modest spheres of football.'

While pace can be a big help, he points out that in the Invincibles side of 1888/89 there was no player with great pace and that the Preston side were superior as a result of the perfect placing of players and a willingness to work as a team, allied to 'pluck' in never knowing when they were beaten. Having the best eleven players does not always win the match, and while getting excited beforehand was only natural, once a player entered the field it was best if he was cool and could keep his wits about him.

Goodall was also a big believer in players ensuring they had lots of rest between games and making sure of not overeating before a match, believing that no player should eat much in the three hours beforehand.

Goodall also offered tips to players about never heeding advice from the spectators, as while 'it is a fact that the people can often seen openings that the players cannot; nevertheless, the player does best when he follows his own dictates.'

He also reminded young footballers that the 'first and last five minutes of a game are just as important as any other' and cautioned against a player losing his temper or becoming frustrated at losing the ball to a good tackle. Well over a century since Goodall wrote his book, it would still prove an interesting read for any young person seeking to know more about how to play football. [N.B. Goodall's book is no longer in print, but the author plans to put its contents online by the end of 2013. Copies can also be viewed at the British Library.]

BRILLIANT 'KEEPING DISPLAY CAN'T STOP TOFFEES

Everton 6 (McKinnon 3, Ross 2, Watson) *v.* Derby 2 (Needham, Plackett)

Nearly 8,000 Everton supporters put in an appearance at Anfield on Saturday to witness the above return fixture. The Derby executive, not being satisfied with their club's decisive defeat by the Liverpoolians resolved on Monday to send the strongest team possible to reverse the previous result; but in this they were disappointed as three of their first men failed to put in an appearance at the last moment and the local team had to supply them with a substitute in Harbour [see under Derby in Gazetteer of Players] who proved worthy of his place.

(The Liverpool Mercury)

Now fully fit, Smalley resumed his place in the Everton goal, and after Ross won the toss Everton elected to play with a strong wind at their backs. Left-back Sugg almost used the conditions to his side's great advantage but twice his well-directed shots came back into play off the crossbar. Yet it was Derby who struck first when Tom Needham beat Smalley with a good shot.

The equaliser, courtesy of Ross, was the result of a powerful drive and then, following a well-placed Farmer corner, McKinnon headed through a second goal for Everton. Marshall in the Derby goal then 'surpassed himself with some remarkable saves' but just before half-time he was to be beaten again, when clearing Weir's corner Watson made it 3-1.

Running, on the restart, towards the Oakfield Road End at Anfield, the Derby 'keeper was warmly applauded for his first-half display but could do nothing to prevent McKinnon adding to the total against his side or Ross then making it 5-1.

And when the pair combined to set up the sixth, McKinnon thus became the first player to score a Football League hat-trick for Everton. He might have had a good few more after that, but Marshall continued to thrill the large crowd with some fine saves before L. Plackett reduced the arrears near the end.

Anfield

Steady progress on and off the field saw Everton, formed in 1878, rent a small field fronting the Anfield Road that belonged to the Orrell Brothers brewers six years later. Enthusiastic followers hammered boards onto stable walls and erected rails around the playing pitch. Everton beat Earlestown 5-0 in the first game held at the new ground, where spectators stood on the grass banks with officials, members, pressmen and the more affluent being housed in a humble stand on the east side of the new ground.

Increasing success saw Everton erect a number of stands for the 8,000 plus who regularly attended matches and the ground was considered at the start of the League season to be capable of holding 20,000 spectators. It was considered good enough to host the British Home Championship match between England and Ireland later in the season. Everton later became Anfield's first League champions at the end of the 1890/91 season before one year later the Toffees, following a dispute that started over rent levels, decamped across Stanley Park to play their matches at Goodison Park. The newly formed Liverpool Football Club played their first match at Anfield in September 1892 and has been there ever since.

THREE IN LAST TEN MINUTES GIVE VILLA AN UNEXPECTED VICTORY

Aston Villa 4 (Allen, Hodgetts, Brown 2) *v.* Accrington 3 (Barbour, Brand, Kirkham)

Knowing that the away side had taken a point from North End, a large body of spectators had assembled to see what Accrington was made of. It didn't take the Reds too long to show their qualities. Kicking towards the Wellington Road End and with the wind behind them the away side took the lead in the first sixty seconds when Kirkham used the conditions to great effect to beat Warner.

Green almost equalised when, following a powerful run and centre from Hodgetts, he headed just over the bar. Warner then turned aside a stinging drive as Accrington pushed for a second, but following a breakaway attack Aston Villa made it 1-1 when Green headed home from a corner.

The home side, though, were to go into the interval a goal down when Accrington scored from a free-kick, after which the game became a fierce tussle between two evenly matched sides.

With the wind now behind them, Villa exerted strong pressure, only for Accrington to break away on sixty minutes to make it 3-1.

Twenty minutes later, Brown ensured a tense finish when he scored to make it 2-3 and there was a huge cheer when Hodgetts equalised. Then, in the final minute, Brown scored his second of the game to give the home side the narrowest of victories at the end of a very exciting match.

SEVEN GOALS IN POOR MATCH

Blackburn 5 (Walton 2, Townley, Fecitt, Southworth) *v.* Stoke City 2 (McSkimming 2)

Dull weather, and despite seven goals this was a poor match littered with mistakes, the first of which was Rowley in the Stoke goal, who allowed a weak Walton shot to beat him after three minutes. The away side fell further behind when Jack Southworth finished off a lovely move. Fecitt then hit a powerful shot just over the crossbar and it was no shock when Southworth set Walton up for his second. Having not been in the game, Stoke did manage to reduce the arrears when, from a corner, McSkimming scored, but just before the break Townley hit a fine, direct shot to restore the home side's three-goal advantage.

A second Stoke goal on the restart seemed certain, only for Beverley to get back beyond Arthur and hack the ball away from the line. The away side did, however, score through Lawton (according to the *Cricket and Football Field*), after which they rarely seemed likely to further reduce the arrears. Just before the end, Fecitt hit Rovers' fifth with a shot that was the best of the afternoon.

JARDINE BECOMES FIRST TO SCORE FIVE IN A LEAGUE MATCH

Notts County 6 (Daft, Jardine 5) *v.* Burnley 1 (Yates)

Having lost the toss and been asked to kick against the wind, Notts County still pushed forward from the off and were two up in eleven minutes. First, Daft scored with a cleverly placed free-kick and two minutes later Jardine doubled County's advantage.

Later in the half, the scorers then combined for Jardine to beat Kay but his effort was promptly disallowed for offside and at half-time the score remained 2-0.

Soon after the restart, Holland in the County goal was injured and when former Accrington man, John Yates, reduced the arrears, the way was open for the away side to snatch at least a draw.

That became more difficult when, on fifty-five minutes, Jardine made it 3-1 before soon after completing his hat-trick with a fine header, finishing off a fine run. Towards the end, Jardine scored his fourth and then in the final minute he notched his fifth, a magnificent achievement, and his side's sixth.

3 November 1888

BLACKBURN THRASHES BURNLEY
Burnley 1 (McKay) *v.* Blackburn 7 (Beresford, Fecitt 2, Forrest, Southworth 3)

The Rovers met with feeble resistance at Turf Moor on Saturday, and walked round the home contingent ... but for some smart work by Poland, the record would have been even more serious than it was.

(*The Burnley Gazette*, Wednesday 3 October 1888)

Having won two and lost six of their opening eight fixtures, the Burnley Club Committee had been searching north of the Border for Scottish players to boost their line-up and it was believed beforehand that three new men had been secured. In the event, only Billy McKay from Edinburgh had travelled south and his performance was to be disparaged in the local paper, reporting that 'he was of very little use, being about the slowest man on the field'. He did, however, score, a feat he was to repeat in his next three games, but after failing to keep his sequence going in the fifth game McKay never played again for Burnley and moved to Newcastle West at the season's end.

After conceding fourteen goals in his last three appearances Kay made way in goal, a move that saw McFettride moved to centre-forward with Poland dropping back to don the 'keeper's jersey.

It was the Blackburn custodian who was first into action though, Arthur fisting away early efforts from Gallocher and Yates. Poland was soon in action, denying Beresford with a smart save. McKay was then too slow to pick up a through pass from Robert McCrae before Poland made 'a save from a magnificent shot from the right wing, amid cheers'.

'After some further pressure the Rovers gained the first goal twenty minutes from the start. On restarting, Forrest collared the ball in midfield and, weeding his way through the home defence, scored with a splendid shot. The home defence was now fairly peppered and the Rovers soon increased their lead.'

Three goals down Burnley did manage to pull a goal back when a slipping McKay recovered his balance to finish off some fine play, in which Gallocher and Yates were prominent. This, however, was to be a temporary blip in an otherwise non-stop procession towards the home goal and 'Poland had some awkward moments to deal with' before on the interval Rovers nabbed 'a fourth goal from the right wing'.

With the wind now behind them, Burnley charged forward when the second forty-five minutes got underway. Blackburn full-backs John Forbes and James Southworth did well to contain the home attack and a disheartened Burnley side were soon under pressure again, with Poland saving a great Jack Southworth shot. The Rovers centre wasn't going to be denied, though, and picking up the ball on the left he cut inside Bury and beat Poland with a hard, low shot to make it 5-1. Two minutes later, Fecitt scored after Beresford had got to the byeline and crossed accurately.

With five minutes of the game remaining, Southworth got what was his third goal of the match, using his explosive pace to get beyond the Burnley backs before beating Poland who, despite having played a fine match, had conceded seven. It was to be the former Dundee Harp's last game for the Clarets, as a few short weeks later he emigrated.

NICK ROSS THUMPS HOME WINNER
Everton 2 (Brown, Ross) *v.* Bolton 1 (Barbour)

After losing the toss, Everton kicked off against the wind and hill. There was a big cheer for George Dobson when he made a fine tackle on Davenport and then Chadwick thrilled the crowd with a powerful run that only ended when he fired just wide. Jim Weir and Barbour were having a real tussle for possession before, early in the second half, Brown beat Gillan in the Bolton goal to put his side ahead. The equalising effort came from Barbour, whose free-kick was powerful enough to beat Smalley.

Down the Everton left, Chadwick and William Brown were combining well but it was Ross, playing at centre-forward, who scored the winner when he hit a hard shot beyond the Bolton 'keeper.

With Everton continuing to press forward, Bolton's only real chance of a second equaliser came when Barbour produced a driving run up the hill that was stopped by a hard, fair challenge by Dobson to leave the home side victors in a hard, keenly fought match.

Players' Wages
Because they were the best-supported club, Everton had been able to attract Nick Ross from Preston North End. It is believed that he was being

paid £10 a month, twice what other top players were receiving at £1.25 a week, or 25 shillings. This was around 25 per cent greater than the average working wage, considerably less than what the top players earn today, but as playing football for a living was much better than working down the pit or a dusty factory, few players would have bemoaned their luck.

Other Earning Opportunities

Although there was no corporate sponsorship of football in 1888 – the first competition to negotiate a sponsorship deal was the League Cup ninety-four years later – some players did benefit from the growing commercial appeal of the game. Ross's teammate George Dobson was an agent for R. Mercer of Bolton, who was famous for manufacturing football goods for many years.

Another Evertonian, Frank Sugg, was even more successful. The international cricketer, who was a brilliant all-round sportsman who also took part in weightlifting, swimming, shotput, billiards and rifle shooting, opened a sports shop in Liverpool with his younger brother Frank in 1894. Over the years, more shops were added and although the brothers split commercially in 1927, they both remained in business until they died within days of each other in 1931. The final link with the business[es] only came to an end in January 2001 when it was announced that 'Sugg Sport is to close its eleven sports stores with the loss of 118 jobs'.

LAMBS TO THE SLAUGHTER

Notts County 0 *v.* PNE 7 (Gordon 3, Goodall 3, Ross)

These sides had first clashed on 31 January 1885 when County had shocked Preston by winning 2-1. Since then, however, the two had clashed on seven further occasions, with the Lancashire side winning the lot including a 14-0 thrashing in November 1886. Any hopes that County had entertained of gaining revenge had disappeared within ten minutes of the start. By then, Goodall had opened the scoring with a fine, low shot and Gordon had doubled the advantage.

When County pressed forward, Trainer made a fine save from a powerful Allin shot and the home side were then unlucky when Russell handled the ball just 3 yards out. From the free-kick, County were unable to put the ball past the North End defenders on the line. At half-time, the game remained 0-2, but in the second period Preston stepped up the pace and their precise passing destroyed the home defence.

'Keeper Hugh Owen, playing what proved to be his only League game, did save Gordon's shot but was then barged over the line by Goodall for a third goal, before spotting his colleague unmarked. Gordon squared a corner to Ross who beat the 'keeper and made it 4-0. Gordon made the score 5-0 before increasing Preston's advantage even further with his hat-trick goal. With County now wilting under the pressure, Goodall beat a number of defenders in a mazy run before scoring to complete his own hat-trick and make it 7-0.

POOR WEATHER AND MATCH
Stoke 1 (Shutt) *v.* Aston Villa 1 (Allen)

Referee – J. J. Bentley.

A heavy pitch and cold, wet weather ensured this was not a match to warm the crowd of 3,000. The players' efforts were honest, but with neither 'keeper having anything to do, it was no surprise that at half-time the score was 0-0. After early home pressure in the second half, Aston Villa then went down the field and Allen put them ahead. A second would undoubtedly have arrived if a lesser 'keeper than Rowley had been in goal; indeed it was his fine saves that set up the home side for a draw, the goal coming when George Shutt rushed the ball home following a corner.

REFEREE ABUSED
WBA 2 (Wilson, Bassett) *v.* Accrington 2 (Barbour 2)

There were only around 1,000 spectators at Stoney Lane. Mackintosh waterproof rain coats had been invented in the early part of the nineteenth century, and the umbrella was conceived by Londoner Samuel Fox in 1852. Even so, few people were willing to risk a heavy soaking in an age with no such thing as central heating; back then, the catching of a cold really could be the 'death of you'. In 1889, a Russian Flu pandemic swept across Europe, and then on to the rest of the world, killing over a million people in the process.

Those who did turn out witnessed a decent game that many felt was ruined by a series of inconsistent decisions by the referee, Mr Armitt of Leek, who was 'hooted by the crowd when he left the field'.

Kicking up the slope, West Brom were ahead on fifteen minutes through Wilson. Stung by going behind, the East Lancashire side pressed forward and Roberts was called into action on several occasions before a hefty clearing kick from full-back Luther Walker was picked up by Wilson and, from his centre Bayliss's header, brought a fine save from Accrington 'keeper Horne.

When the game resumed in the second half, the away side was quickly back on level terms when Lofthouse's centre beat Roberts and Barbour headed home. His second was the result of a long goal-kick by Horne, Barbour showing smart control before beating Roberts. As the goal came only moments after Albion had felt they had taken the lead (Mr Armitt deciding otherwise by the awarding of a foul) there was a sense of injustice among the crowd and even though Bassett later levelled up the scores the referee remained unpopular to the end of the match.

FIRST WOLVES HAT-TRICK
Wolves 4 (Wood 3, Brodie) *v.* Derby 1 (Lees)

The poor weather conditions meant there was only a modest crowd in attendance. They saw Wolves press from the start and it was a surprise that it took half an hour for Wood to put his side one goal ahead, an advantage they doubled when the same player scored just before the interval.

Soon after, Wood secured himself a place in history by becoming the first Wolves player to score a League hat-trick, and although Lees pulled a goal back, Brodie scored to make it 4-1.

ON FIRE BOLTON BLAZE PAST BAGGIES
WBA 1 (Bassett) *v.* Bolton 5 (Barbour 2, Milne, Brogan, Weir)

Both sides were captained by their Bob Roberts for a game that, due to the home side's delayed arrival, started twenty-five minutes late. As a result, the report in that night's *Lancashire Evening Post* only ran as far as half-time with the final result at the end.

A fierce scrimmage in front of the goal was described as 'rugby' rather than football before a Bolton attack that should have seen them take the lead, only for Brogan to head wastefully wide.

With the light already fading, it was clear that the similarity of the teams' jerseys was having an adverse effect on the players, with many wrongly choosing to whom to pass. West Brom were denied twice by magnificent saves from Harrison, before Barbour somehow conspired to miss when just 2 yards out.

Bolton, though, did take the lead before half-time, when Scowcroft dispossessed a dithering Bayliss before taking the ball forward and pushing it forward where it was knocked past Roberts.

In the second half, Bolton continued to dominate, but the big talking-point was a late difference of opinion when Seddons tangled with Hendry. When blows were struck, this led to a small section of the crowd invading the pitch with two minutes remaining. In the event, sanity was quickly restored without any need to request the assistance of the local constabulary. The Football Association later took its own action by suspending both players for a month and Seddons didn't play for Bolton again.

Having won 5-1, it was reported that the away side enjoyed watching a number of fireworks displays as they journeyed home by train.

10 November 1888

ROVERS ROMP HOME
Blackburn 3 (Almond, Walton, own goal) *v.* Everton 0

With the Rovers colours being similar to those of Everton, 'the home team courteously allowed the visitors the privilege of turning out in the famous blue and white by wearing red and black jerseys.'

The game started at a frantic pace, but lost amid the general play appeared to be any idea of how to get the ball into the goal, although a shot from Chadwick raised expectations of better things to come. Forrest and Forbes down the home left were proving too good for Farmer and Watson on the Everton right and it was the home side who then took the lead when Bill Almond's shot proved too powerful for Smalley, leaving Rovers ahead at the interval. With the wind behind them, Everton nevertheless played without spirit in the second half and, after a fine sprinting run, Townley found Walton, who doubled the Rovers' lead. This was to be added to in the final minutes, when Southworth's shot was deflected into his own net by an unidentified Everton defender to make it 3-0.

NEW 'KEEPER INSPIRES CLARETS
Burnley 2 (McKay, unknown) *v.* WBA 0

The home side had a new 'keeper in William Cox from Hibernian. He started well by making a series of confident saves before Burnley grabbed the lead on twenty minutes. Encouraged by their success, the home side made (but unfortunately missed) a number of chances to leave the score at 1-0 at half-time. With debutant McMahon (first name not known) having been injured, Burnley were reduced to ten men for the second half but, despite their advantage, West Brom rarely looked like snatching an equaliser and it was no great surprise when Burnley scored a second goal on seventy minutes.

TOP TWO PLAY OUT EXCITING DRAW
PNE 1 (Goodall) *v.* Aston Villa 1 (Green)

Despite dull weather, it was a large, excited crowd that assembled at Deepdale in November 1888 to watch a match between the top two in the English Football League.

The strong, blustery conditions were sure to test the skills of the players and, with Gordon and Drummond both injured, Edwards and Thomson joined Ross, Goodall and Dewhurst up front as Preston kicked off up the hill. Within two minutes, the League leaders had snatched the lead, when Robertson's forward ball saw Goodall beat Warren amid great cheering.

There was little chance of Aston Villa throwing in the towel, however, and Allen and Hodgetts put Preston right under intense pressure but, when a chance did arrive, Hunter wasted it by failing to even force Trainer into making a save. It was Hodgetts, though, who missed the best chance to equalise when Brown, after a darting run, pulled the ball back, only for the Villa left winger to fluff his shot.

When Preston did attack, the ball was pushed into the middle, where an almighty tussle in which around a dozen players battled for possession was only ended when the ball was cleared for a corner.

The game was becoming increasingly frenetic as the players battled for every ball, the crowd cheering both side's efforts but reserving their greatest applause for the local team. Brown thought he had scored when his shot beat Trainer, only to be left disappointed when the ball bounced just past the post. This was, however, a rare moment of Villa pressure, as by now Preston were showing the finer football, despite playing against the wind.

Ross and Edwards both had efforts at goal, and Goodall was only stopped from making it 2-0 by tackles from Cox and Coulton as Preston's superior passing kept the Villa defence on their toes. At half-time Preston led 1-0.

When the game restarted, Warner made a brilliant save from Ross, touching his fierce shot over the bar amid some excitement. The Villa 'keeper then showed it was no fluke, getting down smartly to keep his side in the game by hanging on to another Ross shot from close in.

Villa seemed certain to equalise when Hunter was clean through, but almost from nowhere Graham appeared to shoulder-charge the attacker off the ball before booting it clear. The visitors' right flank of Brown and Green was now causing the Preston defence all sorts of problems and a keen tussle thrilled the crowd. It seemed that, with the minutes ticking away, Preston would hold on for a famous victory, especially when Hunter's shot grazed the outside of the post with five minutes remaining.

When Warner again saved another Ross effort, this seemed like it would only result in 'keeping the score down, but with two minutes left Aston Villa equalised. The goal came when Archie Goodall's long dropping cross came down in front of Trainer and Green headed through, amid what the *Cricket and Football Field* reported were 'great cheers'. This seems to indicate that there must have been a number of away fans present, but may also indicate that those who turned out to witness matches in the inaugural season were keen to applaud fine play and goals.

When the referee blew his whistle to end the game, both sides were roundly applauded from the field, each earning a point for their considerable efforts.

GOOD GAME ENLIVENED BY THE 'FATTY FOULKES' OF HIS DAY

Notts County 3 (Daft, Jardine, Shelton) *v.* Accrington 3 (Barbour 2, Lofthouse)

For a November's day, the weather was remarkably pleasant, and so too was the football on offer. It was the away side who struck first when Barbour scored, beating Mordecai Sherwin who, at seventeen stone, was the 'Fatty Foulkes' of his day (see Gazetteer of Players). County were soon on level terms when some 'fine combination (team-play)' ended with Daft making it 1-1, the crowd roaring its approval when Sherwin accompanied the success with his trademark celebratory cartwheel.

Accrington then took advantage of some good fortune when, after rattling the crossbar twice, Lofthouse scored. A sturdy forward, the England international during his earlier career at Blackburn had been foolish enough to try and knock over Sherwin during an away game at Trent Bridge. After bouncing off the giant 'keeper, he failed to take the hint and when he tried again Sherwin simply stepped aside and Lofthouse thudded into the goalpost. Sherwin was a wicket-keeper during the summer and a lot more agile and nimble than most. Lofthouse did enjoy a measure of revenge during the 1884 FA Cup semi-final played at the Aston Lower Grounds when he scored the only goal as County lost 1-0 to Blackburn, with the East Lancs man forcing the ball over the goal line as Sherwin dived down to grab it against the post.

When play resumed after the five-minute interval, Charlie Shelton put County level and then Jardine pushed the home side ahead for the first time. Injuries to two home defenders were to leave County at a disadvantage and it was no surprise when Barbour scored his second goal of the game to make it 3-3 at the end.

LAST-GASP WINNER

Wolves 3 (Brodie, Cooper, Knight) *v.* Bolton 2 (Brogan, McGuiness)

With much of Wolverhampton listening to Liberal opposition leader William Gladstone speaking that same afternoon, those who did make it to Dudley Road saw Brogan give the away side an early lead. This was quickly replied to with Brodie equalising before Cooper showed some fine individual skill to dash beyond the Bolton defence before beating Harrison in goal and making it 2-1 at half-time. Bolton levelled the match up through McGuiness, a reward for some earlier near misses but then, towards the end, Knight emerged from the gathering darkness at the back post to complete the scoring by grabbing the winner for the home side.

STOKE'S EFFORTS IN VAIN

Stoke 0 *v.* Preston North End 3 (Thomson, Ross, Robertson)
Monday 12 November 1888.

This League match was played at Stoke on Monday, before a vast assemblage of spectators. North End lost the toss, and commenced to play against the wind. The visitors soon got a corner, which resulted in nothing, and Stoke began to attack, the ball being handed out by Trainer. Stoke still pressed, and Milarvie ran the leather over, as did Edge immediately afterwards.

A foul to North End near the Stoke citadel now occurred, but Smith relieved. North End now attacked, and Ross shot the leather into the hands of Rowley, who fisted the ball out. Twice Stoke assailed the Preston goal, and Lawton gave Sloane a chance, but Trainer cleared.

The home defence raised loud applause by their magnificent display; Goodall had a couple of shots, Clare saving the first, and the second just skimmed the crossbar. A foul to North End looked dangerous, but the attack was stayed, and Graham shot but Rowley saved magnificently. From a foul the home team secured a corner, given by Trainer. From a beautiful shot the Preston defence cleared, and then just upon half-time the Stoke men raised the siege, and had far the best of the play. Just at the call of 'time' North End scored from a corner.

Play recommenced in the Preston half. Ross made a splendid run the length of his wing, and Goodall shot, but Rowley neatly saved it. Thomson and Ross played well on the right, and a shot by the former went over obliquely. Again, the North End put in some fine combined forward play and Ross, with a smart shot from the inside right, beat Rowley and scored the second goal. A fruitless corner followed, but afterwards Thomson sent the leather with a shot that hit the upright, and bounding through, passed Rowley for a third time.

For the remainder of the game, the home team played with only ten men, Ramsey having to retire with a wounded knee. Russell and Sloane came in contact and showed a fighting attitude. Time was drawing near, and Stoke made every effort to equalise. McSkimming, rushing down, was pulled up by Holmes. A corner to the Deepdale men followed, but Thomson put the leather to the wrong side. Some fine passing by Milarvie and Edge resulted in another attempt at a score, but Robertson headed out.

(Report taken from *Preston Herald*, Wednesday 14 November 1888)

17 November 1888

SOUTHWORTH SHOWS ENGLAND FORM

Blackburn 5 (Southworth 3, Fecitt 2) *v.* Aston Villa 1 (Allen)

Minus Townley through injury, Rovers selected Jimmy Brown for the first time in nearly three years and he and Fecitt were to combine superbly down the home left over the ninety minutes.

With the wind swirling around the ground, both sides enjoyed early chances but twenty minutes in, Fecitt headed home a Beresford corner only for the cheers of the crowd to be stifled for offside. Almost immediately afterwards, though, another fine Beresford cross was headed powerfully home by Southworth to huge cheers from the 10,000 spectators. Villa equalised when Hodgetts dodged round Jimmy Douglas and blasted a shot that Allen knocked home on forty minutes, and at half-time the score remained at 1-1. It was Allen's tenth goal of the season.

On the restart, Southworth was guilty of some poor misses but, as both sides tired in the difficult conditions, Rovers re-established their lead when following a desperate scrum in front of goal Fecitt lashed home on seventy minutes and then two minutes later repeated the feat.

It was now Warner, in the Villa goal, versus the home forwards; after making a series of wonderful saves, he was finally beaten with only five minutes remaining when Southworth scored his second goal of the match. Four minutes later, the same man's direct shot had just enough pace on it to beat the 'keeper and thus ensure he recorded his second League hat-trick as he put himself firmly in line for a place in the England side for the 1889 Home International Championships.

THROSTLES FLY HIGH

Bolton 1 (Bullough) *v.* WBA 2 (Hendry, Pearson)

With dark, overcast conditions, it was agreed beforehand that the game would last forty minutes each way, although in the event the referee played forty-eight in the first half! No one knows why. After winning the toss, the away side chose to play with the strong wind in their favour and were quickly into their stride. They would, however, have fallen behind if Roberts hadn't made a great save from a Brogan shot and at half-time the score remained goalless.

Now kicking against the wind, the FA Cup holders showed good form in the second period, but when Bullough found himself free in front of goal he made sure of putting his side a goal ahead. However, even before the cheers of Bolton fans had died down, the away side had equalised through Hendry and towards the end Pearson grabbed the deserved winner for the Baggies who firmly put behind them their 5-1 home thrashing by Bolton less than two weeks earlier.

GOOD CROWD WITNESS FINE MATCH

Burnley 2 (Gallacher, McKay) *v.* Everton 2 (Chadwick, Watson)

Around 200 train excursionists had travelled from Merseyside and they gave a glorious cheer when Everton entered the field of play. Despite the poor weather, muddy pitch and blustery wind the crowd were to witness a good game.

Utilising the slope on the ground, Burnley attempted to grab an early lead, but some strong defending and a long clearance soon had Everton pushing the home side back. The opening goal was only ten minutes in arriving and it was the result of some good close control by Gallocher who then beat Smalley from around 12 yards out. When McKay doubled his side's advantage, the game seemed to be running away from the visitors, but in Sugg they had a player whose never-say-die attitude prevented a third goal. Rallying to the cause, the Everton forwards broke beyond the home defence to leave Watson to reduce the arrears and were confident of success in a second half when they would be kicking down the slope with the wind behind them.

On the resumption, Costley had clearly made his mind up to try and run with the ball straight down the slope, but his progress was quickly ended. When the Everton centre later found Chadwick, his 'spanking shot' left Cox helpless in the Burnley goal.

The remaining portion of the game, despite a heavy shower, was carried on with great energy and brilliancy, both goalkeepers being several times called upon to attend to ticklish shots, but neither side could demonstrate superiority, and a splendidly contested and level match terminated in a draw – 2 goals each.

(Liverpool Mercury)

BATTLING ACCRINGTON GO DOWN TO HONOURABLE DEFEAT
PNE 2 (Gordon, Dewhurst) *v.* Accrington 0

With the two teams having shared the points in the earlier fixture, the crowd of 7,000 was curious to see if Preston could bring down their local neighbours in this return fixture. Despite the short distance to travel, Accrington appeared on the pitch over twenty minutes late and, with a strong wind blowing across the ground, kicked off up the hill.

Accrington's forwards showed some fine passing and Brand, Kirkham and Barbour carved out a great chance, only for Lofthouse to waste it by firing well wide. Dewhurst was a lot closer for Preston, forcing Horne to tip the ball over for a corner. From this Ross, when Accrington failed to clear, should have made them pay but missed from just yards out.

Accrington, however, showed they were not going to be intimidated by Preston's unbeaten run and Brand almost forced the opening goal, only to be denied by a Trainer boot. Lofthouse put the home 'keeper under further pressure, but Trainer showed fine form by smartly collecting a ground shot. There was then joy for Lofthouse when he forced the ball home, only for disappointment to follow when the effort was disallowed for offside.

Horne had had relatively little to do compared with his Preston counterpart, but showed good anticipation when balls were twice pushed through to the home forwards. On thirty-nine minutes, it was Preston who opened the scoring when, following an almighty scrum, Dewhurst whacked the ball past Horne.

Accrington was determined to repair the damage in second half, and Trainer was forced to save a Haworth shot from under the bar. The East Lancashire side's hopes were dashed, though, when Preston scored their second; following some good passing between Goodall and Thomson, the ball found its way to Gordon who struck a hard shot that Horne was nowhere near saving.

Although they probably recognised it wasn't going to be their day, Accrington still tried to push forward. In doing so, the gaps they left might on another day have led to more Preston goals, but whether it was complacency or the conditions, or a combination of both, the home side appeared content to let the clock tick down and make it ten wins and two draws out of twelve.

THIRD CONSECUTIVE VICTORY FOR WOLVES
Stoke 0 *v.* Wolves 1 (Brodie)

Due to Rowley's magnificent form between the posts, Stoke survived early Wolves pressure. Play then swung from one end of the pitch to the other and it was a surprise that the interval arrived without either side having scored. In the second half, Brodie broke beyond the home defence to put his side ahead, after which Stoke pressed frantically for an equaliser but found Baynton in great form. Wolves thus ran off having won their third consecutive match.

24 November 1888

STRONG WIND RUINS MATCH
Accrington 2 (Kirkham, Stevenson) *v.* WBA 1 (Perry)

A crowd of 2,000 witnessed a match played in a gale-force wind. The away side were ahead on twenty-five minutes when Walter Perry forced the ball home. Stern home defence then prevented a second to keep the score at 1-0 at half-time. On the restart Kirkham, who seconds earlier had blasted a fine shot against the post, beat Roberts to tie the scores. Then, on sixty-eight minutes, the Albion 'keeper was left deceived by a wicked long shot from Stevenson for the winning goal.

GOODALL THE GLORIOUS
Aston Villa 2 (Goodall 2) *v.* Wolves 1 (Brodie)

Early home pressure was wasted when Hunter and Harry Devey passed up good scoring opportunities. Warner in the Villa goal then made fine saves from Hunter and Brodie, before Brown crossed and Archie Goodall had home fans cheering the only goal of a tight first half.

With the wind now in their faces, the expectation was that Wolves would have no chance when the second period resumed. Wanderers, though, had other ideas and they scored a fine equalising goal when Brodie crashed home a cross. Inspired by their success, Wolves pressed and only some further fine 'keeping by Warner prevented the away side taking the lead. Then came the moment of the match when Goodall scored the winning goal with what the *Birmingham Daily Post* described as 'one of the finest shots ever made on the ground'.

PRESTON RECOVER FROM HALF-TIME DEFICIT TO WIN IN STYLE

Bolton 2 (Weir, Brogan) *v.* PNE 5 (Ross 2, Dewhurst, Goodall, Robertson)

After winning the toss, Bolton decided to kick with the wind and, urged on by a Pikes Lane crowd of 10,000, the home side started strongly as they aimed to become the first side to beat Preston in the League. At half-time they seemed to have given themselves an outside chance by leading 2-1. It could have been more; Trainer in the Preston goal made fine saves from Brogan and Roberts. With only minutes remaining of the first half, it was the away side that had scored first, only for Goodall's effort to be immediately equalised by Weir. Then, just on the stroke of half-time, and amid tremendous enthusiasm, Brogan put the Wanderers 2-1 in the lead.

The second half was only a minute old when Jimmy Ross levelled scores up and then Robertson, with a fine shot, put Preston back in the lead. Now it was all Preston and it was no surprise when some fine passing and movement on and off the ball opened up the home defence for Dewhurst to make it 4-2. Ross later rounded off the scoring to maintain his side's unbeaten League record.

DERBY'S DROP CONTINUES

Derby 0 *v.* Blackburn 2 (Southworth, Fecitt)

Having won the toss, Blackburn chose to play with the wind and dominated the first fifteen minutes, in which time Southworth and Fecitt put Rovers two goals ahead. It was a lead they rarely looked like surrendering, although L. Plackett did managed to keep the Rovers defenders on their toes. It could, however, have been 3-0 just after half-time, but Walton's shot rebounded from the post before Derby rallied, with Arthur making two fine saves from Bakewell.

TOFFEES HANG ON

Everton 3 (Chadwick, Costley, Coyne) *v.* Burnley 2 (Brady, McKay)

This was a home debut for George Davie at centre-forward. Everton won the toss and chose to make Burnley play into the wind. It was to be a tactic that worked as, after forty-five minutes, Everton were leading 3-0.

Costley had missed a number of good chances before Chadwick opened the scoring – a goal J. Coyne quickly added to. Just before the break, Costley's shot was deflected into his own goal by Bury before Cox made some decent saves to keep his side in with an outside chance.

The goal that brought Burnley back into the game came from a break away on an Everton corner, McKay beating Smalley and the arrears were reduced to just a single goal when Brady scored from a corner. From then to the finish, both goals were in jeopardy, but with no other goals a hard and evenly contested game ended in a win for Everton 3-2.

STOKE DO 'DOUBLE' OVER RE-ELECTION RIVALS
Notts County 0 *v.* Stoke 3 (McSkimming, Milarvie 2)

The poor weather meant the crowd at Trent Bridge was a sparse one. Those present saw Stoke beat County 3-0 for the second time in the season, McSkimming scoring after just four minutes.

Unable to open up the away defence, the home side were grateful for some fine play from their half-back line-up of Harry Cursham (the top scorer in FA Cup history) and the two Shelton brothers, Alf and Charlie, ensuring that when the sides resumed after the break County, with the wind now in their favour, were able to confidently push forward. It was, however, Stoke who scored the next goal, former Hibernian man Bob Milarvie shoulder charging Holland over the line after the 'keeper had blocked Lawton's shot. Then, on seventy-five minutes, Milarvie made it 3-0. Stoke had now won away for the first time in League football.

Dick and Hodgetts Suspended
The commissioners deputed by the English Council to adjudicate in the matter of the allegations of misconduct against Dick (Everton), Hodgetts (Aston Villa), have accomplished their task with completeness and expedition, if not with equity and leniency.

The roving commission sat in Birmingham on Wednesday and in Nottingham on Thursday – an arrangement convenient for Aston Villa and Notts County but not for Everton, who thus had to devote time to two sittings in two different towns – and the upshot of it all is that Dick is suspended for two months and Hodgetts one month.

Football, of course, must be conducted in a respectable manner. The laws of play are readily understood and should be respected, and above all proper behaving ought to be observed but the punishment now inflicted is harsher than the exigencies of the offences seen to warrant.

Hodgetts is not known as a rough player and Dick black as he has generally been painted is not vindictive in his tactics, though he no doubt often raises the ire of even heavier opponents by the effective use of muscular thighs in tackling; and even admitting that both men had committed a grave error under provocation, a strong reprimand would have justly met the case.

Birmingham people while ready to blame Dick are sensitive that great injustice has been doled out to Hodgetts. If this be so, with what greater reason have Evertonians to complain of wrong, for according to the commissioners Hodgetts was declared to have actually delivered a blow whereas Dick could only be proved guilty of an attempt to strike.

However the fist of the commission has gone forth – the law in their eyes has been broken and vindicated, and the opportunity of lunging at the League perhaps gleefully embraced. Will the matter be allowed thus to rest? Violation of rules is not to be tolerated and fighting should be put down in a drastic manner, but the Association must be general and sweeping in their vigilance and remember that roughness is not an exclusive peculiarity of League matches any more than cup ties, but is liable to bubble up at all and sundry contests.

It so happens that the players put through their facing at this latest inquiry belonged to League clubs, while other clubs – outside the twelve – equally involved in misconduct, have been overlooked, and if the Council wish to displace a suspicious of antagonism to the League, they will make haste to apply their power indiscriminately without fear or favour.

The commission having disposed of some cases of infringement of professional rules, wound up their labours by issuing a homily for distribution among clubs, and especially applicable to referees, on a rigid observances of laws and penalties and the desirability of the commission endeavouring to maintain a reasonable demeanor on the part of spectators. Birmingham, Nottingham and other patrons will take note of this latter seasonable advice, it is to be hoped and then there will be small cause for confusions.

(*The Liverpool Mercury*, 26 November 1888)

1 December 1888

REDS' EASY DERBY SUCCESS
Accrington 5 (Barbour 2, Brand 2, Kirkham) *v.* Burnley 1 (Horne, own goal)

The away side were two down in the first five minutes after Arthur Wilkinson, playing in place of Lofthouse, who thus missed his only League game of the season, set up Barbour for the first goal. Some fine passing down the Accrington right then opened up the Burnley defence to allow Brand to make it 2-0.

Things got even tougher for Burnley when McMahon had to limp off after half an hour. The ten remaining players played valiantly and even reduced the arrears when Horne put the ball into his own net. Heavy boots, coarse fitting jerseys and a muddy pitch proved too much of an obstacle for Burnley to overcome and as tiredness set in Kirkham made it 3-1 before Brand and Barbour increased the margin of victory to 5-1.

EASY VICTORY
WBA 4 (Perry, Bassett 2, Hendry) *v.* Everton 1 (Chadwick)

After a bright opening in which Coyne wasted a good opportunity, Everton fell behind in this game when W. Perry headed Bayliss's cross neatly past Smalley. Sugg then forced the home 'keeper Roberts to kick clear before Bassett headed the second after Smalley had saved, but failed to hold onto, the ball. Albion's third came following some 'capital passing' that terminated with Bassett shooting from distance to make it 3-0 at the interval.

There was a further blow for the away side when the game resumed as Sugg, suffering an injury to his right foot, was unable to continue. Things got even worse when, with fifteen minutes remaining, Costley also had to retire injured, leaving Everton with just nine players.

Early in the second half, Chadwick had given his side a glimmer of an opportunity with a beautiful shot from the left, a reward for some earlier efforts that had narrowly missed. Just before the end of the game, though, the home side struck again when, following a 'scrimmage' in front of the goal, Hendry kicked through.

STOKE SQUEEZE HOME
Stoke 2 (McSkimming, Edge) *v.* Blackburn 1 (Beresford)

In order to ensure the game would be completed before darkness set in, the match commenced at 2.30 p.m. and, following early pressure down the Rovers right, Edge put Stoke ahead. This was equalised on thirty-five minutes by Beresford, but the away side's hopes of going into the interval on level terms were ruined when McSkimming put Stoke back ahead on forty-four minutes.

The second half proved a highly entertaining affair. Both attacked in numbers, chances were made and missed and it was something of a miracle that at the end the score remained 2-1 in Stoke's favour.

8 December 1888

POOR 'KEEPING

Blackburn 4 (Townley 2, Beresford, Stothert) *v.* Bolton 4 (Scowcroft, Brogan 2, Milne)

Less than thirty seconds had elapsed before the first goal arrived after Harrison dashed unsuccessfully from his line to try and reach a long ball that Jack Southworth gratefully pushed into an empty goal. Six minutes later, Blackburn were two up when Beresford swept home. Yet Rovers didn't even have eleven men as, shortly afterwards, the late-arriving J. Stothert, asked to deputise for the injured Fecitt, ran on to the pitch.

Blackburn, however, might have done better playing on with ten men, as within sixty seconds of doubling their lead they conceded a goal in ludicrous fashion when Scowcroft's long punt into the box was missed by everyone, including Arthur in the goal. Eight minutes gone and already three goals had been recorded.

Soon after, Southworth shot just wide before Harrison blocked Stothert. Back at the other end Milne, 'with the goal at his mercy', somehow failed to level the scores. With play swinging from one end to another, the ball was cleared from the Bolton goal line before Arthur saved a 'grand one from Brogan and Weir [that] sent another screamer a bit too high'. With ten minutes of the half remaining, Brogan tied up the game before both sides missed further chances to leave the score two all at the interval.

Both sides were denied early goals for offside when the game resumed, before the crowd ridiculed Stothert after he missed an open goal. That appeared to be a costly mistake as first Milne and then Brogan scored to give Wanderers what should have been an unassailable lead.

With time running out, Stothert, playing in what proved to be his only first-team appearance for Rovers, atoned for his earlier miss by scoring to make it 3-4. Failing to clear their lines, Bolton were then made to suffer further disappointment when Townley equalised with only seconds remaining.

'The goalkeeping was bad on both sides.' (*Cricket and Football Field*)

FIERCE BATTLE IN RACE TO AVOID BOTTOM FOUR PLACE
Burnley 2 (Brady, Yates) *v.* Stoke 1 (Edge)

With just three points from their previous eight League matches, the Burnley committee had reinforced their line-up with three new men for the clash between ninth and eighth in the League. Both sides, desiring victory to stay out of the bottom four re-election zone, put in maximum effort with every ball being fiercely fought over before a passionate, committed home crowd who were not above abusing any Stoke players they believed had made fouls.

According to the *Burnley Gazette*, two new signings, eighteen-year-old W. Brady and Mackay, another Scotsman from Gainsborough, did well. According to the paper, the two Bradys linked up well but Mudie, first name not known, from Sunderland 'was not a success' and in fact never made another first-team appearance.

Stoke arrived with just ten men but were at full strength after five minutes when Lawton made an appearance. A no-holds-barred challenge involving Keenan and former Port Vale man Bob Ramsey left the Stoke player injured and it was a few minutes before the game restarted. When it did, W. Brady scored on his debut 'amid cheers'. Rowley was then put under further pressure in the Stoke goal, fisting one shot powerfully away and then enjoying some good fortune when a number of shots fizzed narrowly wide. As a result, the half-time break arrived with the home side just a single goal ahead.

Having withstood further pressure, Stoke fell two goals behind on the hour mark when Yates, continuing to make a case for a first England cap, headed powerfully home. Lang and one of the Stoke forwards then 'had a little unpleasantness' before Alex Brady brought a fine save from Rowley, who was quickly becoming the man of the match and another England contender.

With the game moving into the final quarter, during which time Stoke got back into the game with ten minutes remaining, 'the game reached a high pitch of excitement, players coming to grief every minute, sometimes in groups of three or four.'

'The defences on both sides were exceptionally good.' (*Burnley Gazette*)

FA CUP PRIORITISED

Notts County 2 (Jardine, Weightman) *v.* Aston Villa 4 (Goodall 2, Green, Brown)

Incessant heavy rain had reduced the crowd to 1,500 spectators to witness a match in which County fielded a scratch side, preferring to give precedence to the FA Cup by sending most of the recognised first team to play at Staveley in the fourth qualifying round.

This meant debuts for seven players. For four – Fred Weightman, Herbie Snook, Charles Dobson and Tom Cooke – it proved to be their only League game during their careers, while Alf Shaw managed only one further appearance. And although Haydn Morley later did much better at Sheffield Wednesday, he also played only the twice for County.

In the event, the new boys did well; particularly Tom Widdowson, whose performance in goal was impressive enough to establish himself as a first team regular. The 'keeper was, however, powerless to prevent Brown sweeping Villa ahead after he had parried a fierce Hunter shot.

Cooke almost managed to draw his side level, but was unlucky when twice he drove shots against the post. Then from a Shaw cross Jardine, with a fine effort, was able to force home the equaliser to make it 1-1 at the break.

Goodall restored Villa's lead when he fastened onto a Green shot to beat Widdowson. There was a second equaliser for County when Shaw, dashing through, was bundled to the ground by Warner and when the ball ran free Weightman scored on his debut. There was even a chance for the home side to take the lead, but Cooke missed when well placed. There were to be no second chances after that, however, when first Green and then Goodall scored to make it 4-2. County's reserves had played well, but Villa had deservedly taken both points in a game in which Brown had played particularly well.

FA Cup Result
Staveley 1 – Notts County 3

DEEPDALE MEN WIN WITH EASE

PNE 5 (Inglis, Dewhurst 2, Goodall 2) *v.* Derby 0

On a ground made heavy by recent rains, Derby began kicking up the hill and were behind after two minutes when debutant Jock Inglis finished 'with a beautiful goal'.

This was the start of some serious pressure on the County defence and Marshall did well to block a fast shot from Goodall. The 'keeper repeated the feat a few minutes later before Thomson missed a simple chance to make it 2-0. Inglis then missed when close in, before a fine piece of passing between L. Plackett and Needham gave centre-half J. Smith a chance to test Trainer in the Preston goal. Needham 'had a grand long shot', which the 'keeper saved by kicking it out to the left where Dewhurst made a good run before forcing Marshall to save. At half-time, the score remained 1-0.

The second half was to prove very one-sided, Marshall keeping his side in the game with three early saves. Still just a goal down, Derby pushed forward, forcing Trainer to make a number of saves with his hands. However, when Preston made it 2-0 on seventy minutes through Goodall from a corner, it was clear that the bottom-placed club were not going to win their second League game, especially after a wonderful, dribbling run saw Goodall grab his second of the match to make it 3-0.

It was left to Dewhurst to score two goals in the final ten minutes of the match to maintain Preston's place at the top with twenty-six from a possible twenty-eight points. In comparison, Derby left the field with just three points from eleven matches.

WOLVES SHOW FINE FORM
Wolves 4 (Brodie, Cooper 2, Wykes) *v.* Accrington 0

'The weather was wretched and the conditions of the ground unfavourable to scientific play.' (*Birmingham Daily Post*)

There was an early goal for Wolves, who doubled their lead before half-time when Cooper scored from a Wykes pass. Accrington's recovery chances were hampered when Barbour was forced to leave the field injured after receiving an accidental kick from Baugh. The away side then fell further behind when Cooper scored from a scrimmage under the posts and just before the end Wolves added to their advantage.

15 December 1888

FAIR RESULT

Accrington 1 (Kirkham) *v.* Aston Villa 1 (Brown)

Even before Villa took the lead on seven minutes through Brown, 'Horne had showed his usual abilities as goalkeeper' with a series of good saves. It didn't take the home side long to equalise when Kirkham headed past Warner. Accrington were then unfortunate to see efforts come back into play off the crossbar and post before Goodall shaved the outside of the post as Villa sought to retake the lead. Later, Barbour thought he had scored, only for his effort to be disallowed as offside and, despite some very determined attempts on goal in the second half, the match ended at 1-1 – a fair result.

FOG WINS THE DAY

Blackburn 5 (Southworth 4, unknown) *v.* Notts County 2 (Brown, Hodder)

On a very slippery pitch, Blackburn's initial raids were forced back and Hodder scored for a full-strength Notts. After eight minutes of play, Rovers were denied an equaliser when Gutteridge deliberately handled Townley's shot. From the resultant free-kick, Widdowson showed great bravery by twice blocking the ball on the line. Soon after, however, a thick fog enveloped the ground, leaving the design of the players to only be visible at irregular intervals. At half-time the score remained 1-0 in favour of County.

The second half was played in dense fog. From what could be seen of the play Notts appeared to press most, scoring when play was a quarter of an hour old. The Rovers followed with a goal a minute afterwards, and equalised a little while

later. The Rovers had now the best of the matters and got another goal. Result
– Blackburn Rovers 3 Notts County 2.

(*Birmingham Daily Post,* 17 December 1888)

After the first twenty minutes play the spectators saw little or nothing of the game,
owing to the heavy fog. The ball would suddenly disappear and would not again
be seen by those on the stand for fully a quarter of an hour. The roars of the
cheering gave notice of each goal scored by Rovers.

2-0 down after that Rovers played brilliantly with Brakes ... and Walton reviving
them ... the result was that the first goal was soon scored – or rather it should say
allowed, for the ball went fully 2′ over the bar, but owing to the mist Mr Norris
could not see it and Jimmy Brown claimed vociferously 1-2 – good old Jimmy.

(*Blackburn Times*)

GREAT GAME

Burnley 2 (Brady, McKay) *v.* PNE 2 (Thomson, Ross)

'Best game ever seen at Burnley.' (*Cricket and Football Field*)

This was one of the greatest games ever seen at Turf Moor, with 'the
Invincibles' recovering from twice being a goal down to grab a draw, thus
avoiding a first League defeat.

The largest crowd of the season, 8,000, were in anexpectant mood before
kick-off and both sides were heartily cheered when they entered the arena.
Kicking against the incline, Burnley put Preston on the defensive from the
start. W. Brady's centre was only inches away from being converted by the
on-rushing forwards and Howarth and Holmes did well to contain the home
forwards.

When the ball was moved to the other end, Cox made a fine save from
a Goodall effort. A free-kick close to the Preston goal was knocked wide
before Mills-Roberts saved a powerful shot from W. Brady.

On twenty minutes Mackay, to the 'tremendous cheer' of home fans,
shot the ball past Mills-Roberts to give Burnley the lead. Resuming the
attack, the 'keeper made a diving save to deny Friel before McFetteridge
hit a shot narrowly wide. As half-time approached, Mills-Roberts again
denied Friel and when the ball was cleared Russell, with a fine pass, picked
out Goodall, who quickly found Thomson, and when the Preston man
beat Berry he sent in 'a grand screw shot which went through off Lang and
made the game even'. A brilliant goal.

Burnley, though, were not to be denied a half-time lead and W. Brady
beat Mills-Roberts to make it 2-1 at the interval.

Preston were in a passing mood when the game restarted, but the equaliser
was the result of some brilliant individual play. It came on fifty-three minutes
when Ross dribbled round a couple of defenders and as Cox came diving

out he moved round him before putting the ball into the goal to make it 2-2. Gordon then shot just over before Burnley got themselves back into the game and Holmes was forced to clear quickly. A shot from A. Brady beat the Preston 'keeper but flew just over the bar.

There was then a big appeal for hands by Graham close to the away goal. This being 1888, it would have been only a free-kick, but when the referee Mr Cooper disagreed there were loud shouts of disapproval. Ross then shot over before both Bradys had shots saved by Mills-Roberts, who was having a fine game.

As the game moved towards its conclusion both sides fought to gain a winning advantage, but a 2-2 draw was nevertheless greeted with 'vociferous cheers' by fans of both sides. It had been a great game.

DULL FARE
Stoke 0 *v.* Everton 0

Damp, foggy weather is no friend of football, especially when the pitch is heavy underneath. Despite some vigorous play in the first half, and some decent saves from home 'keeper Rowley, the entertainment on offer was of a mediocre fare.

Soon after the restart, an injury to Costley saw him leave the field for the second time in a month, rendering Everton to ten men for the remainder of the match, which on this occasion was ten minutes less than the ninety after the referee decided that the darkness enveloping the Victoria Ground made it impossible for the players to see the ball properly. Any spectators still present must have heaved a sigh of relief when he sounded the final whistle.

PASSIONATE AFFAIR
Wolves 2 (Hunter, Brodie)[3] *v.* WBA 1 (Pearson)

The above powerful teams met on the Dudley Road ground, Wolverhampton, before two to three thousand spectators. Considerable interest was centered on the contrast of the visitors, being the holders of the English Cup. When the teams have met each other on previous occasions splendid matches have been witnessed.

The Wolves won the toss and kicked off up the hill and immediately an attack was made on the visitors' goal. The play at the commencement was of a very fast nature, the Albion speedily returning the leather. Within a minute from the start they placed the home team's fortress in danger but the goal shot went wide.

The Wolves managed to take the ball up the field but Albion, playing with great dash, rushed it down and once more the scene of the fight was in dangerous proximity to the home goal. Playing up, the Wolves had to fight before the visitors' fortress. They did not, however, manage to score and the Albion transferred the ball. Mason did good service in preventing the downward run.

Both teams played with much determination. The Wolves, playing with much dash, rushed the sphere up the field and a scrimmage took place in front of the Albion goal, the result being, after an exciting minute, a goal to the Wanderers,[4] which was obtained amid great cheering. Wykes was instrumental in running the ball up on the left and it was through this that the goal was scored.

The excitement rose as the Wolves who, up to the time of scoring the goal, had somewhat the worse of the play, got the upper hand of their opponents. Again placing the visitors' goal in danger, they shot out of a scrimmage, but the leather went outside the posts.

The left wing of the Albion did good service. Knight, by a long shot, placed his goal out of a possible danger but, in returning the leather, a foul accrued to the Wolves. Shortly afterwards the game was temporarily stopped owing to Brodie receiving a kick. He, however, resumed play. After this Albion got away with the ball and although they secured a little play in front of the home goal nothing came of it and Brodie ran the sphere up the field again. He kicked off to Wykes who muffed the ball.

The Wolves then took a foul from which Albion took charge of the ball and after some play in the mouth of the home goal they secured a goal from which they equalised.

The Wolves aroused themselves and played with much more determination, repeatedly attacking the visitors' goal. Brodie and Allen respectively made shots for goal, the latter putting just over the bar. Some minutes before half-time the fog had descended so rapidly that it was almost impossible to see the play at the opposite side of the field. Up to half-time the game had been hotly contested.

After the change of ends the Wolves attacked the visitors' citadel, the Albion defence having all its work cut out to protect the goal. The home pets continued to have the better of the play. In the course of several minutes the Albion only had the leather once over the division line. Although the visitors' fortress was continually stormed the Wanderers were unable to score.

The state of affairs continued for fifteen minutes or so after the restart. The Albion then exerted themselves and play became even for a time. The Wolves, however, replied to the challenge, getting the ball down and it was fouled in their favour. Allen made a splendid kick, dropping the leather right in the mouth of the Albion goal. Out of the scrimmage the ball was put through amid great cheering.

The Albion did well but the Wolves showed themselves superior both in passing and alertness. The game became somewhat quieter towards the close.

Wolves: Baynton, Baugh, Mason, Knight, Allen, Lowder, Hunter, Cooper, Brodie, Wood, Wykes.

Albion: Roberts, Horton, Walker, Bayliss, C. Perry, Timmins, Woodhead, Bassett, W. Perry, Wilson, Pearson.

Referee: Mr Brown (Stoke).

(From the *Midland Evening News*)

22 December 1888

PRE-CHRISTMAS CROWD WELL ENTERTAINED
Aston Villa 4 (Green, Goodall, Allen, Hunter) *v.* Burnley 2 (Brady, Mckay)

With Burnley having taken a point off Preston the previous weekend, there was an expectation among the crowd of a close, exciting game. And it was the visitors who scored first after Goodall had seconds earlier flashed a shot just past the Burnley post, Alex Brady hitting a shot from among a mass of attackers that Warner couldn't prevent dropping behind the line.

Defending their lead saw a number of fouls on the Villa forwards by the Burnley full- and half-backs and the crowd showed their displeasure by hooting at the away side. The equaliser was from an incident that today would see the attacker penalised and probably cautioned. Goodall had seen his shot caught by Cox, only for the 'keeper to be shoulder-charged over the line for a goal by Green. Villa then took the lead when Goodall's shot beat Cox and, despite claims for offside, the goal stood to make it 2-1 at half-time.

Hunter was the scorer of Villa's third goal, making space to receive the ball from Allen before hitting a fine shot that Cox had no chance of saving. Goodall, normally so reliable when in front of goal, then missed a real sitter before Allen added to the home side's advantage before McKay rounded off the scoring.

BOLTON IMPROVE
Bolton 4 (Weir 3, Owen) *v.* Accrington 1 (own goal)

Having won just three of their first thirteen League games, this easy victory for the home side moved them within a point of Burnley and Stoke in the struggle to avoid the need to apply for re-election at the season's end.

It was, however, Accrington who started the game brightly, Kirkham shooting just wide and Barbour appealing for a goal when his shot was charged away from the goal line. Bolton then missed chances to take the lead when Milne and Owen shot wide from close in. The Accrington goal then had a remarkable escape when a shot hit both posts before being kicked clear.

When a goal finally arrived, it was a controversial one, Weir's stinging shot was punched away by Horne and after Wanderers successfully appealed for a goal Accrington complained that the ball had in fact gone over rather than under the bar before the 'keeper's intervention. At half-time the score stood at 1-0.

The away side were level soon after the restart, when Hollough directed the ball into his own goal, but Bolton quickly scored twice as Weir, maintaining a bid for an England cap, grabbed another two goals to become the club's first player to score a League hat-trick and the first to ten goals in a season. Towards the end, 'another dash by the home forwards ended in Owen adding a fourth point' and when the final whistle sounded Bolton had won for the first time in five matches.

FIRST HOME WIN
Derby 3 (Bakewell, Higgins, unknown) v. Notts County 2 (Daft, Hodder)

Derby brought a run of eight successive defeats to an end with a first home League victory in a thrilling game between the two bottom sides. The home side had to come from behind when from what looked like an offside[5] position Daft, on fifteen minutes, scored.

Derby's equaliser came from a corner, but remains one of a number of goals from the first League season with no named scorer. The second does, however, with Bakewell making it 2-1. The Derby forward then created the third for his team before Hodder scored to set up a rousing second half contest in which Bakewell saw his shot crash back off the crossbar, Higgins and Cooper missed narrowly for Derby and Hodder and Daft were close to equalising for Notts County.

Victory moved the home side to within a point of their defeated opponents, but with eighth-placed Stoke and ninth-placed Burnley both on ten points, avoiding the need to apply for re-election was going to be difficult.

GOOD HOME PLAY
PNE 3 (Goodall 2, Dewhurst) v. Everton 0

The 800 spectators who had traveled from Merseyside to support their side cheered the Everton side on to the pitch.

Having won the toss, Preston asked Everton to kick against a strong wind in the first period and the away side were immediately forced onto the defensive. Dobson did brilliantly to block a fierce Dewhurst shot, but with just five minutes of the match having gone some fine passing carved open the Everton defence to allow Goodall to open the scoring.

Maintaining the pressure, Gordon was prevented from making it 2-0 when Nick Ross made a great tackle before Dewhurst and Drummond combined to set up Goodall for a shot that flashed over the bar. When Everton did finally break forward, Trainer saved confidently when Brown shot from 20 yards out.

Jimmy Ross was then denied by some fine defending by his brother Nick and Dobson, before Jack Angus hit a fine shot narrowly wide as Everton searched for an equaliser. It was Preston, however, who should had added to their advantage as half-time approached, but Dewhurst was wastefully wide when presented with a scoring opportunity.

Dewhurst didn't waste much time in making amends for his error, heading home an early second half goal and earning the hearty cheers of the Preston fans for doing so.

Everton, though, continued to play some intelligent football and Angus was denied a goal when Trainer saved his powerful drive. The winger was also unfortunate when, following a corner, he shot narrowly wide, before Nick Ross hit a free-kick that only just failed to hit the target.

With Everton continuing to attack, Howarth and Holmes were forced to hack the ball to safety and did so with 'some fine kicking'.

A great side, though, can turn defence into attack in an instant, and after some fine passing Goodall scored a splendid goal, after which Everton continued to push forward without success. Everton had played spiritedly but Preston's greater ability on the ball had won the day.

PEARSON POTS LATE WINNER
WBA 2 (Bassett, Pearson) *v.* Blackburn Rovers 1 (Fecitt)

With Arthur injured, Fergus Suter, one of football's most important historical characters (see Gazetteer of Players) was between the posts for his only Football League match. He could do nothing to prevent the home side taking a 1-0 half-time lead when England international Bassett, receiving the ball from Wilson, drove home from an acute angle. West Brom had earlier been unlucky when a Timmins shot flashed inches wide. Despite plenty of possession, Blackburn fashioned only one chance, which Roberts saved superbly.

When play resumed in the second period, the away side were in a determined mood but again found Roberts in fine form with his punching being particularly inspired. He could not, however, prevent Fecitt making it 1-1 when the Rovers forwards powered their way past the Albion defence. A hoped-for point, however, was denied to the away side when Pearson scored late on to make it 2-1.

WOLVES DO DOUBLE

Wolves 4 (Brodie, Wood 2, Wykes) *v.* Stoke City 1 (Sloane)

Wolves completed the double over Stoke with a comfortable victory after Brodie had scored early on to make it 1-0. While that remained the score after forty-five minutes, the home side scored a second within a minute of the restart when Woods beat Rowley before, according to the *Birmingham Daily Post*, the Stoke centre-forward (thought to have been Sloane) scored to keep his side hopes alive. Despite some fine saves from the Stoke 'keeper – surely a certainty to make his debut for England – thereafter he could do little to prevent Wykes making it 3-1. Just before the end Wood, 'with a clever shot', made the final score 4-1.

League Table

Team	Games	Points
Preston	16	29
Aston Villa	15	22
Wolves	15	20
Blackburn Rovers	15	19
WBA	15	17
Everton	15	16
Accrington	16	15
Stoke	16	10
Burnley	16	10
Bolton	14	9
Notts County	13	6
Derby	12	5

26 December 1888

POOR 'KEEPING GIFTS BOLTON THE POINTS
Derby County 2 (Higgins 2) *v.* Bolton Wanderers 3 (Brogan, Davenport, Milne)

Bolton began the game by kicking towards the canal end. In goal for Derby, Marshall started by failing to hold an Owen shot, an indication of what was to follow over the next ninety minutes.

The Bolton 'keeper, Harrison, was in better form, saving finely from Plackett and when Derby replied Robinson kicked away a low shot only for Higgins to return the ball into the goal amid tremendous cheering.

Higgins then turned provider but Bakewell's shot whistled narrowly wide as the home side maintained their early pressure. Combining well down the Derby left, Needham and Roulstone opened up the Bolton defence for Higgins to score his and Derby's second goal.

Bolton were handed a chance to get back into the game when, on collecting the ball, Marshall threw directly to a Bolton forward and when it was pushed inside Brogan made it 2-1 on twenty-five minutes.

The 'keeper was then too slow in getting down to a Davenport shot, and just five minutes after going 2-0 down the away side had drawn level. A clearly deflated home XI were then forced to defend deeply, although in a rare breakaway Higgins might have given his lead with a close in effort. At half-time the score remained level.

Immediately on the resumption, Derby suffered another reverse and Marshall was again to blame, being too slow in getting down to a Milne shot. The 'keeper then did well to fist away a Davenport effort before the home side attacked vigorously. Harrison saved a good shot from Higgins and then L. Plackett was denied by the Bolton 'keeper who, when he was beaten, saw Roulston's shot come back into play off the crossbar.

With half an hour to go, the drizzling rain that had been falling became torrential and the drenched spectators were, at least, warmed by Derby efforts to rescue the match. Nevertheless, these ultimately failed to be successful and Bolton travelled home with both points in a game that had largely been decided by the performance of the respective 'keepers.

PRESTON AT THEIR VERY BEST
WBA 0 *v.* PNE 5

This was one of Preston's greatest performances during a record-breaking season. Some fine passing, stout defending and lethal shooting saw them heavily beat a West Bromwich Albion side who didn't play badly, but were simply overwhelmed by a great side playing at its the peak.

The game opened at a quick pace, with both sides working to create scoring opportunities and 'keepers Roberts and Trainer being peppered with shots. Bayliss was nearest to scoring, but on ten minutes it was North End who struck first when Goodall created space and from 15 yards beat Roberts in the Albion goal. Warm applause for a fine piece of skill rippled round the ground.

A determined drive by the Throstles was unsuccessful in forcing an equaliser, with Howarth and Holmes showing some fine defensive skills to ensure their side retained the lead. West Brom were, however, unfortunate when Bassett slipped as he attempted to force the ball beyond Trainer from close range.

Under pressure Preston then demonstrated their passing abilities, retaining possession on a difficult surface, and only desperate defending by Timmins prevented Goodall adding to his opening effort. It was to be only a temporary reprieve for Albion, as a few minutes later Gordon grabbed Preston's second. On the restart, Woodhall was unlucky when his shot hit the top of the bar. Moments later, Trainer was up to punch away a dangerous cross before Pearson shot just wide.

There was then a fierce tussle in front of the North End goal, with at least a dozen players trying to kick it clear or belt it into the net. A goal then might have given Albion a chance, but when the ball was hammered upfield Ross dashed clear to beat Roberts and put Preston 3-0 up. A few minutes later Ross scored his second, leaving the score 4-0 at the interval.

On the restart, Gordon and Ross combined down the right only for the latter to miss when well placed as Preston started well before Albion pushed them back. Shot after shot rained down on the away side's goal, but all to no avail and on fifty-five minutes a quick and long pass was seized upon by Goodall who hurtled forward, maintained his balance and rounded Roberts to make it 5-0.

Despite the large deficit, Albion still refused to give up the ghost and continued to pile on the pressure, and might have reduced the arrears in the last half-hour but, though the final scoreline flattered the victors, there was no doubt that the better side had won. When referee Tooks sounded the final whistle, the players were loudly applauded by the Boxing Day crowd.

29 December 1888

ACCRINGTON RECOVER TO WIN ENTERTAINING GAME
Accrington 3 (Brand, Howarth, Lofthouse) *v.* Everton 1 (Brown)

Having won the toss, Everton forced Accrington to kick into the December sun and it was the home side that started in attacking form with Lofthouse sending in a shot that just cleared the bar. It was Everton, though, who scored first when following a fine Chadwick run Brown took the ball on to beat Horne in the Accrington goal.

On the restart, there was a big cheer for Nick Ross when he made a fine tackle before Lofthouse brought a grand save out of Charles Joliffe. Back at the other end, Horne then saved well from Chadwick before Brand thrilled the small crowd with a dribbling run and he then equalised from a free-kick awarded when Ross handled the ball just 6 yards out. Going in at half-time at 1-1, those present gave the players a well-earned cheer as the last of the sun disappeared beyond the horizon.

On the restart, the battle between Stevenson and Howarth down the Accrington left and Watson and Briscoe kept the crowd entertained and it was to be Howarth who scored the next goal when his long shot deceived Joliffe. When Lofthouse then took advantage of a fierce tussle under the Everton posts to fire home, it was clear that the home side were going to take both points and, despite Everton's continued efforts, the final result was a 3-1 home win.

DERBY STAY BOTTOM
Aston Villa 4 (Green 2, Allen, Goodall) *v.* Derby 2 (Spilsbury, Bakewell)

Derby remained firmly anchored to the bottom of the League, and seemed certain to need to apply for re-election, after a ninth defeat in ten matches. Villa were always in control and at half-time had taken a 3-1 lead, Green being found by Brown for the first, and after winning the ball back from the kick-off Allen then made a splendid run down the Derby right before delivering a good centre, which Green pushed home for his second goal.

League debutant Benjamin Spilsbury, scorer of County's first-ever goal back in 1884, got his side back into the match with a fine goal before Marshall, in the Derby goal made some good saves but was helpless to prevent Allen scoring from a Goodall centre.

In the second half, Villa put the game out of their opponents' reach when Goodall scored from a Brown cross before Bakewell reduced the arrears towards the end.

HOME GRIT WINS OUT
Burnley 1 (Abrams) *v.* Notts County 0

'Burnley may be said to have won by sheer determination than by the general superiority of their play.'

A frozen ground ruined any chances of a good game and while Notts County were the better side, and had more chances, it was Burnley who took both points in a game in which both 'keepers performed with distinction.

Cox in the Burnley goal defied an early body charge as he collected a high ball, before throwing out quickly to avoid being barged over the goal line by the onrushing forwards. Three early County corners were poorly delivered before Burnley put Widdowson under pressure, forcing him to punch twice when roughly challenged for crosses. When the 'keeper was beaten, Morley was back to hack clear and at half-time the game remained goalless.

Gallacher celebrated when his shot beat Widdowson, only for his effort to be ruled out for offside. When County replied Yates, back defending in an age when few forwards did so, cleared a goal-bound shot with Cox beaten. Notts then hit the crossbar with a long shot, and when the ball ran loose Cox was brave in rushing out to clear before being bundled to the floor.

On the hour mark John Abrahams, who had hardly had a kick up till then, carefully lifted his shot over Widdowson to put his side ahead. In response, County pushed forward and had a chance to draw level when they were awarded a free-kick for a foul just 6 yards out. Stout defence prevented an equaliser. Burnley were unlucky when a shot from Yates, who many home fans hoped to see playing for England in the forthcoming Home Internationals, hit the bar before another fine piece of 'keeping from Cox denied the onrushing County forwards.

With the game coming to its conclusion, Burnley's determination to hang on to their lead was summed up by Mckay. Left unconscious when he ran into his colleague, W. Brady, he was hauled from the pitch, had water chucked over him and returned for the final few minutes.

THREE WINS IN A ROW
Bolton 2 (Weir, unknown) *v.* Wolves 1 (Cooper)

Bolton completed a merry Christmas with a third consecutive victory that raised real hopes of avoiding the need to apply for re-election at the end of the season. They had to do it by coming from behind after Cooper scored on six minutes for Wolves. It was Weir who scored the equaliser, a flying shot beating Baynton just before the interval.

The winning goal (the name of the scorer remaining unknown) came early in the second period after Bolton 'scored from a determined rush', after which the sides had chances to add to their tally.

PRESTON MADE TO FIGHT ALL THE WAY
PNE 1 (Goodall) *v.* Blackburn 0

This match was brought off at Preston before 8,000 spectators. The Rovers were without Arthur, Fecitt and Beresford. North End kicked off uphill. The game at once became fast, both goals being attacked in turn. Townley and Brown made a great effort for the visitors, and were conceded a corner. William Holden, Darwen's 'keeper who had been drafted in to play in the Rovers goal, saved against the post, and Forbes and James Southworth showed grand back play, but North End obtained two corners. The Rovers were quicker on the ball than their opponents, and their defence seemed impregnable. Trainor had to save, and Holden threw a shot away from Ross. The game continued fast until half-time, when no goals had been scored.

After changing ends, the game was as keenly contested as ever. Trainor soon had to throw away, and both sets of backs showed stubborn defence. The home forwards had not much chance of displaying their usual combination, so determined was the Rovers' tackling. Trainer had to fist out from a corner, and then, from a series of attacks by the home forwards, nine minutes from the finish, Gordon got round Forbes, and cantering off the line, Goodall scored amid great enthusiasm. The home team were very aggressive after this, but Trainor had to save one hot shot from Walton. The game was hotly contested to the finish, the result being a victory for North End by one goal to none.

BRILLIANT 'KEEPING FAILS TO FOIL THE BRILLIANT BASSETT
WBA 2 (Bassett, Wilson) *v.* Stoke 0

In a repeat of the opening-day scoreline, West Brom beat Stoke 2-0. They had to wait to do so after the East Midlanders turned up half an hour late, and when the game got underway the pace was frantic, with the irrepressible Bassett three times testing Rowley, who twice caught and threw the ball out quickly in order to avoid the advancing Albion forwards.

On thirty-five minutes, Bassett got his reward for persistence when, after getting to a loose ball, he hit a well-placed shot. The little winger was as fast as lightning over the short distances of up to 12 yards that matter in top-class football – especially around the goal – and a lesser player would never have scored such a goal.

The second half was virtually all Albion and 'but for the excellent goalkeeping of Rowley the score of the home team would have been increased on several occasions'. Only towards the very end was the Stoke 'keeper beaten when a Wilson cross was caught on the wind and taken beyond him.

5 January 1889

TEN-MAN VILLA SLUMP TO DEFEAT

Burnley 4 (Yates 2, Gallacher, Brady) *v.* Aston Villa 0

Late-arriving Villa had lost three of their players when caught in heavy fog when changing trains at Manchester. Hoping for some post-Christmas charity from referee Mr Cooper of Blackburn, the Midlanders found none and were ordered to get changed quickly and the match kicked off thirty-five minutes late with eleven men against eight.

Burnley was more generous and had failed to exert any pressure when two of the missing players arrived to help their colleagues after ten minutes of play. In the event, Devey was to turn up more than an hour late but was refused permission to take the field by the referee. In his absence Villa, needing to win to keep up some pressure on runaway leaders Preston, chose to play with four forwards, one of whom was Hodgetts, back after a lengthy suspension.

Burnley went ahead on twenty minutes when Yates headed a fine goal. With Villa rarely getting forward, home 'keeper Cox had no shots of note to save in the first period but the Clarets had to wait till the second forty-five minutes before making their advantage seriously count.

Gallacher scored from a scrimmage in front of goal, the referee deciding to overrule Villa's strong appeals for offside. Brown, injured in a strong challenge, battled on bravely for his side, however they should have fallen further behind only for W. Brady to miss when well placed.

There was then a great cheer when a misplaced pass took the referee's hat off his head before A. Brady and Yates grabbed Burnley's third and fourth. The result meant that if Preston had beaten Notts County then the League championship was decided.

PRESTON CLINCH LEAGUE TITLE
PNE 4 (Goodall 2, Edwards 2) *v.* Notts County 1 (Daft)

This match came off at Preston on Saturday before about 3,000 spectators. Notts County kicked off up hill, and at once forced the game in the home ground where it remained for some time. The North Enders, breaking through, took the ball along their line, and Ross sent in a fine long shot. This failing, North End again got off, and Edwards taking from Goodall forced Widdowson to throw out.

Keeping up the pressure, the home team put in several grand shots, the bombardment closing by Edwards shooting through from offside. Another fierce attack was brought about by Edwards making a splendid dash down the field, the effort producing a fruitless corner. Howarth, missing his kick, gave McLean an opening, but a feeble attack nullified it, and Trainer saved easily.

After twenty-five minutes of play, Ross compelled Widdowson to handle, and the ball struck Goodall, the rebound taking it between the posts. Hodder dodged Holmes, but the half-backs were quick to the rescue to prevent danger. At the other end, there was a clean shot to John Clements, and the visiting right-wing smartly ran the ball down until pulled up by Holmes. After some fine centre-forward play, Edwards again scored off Ross. No further goal was made up to half-time.

Seven minutes after the restart, Daft scored for Notts, but the home team then won two corners. A heavy fog now settled on the field and it was impossible to see above 20 yards from the stand. The ball was kept in Notts territory where the brothers Shelton, McLean and Clements defended admirably, but in twenty minutes Goodall scored a third goal for North End.

The visitors were in no way daunted, and continued to play pluckily. They could not, however, make any headway against the fine play of the home halves, and the ball was generally in Notts territory, where another corner was conceded. At last Notts broke away, and for a short time troubled the home defence, but North End retaliated, and five minutes from the finish Edwards scored a fourth goal for Preston, who won by four goals to one.

WOLVES TOO GOOD FOR LOCAL RIVALS
WBA 1 (Woodhall) *v.* Wolves 3 (Brodie, Hunter, Cooper)

Wolves completed the double over their local rivals by coming from behind to collect both points. In the first period the home side played impressively and after Bassett hit a shot just too high there was no surprise when some smart passing between Wilson and Pearson opened up the Wanderers defence to allow Woodhall to make it 1-0.

This was the prelude to fierce Wolves pressure, and Roberts had to be at his best to help preserve his side's lead. It was Brodie, belting home from close range after defenders and forwards fought over the ball, who brought the away side level. Responding Albion forced two quick corners, but to no avail.

Both sides made strong challenges and when Wilson and Woodhall were both injured it was a number of minutes before the game resumed. At half-time the score remained level.

Albion besieged the Wolves goal on the restart, but found Baynton in fine form, and the visitors fought heroically to prevent their local rivals taking the lead. Some of the tackling was fierce, and Bassett suffered a bad kick from fellow England international Charlie Mason that forced him to leave the pitch to receive attention.

'At this point the game was very rough, and the spectators hooted the players who indulged in rough or foul charging.' (*Birmingham Daily Post*)

With a draw looking the most likely result Brodie, Wood and Cooper charged down the field and barged past Roberts to make it 2-1, Cooper getting the final touch.

Shot after shot was then rained down on the Wolves goal before, in the final seconds, a long kick forward saw Hunter run clear to give his side a third goal and a famous victory.

12 January 1889

POOR WEATHER BUT FINE MATCH

Aston Villa 6 (Allen, Hunter, Brown, Hodgetts 2, Goodall) *v.* Bolton Wanderers 2 (Barbour 2)

The crowd at this match was down to just a couple of thousand, the consequence of a wet and miserable afternoon.

Kicking towards the Wellington Road end, the home side were faced by a strong wind. Yet their passing and combination play, often weak in previous games, nevertheless forced Bolton onto the defensive. Brown, receiving from Green, put Villa ahead. This was only maintained by a fine Warner save from a powerful Brogan drive. The 'keeper was fortunate soon after when Davenport's shot beat him but was ruled out for offside. Third time lucky and Barbour equalised with a long shot as half-time approached.

On the restart, Hodgetts was just wide with a hard shot, before he then centred for Allen to make it 2-1. Hodgetts then drove home 'an exceedingly good goal' to double his side's advantage. A downhearted Wanderers side appeared to give up trying as after that Allen, Hunter and Hodgetts quickly added to the home eleven's advantage before a late Barbour effort reduced the arrears.

LUCKY PRESTON MAINTAIN UNBEATEN RUN

Blackburn 2 (Walton, Fecitt) *v.* PNE 2 (Thomson, Dewhurst)

Preston's unbeaten run was to be maintained in this match, but only just; after it appeared the home side had scored a late winner, North End's appeal that the ball had gone out of play was granted by the referee.

Arriving as the manager of the champions, the Preston manager William Sudell could well have cast his mind back almost eight years when Blackburn had travelled to Deepdale to play North End on 26 March 1881. The home side were taught a brutal lesson by the visitors who, with their recruited paid Scottish players of Fergie Suter, Hugh McIntyre and James Douglas, wiped them 16-0.

Sudell took note and within three years virtually the whole of the Preston side were composed of professional, mainly Scottish, players. Nick Ross, the Hearts captain persuaded to travel south, might have found work as a slater with a Mr Bradshaw but his real job was as a footballer – and the best-paid one in the world at the time! When Preston refused to tell lies when asked if their side who played against Upton Park in the 1884 FA Cup match were professionals, it set the scene for a battle that could only ever have one victor.

Once professionalism had been established then the need for regular, guaranteed games to pay player's wages made a Football League almost inevitable.

Played at Blackburn before 11,000 spectators. North End played the same team as at Preston in the first game, while the Rovers had McCowen and Whittaker, of the second team.

North End kicked off, and the Rovers were first to attack, John Southworth heading over the bar. A few minutes later they again swarmed round the visitors' goal, and Trainer saved a hot one from Fecitt on the goal line. Thompson then made tracks, but was pulled up by James Southworth.

Gordon quickly returned, and centring grandly, Thompson headed a little too high. The Rovers then returned to the attack and pressed hotly. At length the visitors' backs relieved, and some pretty passing by their forwards ended in Thompson putting the ball through, amid cries of 'offside'. An appeal was made, but disallowed.

On the ball being restarted, the Rovers secured a free-kick for 'hands'. James Southworth placed the ball splendidly, and Walton forced it home. Gordon was again busy with another good centre, but James Southworth headed the danger away.

A free-kick for 'hands' close in gave North End a good opening, but nothing beyond a useless corner resulted. The Prestonians still kept up the pressure, and debutant 'keeper Billy McOwen had to use his feet. However, the Rovers broke away, and Trainer had again to save. After an appeal for 'offside' by the Rovers when in midfield, the North End forwards played the ball beyond Forbes and James Southworth found no response from the referee. Half-time arrived with the score standing at one goal each.

The second half was opened by North End getting well down, Dewhurst scoring after five minutes' play. The next minute saw the Rovers round Trainer, who only stopped a shot from Townley at the expense of a corner. This came to nothing, but Whittaker gaining possession, and passing to Fecitt, that player, after the ball had crossed in front of the visitors' goal, equalised the game.

Shortly afterwards the Rovers scored again, but a claim that the ball had been out of play was sustained. The Rovers after this pressed and the defence of Holmes and Howarth was taxed to the utmost. Some good half-back transferred matters to the other end, where McOwen saved twice in good fashion. Play, which up to now had been very busy, quietened down considerably.

(Report from *Lancaster Gazetteer*)

ABSENT 'MERCENARY' PLAYERS CAN'T PREVENT ACCRINGTON GRABBING A POINT

Burnley 2 (Yates, Brady) *v.* Accrington 2 (Wilkinson, Kirkham)

It transpired on Friday, however, that Barbour and Brand had disappeared somewhat mysteriously, and Saturday night's telegrams revealed the fact that they played that afternoon for Sunderland Albion, at Sunderland. In their absence the Reds had to enlist Arthur Wilkinson and J. Holden from the reserve.

(*Accrington Times*)

It was the attraction of better wages that had brought Scotsmen Barbour and Brand south at the start of the season to play for Accrington. Now they journeyed north to play in a high-profile friendly match in Sunderland, lured no doubt by a better pay day.

The game was played in damp, murky conditions and kicked off at 2.40 p.m. After some initial exchanges it was Kirkham who raised the spirits with a magnificent run of almost 80 yards before being brought down by Berry for a free-kick. In the away goal, Horne did well to block a Gallacher shot, but was beaten on twenty-five minutes when McKay shot between the uprights amid 'vociferous cheers'. Horne then did brilliantly to keep out a powerful Friel drive, after which the game became tangled down in midfield with some fierce challenges on both sides.

Just before the interval Accrington, to the cheers of their fans, equalised when, following an interchange of passes between Lofthouse and Bonar, the ball was pushed to Wilkinson who 'very neatly got past Lang and Berry and made the score equal'.

It was to take Burnley just eight minutes of the second half to restore their lead when, following a goalmouth tussle, A. Brady made it 2-1. A hard shot almost brought Accrington level, the ball striking the crossbar. Lofthouse was then rudely barged over by a dual challenge from Friel and Keenan (a certain foul and probably at least one booking today), but in 1889 play continued without interruption.

Yates was to be denied by a fine save from Horne before Accrington skipper George Howarth swapped Lofthouse with Wilkinson, the latter taking up the centre-forward's position as the Reds sought a second equaliser.

The change worked a treat when Wilkinson raced down the right before pulling the ball back for Lofthouse to hit a shot that would 'have been a puzzler for any goalkeeper' making it 2-2 amid huge cheering from the away fans.

A tense final fifteen minutes failed to produce a winning goal, Gallacher missing the best chance when left with just Horne to beat. It meant a great game deservedly ended with a point apiece for the local rivals, both of whom had played hard but fair. Wilkinson and Holden had proved themselves as able 'substitutes' for Barbour and Brand and Accrington thus maintained their three-point lead over Burnley in the League table.

DERBY SHOW IMPROVED FORM
Derby 3 (Cooper, Plackett, Higgins) *v.* Wolves 0

With just five points from fourteen games, bottom-placed Derby County gave themselves an outside chance of escaping the bottom four 're-election zone' with a comfortable victory over a poor Wolves side.

Kicking against both the wind and rain, the home side nevertheless scored twice in the first half, Cooper scoring first with a close in effort before L. Plackett doubled the advantage. Derby, though, were grateful to Marshall for maintaining their lead when he made fine saves from efforts by Allen and Knight.

On sixty-seven minutes, Higgins made it 3-0, after which many spectators left early to avoid the heavy rain.

ANGRY ALBION PERSUADED NOT TO LEAVE PITCH
Notts County 2 (Hodder, Cursham) *v.* WBA 1 (Bassett)

Sleet had reduced the crowd to just 2,000 spectators and they saw Roberts make two fine early saves to deny Daft and Jardine. On twenty minutes, though, the Albion 'keeper stood no chance when Alf Shelton crossed and Hodder belted the ball beyond him. Bassett and Wilson both had golden opportunities to level the scores before Cursham doubled the home side's advantage. Having been unlucky with a shot that hit the crossbar Albion left the field at half-time with the score 2-0.

On the restart, a long low shot by Bassett soon reduced the arrears. Albion then felt they had equalised, reported in the *Birmingham Daily Post* on 14 January as follows:

Bayliss led a brilliant attack, and apparently shot through, but the referee ruled that the ball did not pass between the posts. Bayliss was naturally annoyed, and threatened to withdraw his men. The game was completely suspended for five or six minutes and a 'scene' seemed probable. The referee [Mr McIntyre of

Manchester] was so positive that at last Albion gave way and accepted a corner, which proved fruitless.

The game was then vigorously contested to the close without any change, Notts winning by two goals to one.

ROWLEY SHOWS ENGLAND FORM
Everton 2 (Davies, Milward) *v.* Stoke 1 (Milarvie [official records say McSkimming])

Starting with ten men, Stoke were grateful to Rowley who saved good shots from Chadwick and Watson. Chadwick then beat the 'keeper, but his shot flew behind after striking the upright. A fine pass from Watson then set up eighteen-year-old Alf Milward, playing his second League game, for the opening goal before both forwards forced Rowley into further action with fierce shots. Milward was in particularly good form and the Anfield Road spectators were cheering the Buckinghamshire teenager every time he received the ball.

However, the largest cheer was reserved after the interval for Rowley who 'received a magnificent reception from the spectators on taking his place in the goal-mouth'. (*Liverpool Courier*)

Rowley wasn't going to let them down, saving two shots from Chadwick and Milward – who were to forge a fine partnership over the following seasons, helping Everton to win the title in 1890/91 – before Everton scored their second with a header from Joe Davies. The home side then suffered a blow when Weir left the field injured, at which point Stoke took up the attack with McSkimming scoring after a tussle under the posts.

Towards the end of the game, it was though the home side who seemed the most likely to add to the score, Milward missing two good chances before Rowley again foiled Chadwick to earn the applause of the crowd at the end. The Stoke man had never played for England, but that was surely bound to change.

'His display in goal is undoubtedly the finest that has been seen at Anfield enclosure this season.' (*Liverpool Courier*)

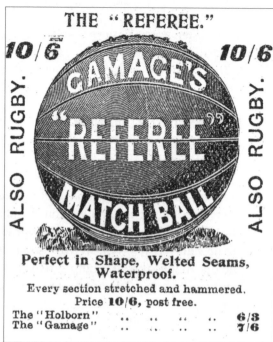

Above left: A statue of Football League founder William McGregor standing outside Villa Park.

Above right: Match ball advert.

Below: Everton advertised widely for players.

Clubs placed adverts in the local press as they sought to boost attendances.

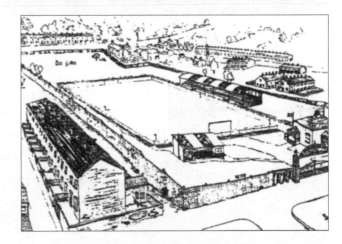

Leamington Road, Blackburn's ground.

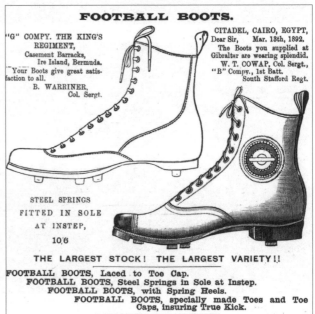

Advert for football boots. (*Cricket and Football Field*)

Pikes Lane, Bolton,
is now covered
by housing.

The Racecourse
Ground, Derby,
remains a cricket
ground today.

Today there is no way
of knowing that Wolves
played their first League
match at this location.

The site of Victoria Ground, Stoke.

Stoney Lane is where West Bromwich played their first League season.

Thorneyholme Road, Accrington, remains a cricket ground today, but the football side that played there in 1888/89 is long since gone.

Above left: Archie Hunter (Aston Villa).

Above right: Charlie Perry (WBA).

Below: Notts County played their 1888/89 fixtures at Trent Bridge, which remains a well-known cricket ground today.

A sketch of Everton's Anfield ground in 1888/89.

An illustration of Trent Bridge in 1889.

A photograph of Trent Bridge in 1889.

Pikes Lane, Bolton, where the first League goal was scored by Kenny Davenport.

Clockwise from top left: Billy Bassett (WBA); Bob Holmes (PNE); Dennis Hodgetts (Aston Villa); James Trainer (PNE); Harry Daft (Notts County); John Goodall, the best player of his era; Alf Milward (Everton).

Above: Preston avenged their defeat at the 1888 FA Cup final by beating their conquerors WBA 1-0 in the 1889 semi-final played at Bramall Lane, Sheffield. (*Cricket and Football Field*)

Below: Wolves were no match for Preston in the 1889 FA Cup final, the Lancashire side winning 3-0.

Above: The Preston North End 'Invincibles', 1888/89. Back row (non-players) R. W. Hanbury MP, Sir W. E. M. Tomlinson MP, W. Sudell (secretary manager). Back row (players): Drummond, Howarth, Russell, Holmes, Graham, Dr Mills-Roberts. Front row: Gordon, Ross, Goodall, Dewhurst, Thomson. (*Image courtesy of the PNE historian*)

Left: Jack Southworth.

Opposite and following page: The match report for the 1888/89 FA Cup final.

THE FINAL OF THE FOOTBALL ASSOCIATION CUP CONTESTS.

Preston North End, about whose foremost position in Association football there has long been but one opinion, secured a deserved victory in the final of the English Cup Competition at the Oval on Saturday. The bad luck which on previous occasions has disappointed them at the last moment, spared them on Saturday, and combination, skill, and training won the day. There were 20,000 persons present at the contest, which was between North End and the Wolverhampton Wanderers, who had defeated the Blackburn Rovers in one of the semi-finals, the Preston team having in turn won their tie against West Bromwich Albion, the holders of the trophy. Preston having selected to defend the Vauxhall goal, which gave them the assistance of the wind, the Wanderers kicked off from the gasworks end. Brodie, who started the ball, was intercepted by Dewhurst, who passed to Thomas, but Hunter saved. The Preston men were soon on the ball again, and play settled in the Wanderers' quarters. Shortly afterwards hands by Ross was of great use to the Wanderers, and they worked right away into Preston's ground, when some fast and exciting play ensued. Allen and Brodie put in some smart work, the latter making a splendid effort to score, but without success. From a foul for Preston in the centre they rushed down, and Thomson sent in a straight shot near the post. Baynton fell on to the ball and just succeeded in averting a goal. Knight and Brodie next got dangerously near the North End citadel, but Holmes saved in splendid style, and again drove the play into neutral ground. Lowder sent the ball well up to Preston's back, but Howarth quickly returned, and, passing to Gordon, the last-named got close in goal; he passed back to Ross, who put in a hot shot, the ball striking the crossbar and rebounding to Dewhurst, who landed a magnificent goal—a very fast shot indeed. The game so far had progressed fifteen minutes. Restarting, the game was not so fast as heretofore, though the men still played a heavy game. The Wolverhampton Wanderers mostly had to act on the defensive, the Preston forwards being very smart indeed. A corner looked like being fruitful, but Allen saved. They, however, could not get away, and after barely half-an-hour's play, Ross brought an enthusiastic cheer by securing a second goal for Preston, though Baynton ought certainly to have saved this point. Throughout the goal-keeping had proved the Wanderers' weak spot. The next event of note was a grand run on the extreme wing by Gordon, but he failed to take a good aim at goal. Hands for Preston right in front of goal looked dangerous, but the ball going right into Baynton's hands he managed to save defeat. The game continued to be keenly fought up to the interval, but nothing further resulted, and Preston crossed over leading by two to nil. So far the League champions had displayed much the best form, and scarcely left the ultimate result in doubt. Resuming, after an interval of about five minutes, the Wanderers were seen to better advantage, and for a quarter of an hour they kept their rivals at bay, and now and again made efforts to score. They, however, passed too long, and gave way to kicking the ball, scarcely any dribbling being done. At length Preston made an incursion, and a shot by Dewhurst almost came off. The Wanderers failed to relieve, and Thomson added a third goal, after rather more than twenty minutes' play. Ross next attempted to pass Baynton, but failed, as also did Thomson. Dewhurst had a favourable opening, but did not succeed. The "Wolves" next got away, and in the last few minutes Preston were pressed somewhat. Howarth cleared from hands right in front of goal amidst tremendous applause, and transferred play into mid-field again; but not for long, as Preston returned to the attack, and right up to the finish the Wanderers played a strictly defensive game. No further points were obtained, so that the Prestonians became the holders of the cup for the first time, winning by three goals to nil. The teams were as follows:—Preston North End: Dr. R. H. Mills-Roberts (goal), R. H. Howarth and R. Holmes (backs), G. Drummond, D. Russell, and J. Graham (half-backs), J. Gordon and J. Ross (right wing), J. Goodall (centre), F. Dewhurst and S. Thomson (left wing) (forwards). Wolverhampton Wanderers: G. Baynton (goal), Baugh and Mason (backs), Fletcher, Allen, and Lowder (half-backs), Hunter and Wykes (right wing), J. Brodie (centre), and Wood and Knight (left wing) (forwards). Umpires: Lord Kinnaird (Old Etonians) and Mr. J. C. Clegg (Sheffield). Referee: Major Marindin, R.E., C.M.G. (President Football Association).

19 January 1889

LARGE CROWD WITNESS FINE SECOND HALF PRESTON DISPLAY
Everton 0 *v.* Preston 2

Everton had won seven in eight games prior to kick-off in a match played on a heavy ground before an Anfield crowd of 15,000.

When the Liverpool side pressed from the off, Holmes was prominent in preventing the opening goal before a marvellous Trainer denied Chadwick a save to the cheers of the large crowd. Holt's clever pass then gave Everton a second chance but Chadwick drove the ball wide of the post. When Angus and Chadwick combined, it was left to Howarth to make a fine tackle to keep the scores level before Angus was guilty of a poor miss as Everton continued to dominate proceedings.

When Preston did finally get forward, the 'demon' Jimmy Ross forced Joliffe to make his first save of the match, and although Everton continued to have the majority of play it was the away side that came closest to open the scoring when, just before half-time, Graham's cross hit the post. At half-time, with the scoreline at 0-0, it was clear that Preston would have to play a lot better in the second forty-five minutes if they were to maintain their season-long unbeaten League run.

Yet, at least at first, Everton continued to play better football, and Bob Kelso missed a glorious chance before Ross scored in the sixtieth minute to put Preston one goal to the good. Holt at centre-half for Everton was certainly not going to go down without a fight, and his fine passes to the wide men constantly kept the Preston backs on their toes. But as the game entered its final stages Preston began to show the skills that had taken them to the League title, passing the ball skilfully in difficult conditions. It was no great surprise when the away side doubled their lead, Dobson being unable to prevent Goodall's run and dribble, leaving the Preston centre-forward to push the ball past Joliffe in the Everton goal.

Although Chadwick had a chance to reduce the arrears, the match ended with Preston two goals to the good and knowing that they were only a game away from completing their League season undefeated. This, however, would entail taking at least a point from Wellington Road, where Aston Villa were not only undefeated but had won all of their ten matches. The match in two weeks time was sure to be a thriller for what was certain to be a packed crowd.

ROVERS WIN LOCAL DERBY
Accrington 0 *v.* Blackburn Rovers 2 (McLellan, own goal, Southworth)

The Rovers came out winners in their match with Accrington, notwithstanding the absence of Arthur, Townley and Fecitt. Beresford returned to his place as Walton's partner on the right wing, but was scarcely up to his usual form.

Bernard Whittaker again appeared on the left, and James Duerden partnered him. McOwen kept his place between the sticks. The 'keeper was to have a great deal of work to do, and the smart way he did it won for him golden opinions as to his skill in goal. To his clear saves is undoubtedly due the fact that Accrington did not score, and so long as he keeps in present form the Rovers will not want for a goalkeeper of the first order.

The backs and half-backs were, as usual, up to the mark. Accrington suffered in this part of the field, McLellan at full-back being clearly responsible for the two goals scored by the Rovers. In fact he kicked the first goal in for them.

Considerable apprehension was felt as to how the forward division would work owing to the absence of Fecitt and Townley and the fact that Beresford was out of practice. It was soon seen that fear on this ground was baseless. Cemented by John Southworth in the centre, the two wings played well, Whittaker and Duerden (the new blood) showing promising form.

The Rovers got both of their goals in the first half and the whole of that time did the most of the pressing. The game was more even in the second half with neither side scoring. It need hardly be said that the Rovers victory was received with great satisfaction in Blackburn, as many were doubtful about the result.

Accrington can scarcely plead that their team was not up to full strength, for they had fetched Barbour back from Sunderland Albion and had gone all the way to Grimsby for McBeth to fill Brand's position. Saturday's result has imparted confidence to the Rovers and their supporters on the issue of the English Cup tie next Saturday between the sides.

(Report taken from *Blackburn Times*)

VILLA SNATCH BOTH POINTS
Aston Villa 2 (Hodgetts, Allen) *v.* WBA 0

'The supporters of each side mustered in strong force.' (*Birmingham Daily Post*, 21 January 1889)

There was beautiful weather for the highly anticipated first League game between the two great West Midlands rivals. Great cheers greeted the arrival of the teams, with the Baggies fans reserving a particular cheer for their 'new' man, Harry Green at full-back.

Having won the toss, it was something of a surprise when the away side chose to kick uphill against the wind. Despite this, West Brom started well enough, but two early corners failed to trouble Warner in the Villa goal.

It was Roberts who made the first save, brilliantly denying Brown from close range before the visitors through Wilson forced Warner to make a fine save.

With the match continuing to thrill the large crowd, Hunter beat Roberts only for the ball to pass just beyond the far post and out for a goal-kick. Warner then again denied Wilson with another good save and then when the ball was kicked clear a strenuous tussle between Hodgetts and Horton was warmly applauded by both sets of supporters.

Bassett was close with a long shot before Villa forced two more corners, both to no avail as the game continued to sparkle. It was the home side who made the breakthrough when all five forwards made a combined dash down the middle and, pushing aside the two West Brom full-backs, it was left to Hodgetts to beat Roberts with a low shot that was accompanied by 'tremendous cheers'.

Wilson, looking to make it third time lucky, was again denied by Warner before Goodall seemed to have extended Villa's lead, only to see his goal bound shot headed over by Allen, his teammate.

Villa were now very much in charge, but corner after corner came to nothing and when half-time arrived and the score remained 1-0. With the wind behind them in the second half, the away side were in with a good chance of earning at least a draw.

A clearly confident West Brom began by pushing Villa back, but Warner was once again in fine form, with Bassett denied by a flying save. On fifty-five minutes, it was the home side who struck, Allen receiving created space around him before hitting a powerful shot for what was a great goal. This had the effect of inspiring his side, who penned West Brom in their own half.

There was some determined defensive play, but when Albion did manage to escape their own half they found the Villa defence impregnable with Burton at right-half making some fine tackles as he continued to break up any attempts by Pearson and Wilson to combine down the West Brom left.

When the referee sounded the whistle, Villa had triumphed 2-0 in what had been a splendid match.

DERBY CERTAIN TO FINISH IN BOTTOM FOUR
Burnley 1 (McKay) *v.* Derby 0

On the opening day of the season, Derby had travelled to Bolton and won 6-3, but this defeat virtually guaranteed that the bottom place club would be applying for re-election in a few weeks time. Kicking with the wind in the first period, Derby had failed to score and although it took until five minutes from the end for McKay to give the home side the lead, this was no more than Burnley deserved. Had it not been for some fine 'keeping by Marshall, the home side would have won a lot more easily.

The first period was a drab affair for the small crowd. Cox racing out to clear some dangerous long balls was about as good as it got, with the inability of both sides to control and pass the ball at speed failing to impress.

On the resumption Burnley, at least, improved and from a number of tussles for the ball Marshall made three decent saves before A. Brady struck the crossbar for the home side. Gallacher blasted wide with the goal at his mercy and with little to do Cox, the Burnley 'keeper, could be seen patrolling the halfway line, safe in the knowledge that the soaking wet leather ball could not be kicked beyond him.

With five minutes to go, McKay beat Marshall, but with Friel standing behind the 'keeper there were strong appeals for offside before the goal was given.

BROGAN GETS JUST DESSERTS WITH LATE EQUALISER
Stoke 2 (Milarvie 2) *v.* Bolton 2 (Owen, Brogan)

After kicking off, Bolton were soon forced to defend deeply and fell behind on ten minutes when Harrison made a mess of a Milarvie shot.

Debutant Wilf Merrit kept his side ahead with a great save from a Brogan effort, before Weir was denied a goal when Stoke's appeal for offside was allowed.

Bolton equalised when Ramsey kicked Owen's shot into his own net and they might have taken a half-time lead, had Brogan not fired over when well placed.

The Bolton forward was desperately unlucky on the restart, his shot hitting one post and bouncing across the goalmouth to hit the other before a grateful Merrit pounced on the ball. When Milarvie then restored Stoke's lead, the Lancashire side were not going to take it lying down and, just thirty seconds later, Brogan got his reward for a fine performance by making it 2-2.

After the match the new owners of the nearby Hanley Music Hall entertained the teams.

GOOD TWO POINTS FOR HOME TEAM

Notts County 3 (May 2, Cursham) *v.* Wolves 0

Wolves arrived without Brodie and Harry Lowder, who were playing for the North against the South in a match used by the England selectors as the base to choose the side for the forthcoming Home International matches against Ireland, Wales and Scotland.

The South was to win the match 2-1 before a 10,000 crowd at Sunderland's Newcastle Road ground. Charles Wreford-Brown of the amateur side Old Carthusians opened the scoring.

Despite the absence of the two players, and with William Rose making his debut in goal, it was Wanderers who started the more brightly on a dull day. McLean at full-back twice intervened to clear, before Notts attacked down the left, with Daft and May combining well, and the latter scored with a fine shot after the Shelton brothers had worked an opening. A shot that smacked against the crossbar maintained the home side's pressure and, with forty-three minutes gone, Cursham made it 2-0, which is how the score remained when the sides took their five-minute interval break.

Rose had made many fine saves in the Wolves goal but was unable to prevent May scoring his second of the match after the left winger came in from out wide to meet Hodder's cross and make it 3-0.

Brodie's loss at centre-forward meant there was never any serious possibility of Wolves getting back into the game, and it was no surprise when the game finished in a fine victory for the home XI.

Origins of the Term 'Soccer'

Charles Wreford-Brown is the man responsible for the term soccer, derived from *rugger* in rugby and as-*soc*-iation football. Brown was a member of the Football Association council from 1892 until his death fifty-nine years later, serving the last ten years as vice president.

26 January 1889

ROBBERY

Accrington 1 (Kirkham) *v.* Notts County 2 (Daft, own goal)

A reshuffled Accrington side, with McLennan at half-back and Stephen Singleton partnering Stevenson, were to dominate this match before a battling County side grabbed two goals in the final ninety seconds of the game to snatch both points.

The man of the match was Widdowson in the Notts goal, and in the first half, with a strong wind behind them, the 'Reds' pounded his goal; within fifteen minutes of the start the 'keeper had already made fine saves from Lofthouse, Barbour and Kirkham. Corner after corner was defended stoutly by the away defence but, just as it seemed they might escape without conceding a goal in the first forty-five minutes, Kirkham gave his side the lead in the forty-third minute.

On the restart, Gutteridge finally made Horne earn his wages in the Accrington goal before the home side returned to the attack, which would today have earned a penalty – the ball was handled just 3 yards out, the resulting free-kick being blocked by the County defenders on the line.

On eighty-nine minutes Daft, largely anonymous until then, managed to make space but his shot was poor. Inexplicably, Horne seemed to not realise the danger and the ball trickled past him and over the line to make it 1-1. Worse still, ninety seconds later, with no one around him, McLennan preferred to pass the ball back to his 'keeper rather than plant it forward and it sailed into the goal to give County a 2-1 victory.

Oh what a surprise! For Accrington to have had pretty nearly all the play this afternoon and allow the Lacemen[6] to get the verdict in the last minute or two was indeed unfortunate.

(*Cricket and Football Field,* 26 January 1889)

BOLTON PUSH ON
Bolton 3 (Weir 2, Owen) *v.* Blackburn 2 (Walton, Southworth)

Kicking with a strong wind behind them, the home side, whose players wore armbands in memory of the club's groundsman who had died during the week, was ahead within two minutes when Weir scored with a great shot. McOwen then kept Rovers in contention with a series of good saves, as the away defence came under stern pressure when Bolton forced five corners in as many minutes.

On the stroke of half-time, Bolton doubled their advantage when Owen swept home the rebound after McOwen had brilliantly saved a Roberts shot. On the restart, Forrest shot just wide, before on fifty minutes Walton reduced the arrears.

Resuming the attack, Barbour was checked by Forbes, but when the ball ran loose Weir scored Bolton's third 'amid ear-splitting cheers'. Then Jack Southworth beat Harrison to set up a tight finish, before the referee came in for 'considerable hostility' after he disallowed a Weir effort for offside. At the end 'a mighty cheer heralded the Wanderers' victory'.

BAKEWELL GRABS LAST-GASP WINNER
Derby 2 (Bakewell, Cooper) *v.* Stoke 1 (Edge)

This was a poor match, in which the home side overcame the early loss of Needham to beat a disappointing Stoke side. The game only came to life when Edge scored five minutes before the break, neatly finishing a cross from Billy Hutchinson, playing his only League game, after which Derby pushed forward.

On the restart, a quick series of corners failed to produce the equaliser and, just as it appeared Stoke were to leave with both points, Cooper made it 1-1 on seventy-five minutes. Rowley then made a number of good saves, but at the death he was beaten by Bakewell, the final whistle sounding even before Stoke had time to resume the match.

VILLA RECOVER FROM THREE DOWN TO TAKE A POINT
WBA 3 (Bassett, Pearson 2) *v.* Aston Villa 3 (Allen 2, Green)

After the exciting match between the sides on the previous Saturday, it was natural that their return would arouse a lively interest. The 'immense crowd' was also blessed with some remarkably warm weather for the time of year. There were several changes in the sides; Goodall dropped to right back and Devey took the centre-half position for Villa, while for Albion, Hendry went to right back and W. Perry was moved to partner Bassett on the right wing.

Brown was just wide as the game started at a gallop. Only five minutes had elapsed when a fine Timmins ball found Bassett unmarked, and from close in he easily beat Warner to put his side ahead. It was the England international's twelfth League goal and surely confirmed that he would again be representing his country in 1889. There was almost an immediate equaliser, but Hodgetts saw his shot kicked off the line by H. Green.

On nine minutes, Bayliss was celebrating when his shot beat Warner but his effort was disallowed for offside. However, just three minutes later West Brom did extend their lead when Pearson scored. There was then further trouble for Villa when Harry Yates twisted his knee, thus rendering him a virtual passenger for the rest of the game.

The away side's chances looked to be over soon after when Pearson, with his twelfth League goal, made it 3-0 to the huge cheers of the home supporters.

Villa got back into the match with a goal that would not be permitted today. Collecting the ball in his hands, Roberts was so heavily charged by Hodgetts that he ended up smashing into the boards behind the goal, and with the ball running loose Allen put it between the posts. With the 'keeper injured, a good few minutes' break was needed before the match resumed at 3-1, which was the score at the interval.

On forty-eight minutes, Hodgetts found himself unmarked and his header made it 3-2. Now playing with the wind, Villa pushed back their opponents, and only some fine saves by Roberts prevented the equaliser.

However, 'at length T. Green, by a neat shot, made the score equal, amid vociferous cheers from the Villa supporters'.

A stung West Brom pushed forward, but a handball just 6 yards out from the goal was of little avail as Villa packed their goal with every player. A few minutes later, a great tackle by Devey blocked Perry, before Hodgetts cracked a shot that beat Roberts but not the post. As a result, the game ended all square at three goals each.

'KEEPER'S EFFORTS KEEP SCORE DOWN

Wolves 5 (Lowder, Brodie, Wood 2, Knight) *v.* Everton 0

Returning to the Everton goal for the first time in a number of weeks, Smalley suffered an uncomfortable afternoon and was beaten within ten minutes; when a rush forward by the Wolves forwards overpowered the Everton backs, he was helpless to prevent Lowder scoring. Wood then beat the Everton 'keeper to double his side's advantage, and although he then saved a Brodie grass-cutter in the follow up, Knight hit a high shot out of his reach to make it 3-0. Now it seemed like the 'keeper was playing Wolves on his own and, try as he might, it was no surprise when Wood made it 4-0 before the break.

Playing with the wind in the second half, Everton had much more of the play and Wolves were grateful for some fine saves from Rose, but when Brodie made it 5-0 the game as a contest faded.

DERBY DOUBLE DELIGHT FOR ROVERS

Blackburn 4 (Southworth 2, Townley, Walton) *v.* Burnley 2 (Gallacher, Brady)

After winning the toss, Blackburn kicked with the wind behind them towards the Preston Road goal. Cox, in the Burnley goal, had to be alert, as three shots from distance were driven towards him in quick succession. The home side's pressure continued with two corners and when the ball ran loose Townley failed to control it when left unmarked.

In an age when full-backs rarely ventured beyond the halfway line, the crowd were amused when James Southworth came forward before releasing the ball. He'd clearly enjoyed the experience, because a few minutes later he repeated it and when he crossed the ball his brother, Jack, made the score 1-0 with a great shot. The Blackburn centre then hit a fine shot that whistled home to put his side deservedly 2-0 ahead. It was his sixteenth League goal of the campaign.

Having hardly been anywhere near their opponents' goal, Burnley got back into the game when Gallacher rattled home a great shot and then, to the shock of the Blackburn partisans, equalised with another fine effort, this time from A. Brady. It was his seventh of the season, making him Burnley's top scorer in their first League season.

Having hauled themselves back into the game, Burnley were then disappointed to go into half-time a goal down when, after a centre from Townley, Walton made it 3-2.

On the restart Blackburn, now playing with ten men due to an injury to James Southworth, continued to look the more likely to score again and Fecitt should have done so when he was sent clear, only to fluff his shot as Cox moved towards him. The home side did, however, make it 4-2 when, if the reports are believed to be true, Walton scored 'a clever goal' before Douglas and Yates collided with each other and both had to be taken off for treatment. With the Rovers man bleeding profusely, the home side were now, with Yates returning to the field, playing with two players less than their opponents.

'The game was by no means a pleasant character, an all-together unnecessary amount of brute force being used, and there being far too much going for the man instead of playing the ball,' reported the *Burnley Gazette*.

The competitive nature of this fixture has been maintained ever since. In December 1891, Burnley were beating Blackburn 3-0 at Turf Moor in a match that had seen the teams reduced to ten men each after the dismissal of two players for fighting. At this point the Rovers team, after complaining unsuccessfully to referee J. C. Clegg, walked off the pitch (with the exception of 'keeper Arthur). Burnley kicked off again, scored and the match was abandoned. This was the first League game of a handful of first class games left uncompleted. Afterwards, the Football League insisted the result was 3-0.

9 February 1889

'THE INVINCIBLES'
Aston Villa 0 *v.* Preston 2

When these sides had last clashed at Wellington Road during the previous season's FA Cup competition it proved a historic occasion when the game was abandoned after the crowd invaded the pitch with North 3-1 to the good. Although a replay date was agreed the FA intervened to order the result to stand. This was the first of a handful of first-class games in English football to remain uncompleted.

Immense interest attached to the visit of the Preston team to Birmingham today. It was their last League match and they were to meet the only one of the other eleven members of the League whom they had not beaten in the tournament. When the Villa were at Deepdale the score was a goal each, so that today's game was expected to be the greatest of the series. Unfortunately the North End were without the valuable services of Robertson, who fractured his collarbone at Bootle a week ago.

Ten thousand spectators gathered. The ground had a thin covering of snow and there was a wind blowing. The North End kicked off with the sun in their eyes, and the game became fast. Hodgetts and Allen darted down the left, but were pulled up by Drummond and shot over and play of a give and take character followed. After pretty passing Dewhurst centred, Goodall shooting over, and a beautiful centre by Gordon missed right in front. North End was now pressing and from a corner Thompson headed against the bar.

An excellent run followed by the Villa forwards, but Howarth pulled them up and the visitors' right made away, the ball again being put wide of the Villa posts. The home backs were in rare trim, and their forwards were very speedy. Ross won another corner, Gordon heading by the upright. Green and Allen were then rather dangerous, and made Holmes kick out, but the ball was soon again near Warner, who had to stop a shot from Ross. Brown and Hunter were let in through misunderstanding and Mills-Roberts conceded a corner. The Villains were playing desperately hard, but kept in check by the North End backs. The ball was frequently in touch through the wind.

A grand attempt by Brown made Dr Robert Mills-Roberts give a corner away from under the bar. Play was now very even. From a free-kick Brown was again looking dangerous but was again repulsed by Howarth and Thomson. Thomson coming away, he and Goodall got right through the Villa backs, but the latter shot over the bar. A corner then fell to North End, and the game was taken in midfield. North End got a free-kick for a foul, but soon Holmes had to head away, and Green shot over. At the interval no goals were scored.

No time was lost in crossing over and after Devey had kicked out Gordon won a corner. In a minute Dewhurst scored a goal with a splendid shot. North End had a free-kick near Warner, but Hodgetts got clear away, but the game was soon again near Trainer, where beautiful passing ended in Thomson shooting wide and after another run by Hodgetts Ross shot wide. Give and take play now became the order, the halfbacks on both sides showing up well until Ross again shot. Howarth neatly robbed Hodgetts and Allen, but Green centred from the right and Hodgetts missed another chance. Gordon ran down the right, but was floored by Cox, but Ross centred and Thomson just missing. Dewhurst again putting the ball through. The point was protested against for offside, and after some consideration the goal was allowed. This was after sixteen minutes' play. On restarting Gordon again centred and Ross put the ball wide.

Villa seemed to fall off, but from a pass by Hunter, Hodgetts struck the crossbar and Mills-Roberts put over, the corner coming to nothing. North End was again threatening when they were ruled offside. Repeated efforts of the Villa forwards were nullified and from a pass by Gordon, Goodall nearly scored another. North End continued to have the best of matters, and was very aggressive, winning two more corners and winning a good game by two to none.

(Report from *Cricket and Football Field*, 9 February 1889)

Brilliant Display

North End arrived at New Street Station at seven minutes to three and had dressed in the saloon, so no time was lost in starting. From the start it was obvious that the Villa were carefully trained and they exhibited some fine fast runs. On the other hand North End relied on their passing, but though favoured by the wind could do nothing to half-time in the way of shooting. In fact at the interval it was difficult to surmise which way fortune would turn.

However, in the second half the Prestonians soon showed their superiority and played a grand passing game to the finish.

The Villa appeared to have been over-trained and fell away greatly towards the end. Their forwards showed poor combination, Brown, Green and Hodgetts being the best. Devey was the best of the halves. Both backs played well. Warner could not have stopped either goal of the winners, who all played grandly. Drummond was a good substitute for Robertson. The defence was very safe, and the forward play much admired.

Among the Preston North End it was a case of superlatively fine individual and collective work. Nothing grander than the North End play in the second half of the game has ever been seen at Perry Barr.

The perfection of unity of action, through the command over the ball, dashing attack, impregnable defence, and untiring physical exertion were all seen at their best in this grand eleven.

Every pass those forwards made had some intent and purpose; each man knew where the ball would go, why it was sent there, and who would receive it.

There were lessons given at Perry Barr on Saturday for even the Villa to take to heart. It was combination of the highest order; a picture and poem of football motion. The Prestonians have left a magnificent impression behind them on that huge assemblage who saw them beat the Villa.

(Birmingham Daily Times)

The general expression of opinion after the match was that Preston North End was the cleverest Association team in the world; and after Saturday's display I am bound to concur in this opinion.

(Birmingham Correspondent, Athletic News)

The feat North End have accomplished, gaining eighteen victories and four draws – a record for which no comparison can fairly be found at English Association football. Attention will now be directed towards the progress of Preston in the competition for the Association Cup. On public form Preston once more look to have a better chance of ultimate success than any other eleven and whether they win or not, their record in the League matches must stamp them, as the champion club of 1888/89.

(Daily News)

EVERTON FAIL TO EXACT REVENGE
Everton 1 (Chadwick) *v.* Wolves 2 (Wood, Knight)

Everton were deprived of Ross's service, who was away on County duty for Lancashire against Staffordshire. His absence had a big impact and Everton failed to avenge their heavy defeat at Wolves two weekends previously on a frosty pitch that would today be declared unplayable.

Brown missed narrowly in the early moments, before Albert and Edgar Chadwick combined to force Baugh into conceding a corner. Rose, in the Wolves goal, then saved a number of shots, and when the away side attacked Smalley fisted the ball away under pressure from Woods. Some fine passing, especially considering the conditions, was ended when Chadwick put Everton ahead at half-time with his sixth League goal.

Playing downhill, Wolves put Everton under early pressure. Indeed, they might have fallen further into arrears had Rose not stopped a splendid shot from Watson. The 'keeper continued to deny the Everton forwards and was rewarded when, in the final quarter of the game, Hunter and Cooper combined to set Wood up to level up the scores before Knight hit a late winner, with Everton's appeals for offside being overruled by the referee.

23 February 1889

EVERTON ON THE SLIDE
Everton 0 *v.* WBA 1 (Bayliss)

The away side was missing Bassett, on international duty at Stoke against Wales. For Everton, Waugh was back after a long-term injury and he received a good reception from the 10,000-strong crowd. The first half was a scrappy affair, Dick providing some entertainment with his long punts forward, but there was disappointment when Davies missed an excellent chance after Ross set him up. Pearson and Wilson combined in the best moment for West Brom to force Smalley into saving in order to keep the score level at the interval.

Within three minutes of restarting, the away side had taken the lead when Bayliss received a return pass from Timmins before hitting home. Pearson who, like Bayliss, completed the first season having played all twenty-two League matches, then tested Smalley from a free-kick before Davies again missed when well placed. Towards the very end, Ross was unlucky when his fine shot hit the crossbar, only for the ball to fly behind into the crowd. West Brom's fine defence had held up to anything Everton could throw at them and both points were heading south.

POOR SHOW BY COUNTY
Wolves 2 (Wood, Knight) *v.* Notts County 1 (Jackson)

A depleted home side still had too much for a poor County side as Wolves wrapped up their League season with two points. Having won the toss, the Wanderers began with the wind behind their backs, but kicking uphill.

County were close with the first serious effort at goal, but the ball passed just over the bar. Wood then did well with a header and from a free-kick Widdowson in goal stopped a fine shot. A disallowed offside goal failed to dent the home side's confidence and it was no surprise when Wood, with his thirteenth League goal of the season, put them in front. A riled County then piled forward, and it was only thanks to some fine 'keeping by Rose that Wolves went into the half-time break in the lead.

In the second half, Knight doubled his side's advantage before a Harry Jackson goal at least had the benefit of keeping the game alive for the small crowd.

2 March 1889

BURNLEY'S DEFEAT PUSHES THEM INTO DEEPER DANGER
Derby 1 (Cooper) *v.* Burnley 0

In their final League match of the season, Burnley were missing Yates. The outside-left had played in every League game, but now his presence was needed for England in their game against Ireland (where he scored a hat-trick). His absence, which left Friel as Burnley's only constant presence, was certain to be a big loss to a side that needed to win to remain outside the bottom four. Derby's chances of doing so were remote but with four games still to play, victory would give a glimmer of an opportunity.

The game was to be fiercely contested with the home side scoring a late winner. Debutant John Pitman made a good early save from McKay, and in response County fashioned a good opportunity, only for Bakewell to push the ball over the bar. Roulston was having a fine game in defence for Derby and made a number of important interceptions, but Burnley were also grateful when Needham failed to beat Cox when left unmarked from close-in.

On seventy minutes, Derby grabbed the all-important goal when, following a darting run, Bakewell centred accurately and Cooper finished with great skill from a range of around 12 yards. Intense pressure from Burnley followed, but Pitman in goal was in good form and helped ensure his side won the match by the tightest of margins. Both sides now seemed certain to finish in the bottom four.

5 March 1889

EASY FOR BOLTON

Notts County 0 *v.* Bolton 4 (Brogan 2, Davenport, Barbour)
Played at Castle Ground.

The first of two games between the sides in five days, with both lying in the bottom four, victory was essential to avoid applying for re-election. Victory would take Bolton from ninth up to sixth, while a home victory would give them an outside chance of finishing in eighth place.

Defending the Pavilion end, Notts were the first to show and Bolton 'keeper Harrison had to be alert to a number of high crosses. Brogan then beat Widdowson, but County's appeals for offside were granted and the game remained at 0-0, before the home side also had a 'goal' for offside chalked off following a May shot. Davenport then got beyond Gutteridge and, although Widdowson got his hands to the ball, the shot was strong enough to put Bolton 1-0 in the lead, which is how the score remained at the interval.

With a slight wind in their favour, Bolton forced Widdowson into making three early saves, before Daft hit a tame shot when well placed to give his side an equalising goal. Hodder then hit a shot which only the outstretched boot of Harrison prevented from entering the goal, but soon after the County forward was guilty of a poor miss when he had only the 'keeper to beat.

Under pressure Bolton responded, and Barbour fired just wide before George Brown, playing at centre-half for County, held on to the ball for too long. When he was dispossessed, Bolton doubled their advantage. With the game now won, Bolton stepped up the pressure and Brogan scored with a fine free-kick before a final effort made it a comfortable away victory, thus ensuring that Notts County would be applying for re-election.

9 March 1889

BOLTON OUT OF DANGER IN FINE HOME WIN

Bolton 7 (Turner, Brogan, Barbour 2, Davenport 3) *v.* Notts County 3 (May, Jackson, unknown)

Having beaten their opponents in midweek, Bolton were 'cocksure' of repeating their success, and had the incentive of knowing that victory would not only take them out of the bottom four, but up the table to fifth.

The Wanderers and County had first locked swords competitively during the 1883/84 FA Cup, when Bolton recovered from two down to grab a draw at Trent Bridge and force a replay. Back at Pikes Lane, a huge crowd of 20,000 assembled and gate receipts totalled £468. This didn't include the money taken by an enterprising local farmer, who charged to watch the match from a hill he owned overlooking the ground. With Billy Gunn in great form, County won a tense thriller 2-1 watched, according to J. A. H. Catton, by a 'mass of folks at a fever heat never matched' by any game he witnessed during his fifty years watching football. County lost to Blackburn in the semi-final. County and Bolton were to play each other at the 1894 FA Cup final when, inspired by a hat-trick from William Logan, County won 4-1. 'The Notts men had the journey on them'.

For Bolton, Tyrer was left out with Turner of Black-Lane Rovers making his League debut after scoring in a friendly against Helliwell the previous week. It was the new man who gave his side the lead on just three minutes before County almost immediately equalised. Following a scrimmage, Davenport restored his side's advantage before Brogan made it 3-1 with a shot that Clements blocked with his feet but couldn't prevent from entering the goal. Now on the wrack, the away side fell further behind when, with Davenport barging Widdowson out of the way, Barbour shot home into an empty goal. It was an effort that would not be allowed in today's football, but that gave Bolton a 4-1 half-time lead.

The County 'keeper, this time left unimpeded, brilliantly denied Brogan when the game recommenced in the second half, before Flitcroft made a lovely tackle on Daft to deny the County centre-forward a chance to reduce his side's arrears. Back on the attack, a fine save again denied Brogan from Widdowson, but on sixty-five minutes a fine goal reduced the County deficit to just two at 4-2.

A pinpoint Barbour pass then gave Weir an unstoppable opportunity, and even though Jackson almost immediately made it 5-3, the game as a contest was ended on eighty minutes when Weir got his second goal of the match to make it 6-3.

Clearly dispirited, County wilted and close to time the home side notched a seventh to win the match 7-3, thus completing a League 'double' over their opponents in four days.

Considering the heavy, muddy conditions, the game had been a fast one, at the end of which both teams 'presented the appearance of veritable mud-larks'.

DERBY SHOW SOME FINE TOUCHES
Derby 5 (Higgins 4, Cooper) *v.* Aston Villa 2 (Allen 2)

Both sides were missing key players, with Bakewell and Ferguson out injured for the home side and Hunter, Green, Coulson and Yates absent for Villa. As was the tradition at the time, on winning the toss the visitors chose to kick with the sun and wind at their backs. However, an early corner proved unproductive before Hodgetts brought a fine block by Haydn Morley.

At the other end, Warner did well to save a Smith shot before H. Plackett shot over the bar when well placed. Returning to the attack, Villa's Devey and Hodgetts both missed narrowly before Allen's shot beat Pitman and, despite strong appeals from Derby that the ball had failed to go between the posts, the goal was given.

Stout defence initially held up a vigorous Derby response before Higgins equalised with a powerful dive, only for Villa to restore their lead just before the interval when Allen pushed home a good Brown cross.

It didn't take the home side long to again equalise, with Cooper scoring with a low drive before from a John Lees cross Higgins, exhibiting good control of the ball, put his side ahead for the first time in the game. The response of the away side was a good one, and with both sides committed to attack, Pitman and Warner in the respective goals needed to be in fine form.

Towards the end, however, Hodgetts was forced off after a heavy collision and this seemed to take the sting out of his side's confidence. In the final few minutes, Higgins rattled home two more to take his personal total to four and Derby's to five.

16 March 1889

DERBY PUSH ON AT LOCAL RIVAL'S EXPENSE

Notts County 3 (Bailey, Daft, Jackson) *v*. Derby 5 (Bakewell 2, Higgins 2, Cooper)

Played at Castle Ground.

Despite heavy flooding in Nottingham the previous week, the ground was in fine condition for the last County game of the season. There was a chance for Bailey, a youngster from Melton Mowbray with experience at Loughborough Town and Long Eaton Rangers, to impress as the Notts executive committee looked to the following season.

With the pitch being used for a game that overran and the referee Mr Jope late, there was a delay to the advertised start. Derby started brightly and Lees fired narrowly wide, before Bakewell gave his side the lead. In response, Wardle shot just over, but soon after Brown's fine pass was swept home by Higgins to put the away side two goals ahead. It was soon three; Bakewell beating Widdowson with a well placed effort. Swapping to inside right from the centre, Bailey got his side back into the game with a headed effort to leave his side 3-1 down at the interval.

After early pressure at the start of the second period, the home side further reduced the arrears when Daft hit home. A great McLean run, however, soon restored Derby's two-goal advantage as Cooper swept his final pass home. 'This success was heartily applauded by the Derby supporters', reported the *Nottingham Daily Express*.

Now sure of victory, Derby showed some nice touches before Higgins with a cross shot made it 5-2. It was his twelfth League goal of the season. In the final few minutes of the game, Jackson headed home Notts' third to round off a fine game.

23 March 1889

AWAY FANS SEE SIDE GRAB LATE WINNER
Accrington 2 (Kirkham 2) *v.* Bolton 3 (Brogan, Roberts, Davenport)

A 1.45 p.m. special train from Bolton meant the Wanderers had plenty of fans behind the ropes when the match got underway, but after early home pressure the travellers would have been disappointed when Accrington struck first on eighteen minutes through Kirkham.

Soon after, Lofthouse had a chance to make it 2-0, but reacted too slowly to a loose ball before Barbour missed a great chance and Bolton escaped at half-time by being only a goal down.

Lofthouse compounded his earlier failure by missing an open goal on forty-seven minutes and then, two minutes later, Bolton took their chance to draw level, with Brogan hitting home. It was his thirteenth League goal of the season, equal with Weir. Two minutes later, the Wanderers were ahead when Roberts cut inside to hit a fine shot between the posts. Soon after, Horne in the Accrington goal, in making a save, crashed into the post and needed to be revived after being knocked out cold. To the cheers of all, he then made a good save from Brogan before Kirkham, from a scrimmage in front of goal, made it 2-2.

That seemed certain to be the final score but, with just seconds remaining, Davenport beat Horne to give his side both points in what had been a tight, hard-fought encounter.

30 March 1889

GOOD TWO POINTS FOR EVERTON

Everton 3 (Davies, Milward, Waugh) *v.* Blackburn Rovers 1 (Whittaker)

This game had originally taken place on the first Saturday in January when, with the ground in a dangerous condition, the sides had agreed to provide entertainment for the crowd that had assembled, on the basis that whatever the result the match was to be declared a draw. In the event Everton had won 1-0 and the Football League committee had instructed the sides to replay the game.

In this replayed game, Blackburn-born Chadwick's appearance meant he became the first Everton player to play in every League game in a season. Milward opened the scoring with a fine shot but Whittaker made it 1-1 at half-time with a free-kick awarded close to the goal. Waugh, with a neat shot, restored Everton's advantage in the second half, after which the home side dominated the game. Davies added to the score after Forbes brought down Brown close to the Rovers goal. In the final quarter, Barton's heavy handling of Waugh was the occasion for retaliation, after which the pair appeared to conduct their own personal duel that kept many of the crowd entertained to the very end of the match.

6 April 1889

BOTTOM FOUR BATTLE LEAVES NEITHER SIDE SATISFIED
Stoke 1 (Sawyer) *v.* Derby 1 (Plackett)

With bottom-placed Stoke guaranteed to finish in the bottom four, interest in this game centred on whether the visitors could take both points and give themselves an outside chance of overtaking eighth-placed Accrington in the race to avoid needing to apply for re-election.

Accompanied by a number of supporters, Derby left Midland Station at 2.00 p.m. and were greeted with warm weather when they ran out at the Victoria Ground to kick-off at 4.00 p.m. Within a minute, they were ahead when Plackett scored, but with Roulstone out injured and a number of players carrying knocks, they rarely looked like adding to their lead in a poor first half.

Early second-half chances for H. Plackett and Cooper were missed and the Rams were grateful to debutant Enos Bromage, who made a number of good saves to preserve his side's lead. Just as it seemed Derby would escape with a clean sheet, Sayer beat the 'keeper and, despite appeals that the goal had gone in just as the referee sounded the final whistle, it was of no avail as a vital, precious point was lost. Derby now had to win their final game at Blackburn and hope Accrington lost theirs against Stoke at home, to avoid a re-election application.

With this match the County concluded their home League engagements, and though their position on the list is considerably below what we might have expected six months ago, it is undoubtedly better than could have been hoped for at Christmas. We believe we are expressing the sentiments of Derbyshire footballers when we say that they have earned the right to be considered one of the best twelve clubs in England, and we hope that the League will again award them a place in the competition.

(Derby and Chesterfield Reporter)

15 April 1889

ONE GAME, TWO GOALS AND ONE STRIKER NEVER SEEN AGAIN!
Blackburn 3 (Mitchell 2, Haresnape) *v.* Derby 0

Once debutant Mitchell (first name not known) had opened the scoring on five minutes, there was never any chance of Derby taking both points to give themselves a chance of finishing in eighth place in the League. Jack Southworth missed an easy chance to double Rovers' advantage, but it was not until the second period that the game was made safe, Mitchell scoring from a free-kick and Haresnape after a scramble in front of the goal. The result meant that fourth-placed Blackburn had gone through the inaugural Football League season unbeaten at home, with seven wins and four draws. This proved to be Mitchell's only game for Blackburn Rovers. One League game, two goals but never heard of again!

20 April 1889

THE LAST MATCH
Accrington 2 *v.* Stoke 0

The last of this season's League fixtures came off at Accrington this afternoon, when Accrington played Singleton instead of Pemberton, while Sayer and McSkimming reinforced Stoke.

Accrington took the wind in the first half, and only twelve minutes went by when Gallacher scored with a fine shot after capital work among the forwards. Up to the interval the game was in Accrington's favour. Barbour missed a goal when right in front, and Tattersall followed up with a shot that took Rowley all his time to clear.

Three times the ball was sent against the crossbar. Rowley's goalkeeping was wonderful. Horne only had one dangerous shot to stop up to half-time, and when Accrington crossed over they played a fine game against the wind. Barbour scored in five minutes after a capital run by Lofthouse and Kirkham.

Stoke rushed up and Milarvie shot an offside goal. Other attempts were very near but Accrington managed to keep their end to the finish and won by 2 to 0. So finished the League programme of 1888/89 and the 'reds' by this victory now have slightly the best of Everton on the list.

(Report from *Cricket and Football Field,* 20 April 1889)

Thorneyholme Road
The pitch at Thorneyholme Road Cricket Ground was possibly the best in the Football League in 1888. Firstly, it was flat; unlike in reports from other grounds, there are therefore no references to sides kicking off 'up the hill'.

Pitches in 1888/89 had very few markings on them. Boundary lines had been introduced in 1870, before which only two goal posts and four corner flag posts were the order of the day. In 1888, the goal area was two arcs of 6 yards radius from the goalposts, and when the penalty kick was introduced it could be taken anywhere along the newly introduced line of 12 yards. In 1902, the penalty box was introduced, along with the penalty spot and goal area. The 'D' on the edge of the box was introduced in 1937/38 to ensure all players were 10 yards away from a penalty taker.

At the start of the 1888/89 season, Accrington had promised their fans they would construct a new pavilion but failed to do so. Thorneyholme Road is still a cricket ground today.

Final League Table – 22 Games Played

Team	W	D	L	F-A	Pts	
Preston	18	4	0	74-15	40	(Champions)
Aston Villa	12	5	5	61-43	29	
Wolves	12	4	6	50-37	26	
Blackburn	10	6	6	66-45	26	
Bolton	10	2	10	63-59	22	
WBA	10	2	10	40-46	22	
Accrington	6	8	8	48-48	20	
Everton	9	2	11	35-46	20	

Applying for Re-Election

Team	W	D	L	F-A	Pts
Burnley	7	3	12	42-62	17
Derby	7	2	13	41-61	16
Notts Co	5	2	17	40-73	12
Stoke	4	4	14	26-51	12

[N.B. Where teams were tied on points, goal average was used to decide the final position.]

Re-Election

This was held on 3 May 1889 at the Douglas Hotel, Manchester.

The main business of the day was the re-election process. It was agreed that the four clubs who had finished at the bottom of the League (Burnley, Derby, Notts County and Stoke) should be allowed to vote, putting those from outside the League at a considerable disadvantage.

Applications were submitted from Sunderland Albion, South Shore, Sunderland, Bootle, Newton Heath, Sheffield Wednesday, Birmingham St George's, Grimsby Town and Walsall Town Swifts. The very fact that nine clubs were keen to join demonstrated that the Football League was here to stay, although, significantly, none were from the south and it was only when Arsenal joined in 1893 that the League moved to be truly national.

In the re-election vote, Stoke collected ten votes, Burnley nine, Derby eight and Notts County seven. All were subsequently re-elected, with St George's attracting the next highest vote with five.

The AGM also agreed that, having no trophy to be presented to League champions Preston, they should instead be presented with 'a flag bearing the winner's name, together with the English coat of arms and the town motto'. It was not to be until 1891 that a championship trophy was purchased and Everton became the first to be awarded it when they pipped twice-champions Preston to the title.

The 1888/89 FA Cup

The most famous cup competition in the world had a new format for the 1888/89 season. With the League having been reared on the permanence of its fixtures, FA council member R. P. Gregson proposed that qualifying rounds be introduced, with exceptions given to the vast majority of League clubs – the exceptions being in 1888/89 Bolton Wanderers, Notts County and Everton.

However, when the latter found themselves drawn to play Ulster away in the first qualifying round, the Merseysiders withdrew rather than make an expensive trip across the Irish Sea. The 1888/89 tournament saw its only game ever played on Christmas Day when Linfield Athletic beat Cliftonville 7-0 in a fourth qualifying round second replay. It meant that the Belfast club joined the other qualifiers in the draw for the first round (Wrexham, Notts County, Sheffield Heeley, Chatham, Grimsby Town, South Shore, Old Brightonians, Small Heath and Sunderland Albion), who had seen Sunderland prefer to withdraw rather than give them a much-needed revenue boost in the form of a good crowd for a fourth qualifying-round game. This was a shrewd move that ultimately starved Albion of funds and left Sunderland the winners when the former went out of business.

The holders of the FA Cup were West Bromwich Albion, who had beaten Preston North End 2-1 in the 1888 FA Cup final played at the Kennington Oval. The key question was: could Preston go one better and win the competition? Such was the reverence in which the FA Cup was then (and for many years afterwards) held that a failure to do so would have rendered their League success as almost worthless among some fans.

The 1888/89 FA Cup was the eighteenth time that the competition had been held. Wanderers had won the first two and by also capturing the Trophy in 1876, 1877 and 1878 they became the first to win it three seasons running. In 1882, Blackburn Rovers became the first side from the North to get to the final played at Kennington Oval. Around 1,200 spectators, who journeyed south on two special trains, accompanied them.

What a fantastic occasion that must have been for all those lucky enough to make the trip! Their arrival in the capital caused a real stir, with a snobbish article published in the *Pall Mall Gazette* attacking – and not for the last time – football fans' uncouth manners and broad accents. London, it suggested, had been invaded by a 'Northern horde' – and quite right too, as football began its journey towards becoming the nation's favourite sport by 1946.

Rovers lost in the 1882 final to amateurs Old Etonians, but after Blackburn Olympic beat the holders in the following season's final, Rovers then returned to win the Trophy for three seasons in a row before Aston Villa beat West Bromwich Albion 2-0 at the 1887 cup final.

First-Round Results – 2 February 1889
Burnley 4 *v.* Old Westminsters 3
Swifts 3 *v.* Wrexham 1
Notts County 2 *v.* Old Brightonians 0
Nottingham Forest 2 *v.* Linfield Athletic 2
Aston Villa 3 *v.* Witton 2
Accrington 1 *v.* Blackburn Rovers 1
R Blackburn 5 *v.* Accrington 0
Chatham 2 *v.* South Shore 1
Grimsby Town 3 *v.* Sunderland Albion 1
Halliwell 2 *v.* Crewe Alexandra 2
R Crewe 1 *v.* Halliwell 5
Wolverhampton Wanderers 4 *v.* Old Carthusians 3
Derby County 1 *v.* Derby Junction 0
Notts Rangers 1 *v.* Sheffield Wednesday 1
R Sheffield Wednesday 3 *v.* Notts Rangers 0
Birmingham St George's 3 *v.* Long Eaton Rangers 2
Small Heath 2 *v.* WBA 3
Walsall Town Swifts 5 *v.* Sheffield Heeley 1
Bootle 0 *v.* Preston 3

FINE FIRST-HALF PERFORMANCE BY LEAGUE SIDE
Bootle 0 *v.* Preston North End 3

Both teams were fully represented, Mills-Roberts keeping goal for North End. Bootle kicked-off against a strong wind, and the visitors at once pressed. F. Woods relieved and the home right carried play to the other end. The visit was only momentary, and play was in the Bootle half, Gordon scoring, and a few minutes later Thompson placed a second.

The home goal was again in danger through some misunderstanding by Alsop and Macfarlane. Gordon, however, shot wide. Play was all at the Bootle end,

Jackson saving a couple of headers by Dewhurst. The visitors showed grand passing, and Gordon scored a third goal.

The home left wing again took play to the other end, and Ferguson troubled Mills-Roberts. The attack was repulsed, and Goodall was prominent with a good dribble, and up to half-time the play was in the home half.

With the strong wind Bootle attacked, and from a corner an exciting scrimmage took place close on goal. This was cleared, and Ross was knocked off the ball when nicely underway, and the Preston goal was again in danger.

Play was more open, the visitors' right frequently breaking away. Mills-Roberts saved well, and at the other end Ross compelled Jackson to concede a corner. The home lot still had the best of matters, and Howard saved a shot by Hughes. With close on twenty minutes still to play MacFarlane retired owing to a bad sprain. On resuming North End attacked and gained a corner, Jamieson relieving, and to the close the game was evenly contested.

Early in the second half Robertson had his collarbone broken, but was not aware until after the game, when Dr Mills-Roberts examined him.

(Report from *Birmingham Daily Post,* 4 February 1889)

Second-Round Results – 16 February 1889

Blackburn Rovers walk over Swifts.
Aston Villa 5 *v.* Derby County 3
Sheffield Wednesday 3 *v.* Notts County 2
Chatham 1 *v.* Nottingham Forest 1
R Forest 2 *v.* Chatham 2
2R Chatham 3 *v.* Forest 2
Halliwell 2 *v.* Birmingham St George's 3
Wolverhampton Wanderers 6 *v.* Walsall Town Swifts 1
WBA 5 *v.* Burnley 1

NON-LEAGUE SIDE PUSH CHAMPIONS ALL THE WAY

Grimsby Town 0 *v.* Preston North End 2

Played at Clee Park on Saturday, in the presence of 8,000 spectators. During the morning there was a small snowstorm, which settled into steady drizzling rain. The ground, notwithstanding, was in fair condition.

Grimsby won the toss, and Goodall kicked off for Preston, who had the wind in their favour. Goodall at once passed to Ross who, with Gordon, made a nice run, but Doyle pulled them up. Preston did not have all the game. On the other hand, Grimsby pressed continuously for a long time. When half-time was called, no goals had been scored.

On commencing the second half, Preston at once pressed, but they could not score for some fifteen minutes, when Goodall shot a beautiful goal, which was appealed against and disallowed for offside. Grimsby worked hard, and was rewarded with a grand goal by Macbeth, but it was disallowed on the plea of 'hands'.

Preston, who was now looking very anxious, again came, and for some time the Grimsby goal was in jeopardy. Fifteen minutes from the finish Goodall secured the first goal for Preston, and five minutes later Gordon notched another with a beautiful oblique shot that completely puzzled the goalkeeper. Grimsby again pressed severely, but could not score, and was finally defeated by two goals to nil.

(Report from *Lancaster Gazetteer*)

Third Round Results – 2 March 1889

Blackburn Rovers 8 *v.* Aston Villa 1
Chatham 1 *v.* WBA 10
Wolverhampton Wanderers 3 *v.* Sheffield Wednesday 0

LATE GOALS TAKE NORTH END INTO LAST FOUR

Preston North End 2 *v.* Birmingham St George's 0

Played on Saturday at Deepdale, before 8,000 spectators. The weather was fine, and the ground in good going condition.

Play was of a give-and-take character for some time, both custodians clearing easy shots. The first real danger came from the 'Saints', Blackburn giving Mills-Roberts a low shot to stop, and for a few minutes the North End goal was in jeopardy. This roused the home team, and the ball was kept mostly near Hadley. Dewhurst hit the crossbar with an excellent shot, and two corners were conceded to North End, but the defence of Siddons, Gray, and all the half-backs continued of the best descriptions. Half-time arrived without goals to either side.

North End forwards improved, Goodall and Gordon being very dangerous, but Siddons continued to play a splendid back game. Dean and Blackham won the first corner for the 'Saints', a hot scrimmage resulting, but the ball soon got near Hadley, when Goodall and Ross hit an upright.

Play on both sides continued of the most stubborn description. Matters were not looking very promising when Gordon forced a corner, and the same player directly after centring the ball, it was scrimmaged through, thus scoring the first goal for North End after half-an-hour's play (seventy-five minutes). The game continued to be well fought, both lots of forwards attacking, but North End were now having the best of matters, and, after Dewhurst had made Hadley save, Thomson scored with a splendid shot. The North End won another corner, and the final result was a victory for Preston North End by two goals to nil.

(Report from *Lancaster Gazetteer*)

1888/89 FA CUP SEMI-FINALS – 16 MARCH 1889

Wolverhampton Wanderers 1 *v.* Blackburn Rovers 1
At Alexandra Road, Crewe.

R Wolves 3 *v.* Blackburn Rovers 1
At Alexandra Road, Crewe.

REVENGE

Preston North End 1 *v.* West Bromwich Albion 0
At Bramall Lane.

Perhaps of the two great semi-final ties for the FA Cup set for today that at Sheffield between the Preston North End and West Bromwich Albion commanded the most attention. The two clubs have run such a close race for the past few years that to meet at any time and anywhere means a deadly struggle. Twice before they have contested in the latter stages of the competition and twice victory has rested with the clever West Bromwich players. They knocked their famous rivals out of the semi-final at Trent Bridge two seasons ago, and when fate brought them together again last year, this time in the last round of all at the Oval, the Preston team were once more compelled to strike their flag.

In the League fixtures this season, however, the North End have had a big pull over their skilful, antagonists, defeating them on both occasions and scoring eight goals to none.

Also on the doings of the present season, as a whole, the North End have a far better record of won 36, lost 5, drawn 5 with 153 scored and 41 conceded, West Bromwich Albion having won 22, lost 11, drawn 5 and scored 109 against 66.

Both teams have been quietly training for the big battle, but their training in each case has been wisely done at home. As will be learnt from a perusal of the names, the Albion again had the assistance of Bethell Robinson of the Bolton Wanderers, who joined them on Thursday, and who had the somewhat anomalous experience of appearing against his own townsmen in an important cup tie.

The weather at Sheffield today was as balmy as could be wished for in spring, and from an early hour in the afternoon the great match at Bramall Lane was the sole topic of conversation.

Two hours before the match started crowds began to gather at the ground and shortly before kick-off there were fully 20,000. The stands were packed inside and out, and the various shouts of residents from at least a dozen towns made a Babel of sounds.

At twenty minutes past three, Bob Howarth led on the North End amid a roar of applause. The crowd was no less than 23,000. Just on half-past three Mr Clegg appeared and then came the Throstles and the shaking of hands between the teams ensued. Then the crowd broke into the goal line.

Bayliss kicked off at 3.40 and at once Parry tripped Goodall. The Albion playing against the wind and sun. Goodall a minute later kicked over the bar. Tackling by Drummond and grand passing by the North End right followed, and Thomson shot the ball through, but the goal was disallowed for offside.

The game was now stopped through the crowd breaking in, and after some delay the players threatened to leave the field. Play was stopped for sixteen minutes and on the restart Thompson missed an easy chance.

Horton, Bassett and Perry tried to pass Holmes, (who had been given permission by the FA to play after originally having been selected to represent England against Ireland the same day) but Gordon won a corner and after some pressing Bassett got away and then obtained a corner, Mills-Roberts and Holmes each making mistakes. For a minute West Bromwich were dangerous, but Green had to stop Gordon. Give and take play now ensued, and the spectators began to think that it was no cup tie. [Rumour had taken hold that due to the stoppage in play it has been decided to make the game a friendly – editor.]

Robinson neatly robbed the North End right. Two corners followed to Preston, and a splendid run by W Perry and Bassett. From a free-kick Russell scored on 30 minutes. Mills-Roberts saved and Preston then pressed to the interval.

Half-time 1-0.

The reporters were told at the interval that the game was a cup tie. On the restart North End had both the sun and wind against them, but they were very aggressive and Roberts had to save several times. The Albion retaliated and Mills-Roberts saved by falling on the ball.

The game was much faster than in the first half, and Robinson showed splendid defence on the one side, and all the Preston backs. Ross missed a good chance, and the play thus became even.

Russell, Graham and the two backs repelled a fine attempt at scoring by Bassett and Perry, and Timmins showed up well against the North End right.

After some pretty passing by the Albion forwards Bassett just skimmed the bar. Amid much excitement Wilson put in a fine run, but Robinson pulled him up, and another attack followed on the Preston goal. Grand tackling was being shown on both sides, but the forwards seemed to lag. Wilson next shot over the Preston bar.

Towards the finish both sides seemed to fall off considerably and there was some wild shooting and passing by both sets of forwards. All the backs defended first rate, and were very safe. Thomson made one or two good attempts to score, but the remainder of the forwards dallied too much. After a spell of pressure by North End, Bassett and Perry made an attempt, but Howarth relieved. The Albion won a corner and the game soon ended.

The crowd spoiled the game at Bramall Lane, where there could be no less than 25,000 people. In the first half the North End had far the best of the game, and were many times within an ace of scoring, but were somewhat unlucky.

The goal they got was very smart from a free-kick. The stoppage in the first half through the crowd seemed to unsettle both sides, and they never seemed to thoroughly recover themselves. It was thought that Albion would have been able to equalise when they got the benefit of the wind and sun, but they did not come up to expectation and had to submit to defeat. All their backs played stubbornly, and the same may be said of the North End. The Albion forwards were not combined in front of goal, and the Preston forwards rambled too much.

(Report from *Cricket and Football Field,* 16 March 1889)

The FA Cup Final up Until 1889

When the first FA Cup final took place in 1872 there were an estimated 2,000 spectators. The entry fee of 1*s* (5p) was felt to be prohibitive and the *Bell's Life sporting newspaper* of the time wrote, 'That the Association code can ever rival the Rugby Union game in public estimation can hardly be hoped for by its most sanguine admirers.'

And while it took over a decade to do so, in 1885 the final attracted a crowd of over five figures for the first time when 12,500 witnessed Blackburn Rovers beating Scottish side Queen's Park 2-0 to retain the cup. The 'death or glory' nature of the competition was fast turning it into the most famous in the world such that by the 1920s the final had overtaken the England *v.* Scotland match each season as the biggest game in the world.

1889 FA CUP FINAL

Preston North End 3 *v.* Wolves 0 (See match report, pp. 125/26)

The Home International Championship 1888/89

This was the sixth time the championship had been played for. Holders England had won it outright for the first time in the previous season, before which Scotland had triumphed three times with England and Scotland tying in 1885/86. The Ireland side – representing north and south – had won just one game in the five years.

The tournament began with England at home to Wales. The England side, which was selected by a committee, was composed of three amateurs in the 'keeper and two full-backs. One of these, Percy Melmoth Walters, was selected as captain on his tenth international appearance. Five players were handed their debuts with the Wolves half-back pairing of Albert Fletcher and Arthur Lowder given a chance to show their League form at a higher level. Up front, his Blackburn Rovers colleague William Townley joined John Southworth and there was also a debut for Billy Betts of Sheffield Wednesday at centre-half.

THURSDAY 28 FEBRUARY 1889
ENGLAND RECOVER FROM GOING A GOAL DOWN TO WIN HANDSOMELY
England 4 (Goodall, Bassett, Dewhurst, Southworth) v. Wales 1 (Owen)

Half-time 1-1.

Many thousands of spectators witnessed the annual encounter between England and Wales, played on Saturday under Association rules at Stoke.

The visitors at first had the wind in their favour, but England at the outset kept the ball well in their rivals' quarters. They made two excellent shots at goal; but Trainer dexterously turned both of these on one side. Wales now played up with greater determination, and when Moon had well met one attack, another was made, which ended in Owen scoring the first goal, after a quarter of an hour's play.

The English, aroused by this reverse, displayed excellent form, the feature of their play being capital passing. After a couple of ineffectual attempts to put the ball through, Goodall, who received it from Bassett, kicked a goal, and thus brought the scores level. Some interesting play was witnessed from this stage until the arrival of half-time; but no further point was gained, and when the teams crossed over the record stood at 'one goal all'.

England now had the advantage of the wind, and turned it to good account. A corner-kick fell to them, and this was so well made that Bassett registered a second goal.

Other attacks were well met by Trainer, but at length Dewhurst, who had scored twice when the sides last met in 1888, shot the ball between the posts, thus gaining a third point for the home eleven.

The Welsh forwards now went over in a body; they were well met by the opposing backs, and P. M. Walters kicked the ball out of danger. England then made persistent attacks in their rivals' posts. Townley affected a good run and passed to Bassett, who in turn sent the ball over to Southworth, and the last-named shot it between the posts for his first international goal. Wales were unable to add to the solitary item mentioned in the early part of the game, and thus England were victorious by four goals to one.

All of which means in the eleven matches now played England have won eight, Wales two and in 1884/85 the match was drawn.

England: W. R. Moon [Old Westminsters], A. M. Walters and P. M. Walters [Old Carthusians] [backs], A. Fletcher [Wolves], A. Lowder [Wolves] and W. Betts [Sheffield Wednesday], A. Bassett [WBA] and J. Goodall [PNE], Southworth [Blackburn Rovers], F. Dewhurst [PNE] and W. J. Townley [Blackburn Rovers].

Wales: J. Trainer [Wrexham and PNE], W. P. Jones [Druids] and D. Jones [Chirk/Bolton Wanderers], P. W. Hughes [Bangor], R. Roberts [Druids] and Bolton Wanderers], Humphrey-Jones [Wrexham], J. Hallam [Oswestry] and R. Jones [Bangor], W. Owen [Chirk], A. Lea [Wrexham] and W. Lewis [Bangor].

Umpires – C. Crump [Birmingham Association], A. H. Hunter [Oswestry].

Referee J. Campbell [Scottish FA treasurer].

(Report from *Lancaster Gazetteer*)

SATURDAY 2 MARCH 1889
IN A REPEAT OF THE WALES GAME, ENGLAND RECOVER FROM A GOAL DOWN TO WIN

England 6 (Shelton, Yates, Yates, Lofthouse, Yates, Brodie) *v.* Ireland 1 (Wilton)

The England side against Ireland contained nine players making their debut, with only Joe Lofthouse and Albert Aldridge having previously played for their country, and in the latter's case only the once. In goal the superb form shown by Billy Rowley in the Stoke goal was rewarded with the first of what were to be just two caps. Team colleague Tommy Clare joined him in front of him at full-back. Wolves John Brodie, a professional, was made captain for the match.

With the Irish Football Association sticking to its rules that non-resident players were ineligible for selection there was no place for Aston Villa's Archie Goodall, who was forced to wait until the rules changed to make his debut in March 1899.

Played at Everton, before 8,000 spectators. From the onset play was exciting, the Irish forwards playing up, and at last they scored. Play was even, and Weir equalised. The English pressed and Yates scored a second goal, and shortly after Yates added a third - a doubtful point. To the interval play was slightly in favour of England.

From the restart, Daft and Yates came away, but Daft shot wide. With the exception of an occasional burst play was in the visitors' half, and Lofthouse scored a fourth, and a little later Brodie a fifth and Yates a sixth. From the kick-off Rowley was troubled, and after Clugston had stopped two shots Rowley threw out one from Wilson. Give-and-take play was the order, and then the Irishmen sustained a fierce attack with Crawford eventually kicking wide. Play to the close was tame, and in favour of England.

Yates is one of five players to have scored a hat-trick on his England debut, yet not make a second appearance.

England: Billy Rowley [Stoke], Tommy Clare [Stoke], Albert James Aldridge [Walsall Town Swifts], Charles Wreford-Brown [Oxford University], Davie Weir [Bolton], Alf Shelton [Notts County], Joe Lofthouse [Accrington], Frank Burton [Nottingham Forest], John Brodie [Wolves] Harry Daft [Notts County], Jack Yates [Burnley].

Ireland: John Clugston, Manliffe Goodbody, James Watson, Alex Crawford and Archie Rosbotham and Sam Cooke, Arthur Gaussen, Olphie Stanfield, Jack Barry, James Wilton and John Peden.

Attendance 6, 500.

(Report from *Lancaster Gazetteer*)

SATURDAY 9 MARCH 1889
Scotland 7 (Watt 2, Black, Groves 3, McInnes) *v.* Ireland 0
Played at Ibrox, Glasgow.

Scotland: Doig, Arbroath, J. Adams [Heart of Midlothian] and McKeown [Celtic], Robertson [Queen's Park] captain, Calderhead [Queen of the South], J. Buchanan [Cambulsang], F. Watt, Kilbarnie and McInnes [Cowlairs], W. Groves [Celtic], R. Boyd [Mossend Swifts] and D. Black [Hurlford].

Ireland: Clugston [Cliftonville], McVicker [Glentoran] and R. Crone [Distillery], Thompson [Belfast Athletics], Christian [Linfield], S. Torrens [Linfield], Stanfield [Distillery] Peyden [Linfield], Wilton [St Columbs Court] and Gibb [Cliftonville].

Umpires – J. Campbell, Ulster, J. Campbell [SFA treasurer], W. H. Stacey – Sheffield. This was the sixth game between the two countries and the sixth victory for Scotland.

SATURDAY 13 APRIL 1889
SCOTS FIGHT BACK WINS THE DAY
England 2 (Bassett 2) *v.* Scotland 3 (Munro, Oswald, McLaren)

When these sides had clashed at Cathkin Park [First Hampden] on 15 March 1884 it was the occasion for the first all-ticket football match when all 10,00 tickets were sold for a game that Scotland won 1-0, their fifth consecutive home success in a series that had kicked off in 1872 with a 0-0 draw at Hamilton Crescent, Scotland. Victory had given the Scots top spot in the first British Home Championship.

England had won for the first time in Scotland in 1888 when a powerful, well-built English forward line of George Woodall, Johnny Goodall, Tinsley Lindley, Dennis Hodgetts and Fred Dewhurst had overpowered the Scottish back line to win by a handsome 5-0.

In 1889 Goodall and Lindley were again selected and there was a debut for Henry Hammond of Oxford University, one of five amateur players' in the England XI. With Scotland's selectors sticking strictly to a policy of not selecting Scots playing in England there were no places for the Ross brothers, Jimmy of Preston and Nick of Everton or the many Scots that formed the backbone of the North End Invincibles. England was looking for only their third home success, the Scots having won four of the matches played with two draws. The match was played at the Kennington Oval, London.

In somewhat objectionable weather, as far as visitors were concerned, this great international Association match between the sister countries was decided at Kennington Oval, and after a well-fought and obstinately disputed contest, ultimately resulted in a grand victory for Scotland 3-2.

The afternoon was dull and unpromising, and the turf, through recent rains, was in very sorry condition – falls being frequent, to the detriment of the neat costumes that adorned both teams; nevertheless, both played on with untiring vigour from first to last.

Two Strong Sides
England decidedly stood first in the betting at the starting, P. M. Walters bringing into the field an unusually strong team; but the Scots as the game went on improved so unmistakably that few were surprised at their victory when the whistle sounded the retreat at the close of proceedings.

England having gained the choice of positions, Walters drew up his followers on the Clayton Street side of the enclosure, and at three minutes after three Brodie made a start from the Vauxhall end.

The Scots, following up, made a strong attack on the English quarters, but soon had to retreat before the unified efforts of the brothers Walters. By way of exchange, however, Bassett now headed an assault on the enemy's lines, when, out of a loose scrimmage, the ball, hitting the bar, flew back into play again, and the battle was resumed.

A good run by Brodie, which took him well across the ground, failed to prove effective, as the ball flew over. A strong assault by the Scots, in which Berry, Munro, Macpherson, and Oswald particularly distinguished themselves, failed through the energy displayed by the English backs; and a corner by the Scots fell harmlessly as Moon was all there, and punched the ball away.

P. M. Walters cleverly repelled a good attack by the Scots, and the ball was almost instantaneously thrown in again from a mistaken shot by a Scot. A good run and a kick by Lindley were well disposed of by Munro, but Bassett and Hammond together soon made amends for the comparative failure by forcing the Scots back on their own lines.

England Opens a Two-Goal Lead

Forrest and Goodall also troubled their foes severely, and put Wilson to a considerable amount of trouble in keeping his goal intact. At length, after the game had lasted twenty minutes from a fine dribbling run by Bassett, England scored their first goal, and two minutes later, from a pass by Goodall, Bassett was credited with a second, amid immense cheering from the natives.

A corner by the Scots fell through, a miskick having been made by Kelly, and a strong assault by the Scots' forwards was fisted away by Moon. A good combination attack by Goodall, Bassett and Hammond looked threatening for the peace of the heroes of the Thistle, but MacPherson was in the way, and turned the threatened danger aside. A claim of hands by the Scots failed by a miskick by Smellie, and Moon had again to use his hands to save his goal from danger. Half-time having arrived, ends were reversed, the score standing at England 2 – Scotland 0.

On recommencing, from a corner by Smellie nothing resulted, and an attack by the English forwards was made. Wilson put forth his strength, sent them to the right about, and shortly afterwards Wilson, from a like attack, went through in a similar performance. Up to this time the action had been carried on under very equal circumstances, both teams doing their duty splendidly; but the Scots seemed to improve rapidly, and England had to do all they knew to hold their own.

At last, after some desperate onslaughts on both sides and run by Bassett, who passed to Goodall, who in turn sent the ball over to Brodie, the latter kicked over, and, after a splendid attack by the Scots, Munro scored the first goal for Scotland.

A shot by Oswald was finely fisted by Moon, but the attack being instantly repeated, the ball glancing off Allen went through the posts, and finally, a strenuous shot by McLaren brought this magnificent encounter to a conclusion, as previously recorded.

Scotland: J. Wilson [Vale of Leven] [goal], W. Arnott and R. Smellie [captain] [Queen's Park] [backs]; J. Kelly [Celtic], J. Dewar [Dumbarton] and J. McLaren [Celtic] [half-backs], A. Latta [Dumbarton Athletic] and W. Berry [Queen's Park]. Right-wing, J. Oswald [Third Lanark] [centre], J. Macpherson [Cowlairs] and N. Munro [Abercorn] [left wing].

England: W. R. Moon [Old Westminsters], Arthur Melmoth Walters and Percy Melmoth Walters [Old Carthusians] captain][backs], H. E. D. Hammond [Oxford University], H. Allen [Wolverhampton Wanderers] and J. Forrest [Blackburn Rovers] half-backs, W. J. Bassett [WBA] and J. Goodall [PNE] [right wing], J. Brodie [Wolverhampton Wanderers] [centre], D. Weir [Bolton Wanderers] and T. Lindley [Notts Forest] [left wing].

J. C. Clegg – umpire and J. Crerar [SFA president].

Referee – J. Sinclair, Irish FA .

(Report from *Derby and Chesterfield Reporter*)

Of the England players, Davie Weir had made the final of his two international appearances while Hammond never played for England again. Bassett though was to go on and make another thirteen appearances – in which he often played superbly against the Scots – to tally up sixteen international appearances in which he scored eight goals.

John Goodall, whose father was Scottish, was to make a further ten England appearances in a total of fourteen, in which he scored twelve times. Two of these came in a 4-1 success at Ibrox Park, Glasgow in 1892 and when England then beat their great rivals 5-2 at home the following season it was their third consecutive victory. A draw in 1894 and a fourth English victory in five matches in 1895 saw Scotland abandon the policy of playing only home-based players.

SATURDAY 15 APRIL 1889
SCOTLAND CAPTURE CHAMPIONSHIP CROWN
Wales 0 *v.* Scotland 0
At Wrexham.

Scotland: W. Macleod [Dumbarton Athletic], A. Thomson and G. Rae [Third Lanark], A. Stewart, Queen's Park, J. Auld [Third Lanark] A. Lochhead [Third Lanark], F. Watt [Kilbrinie] and H. Campbell [Renton] right, W. Paul [Partick Thistle] centre, A. Johnstone and A. Hannah [Third Lanark] left-forwards.

Wales: J. Gillam [Wrexham], A. O. Davies [Wrexham] and D. Jones [Chirk/Bolton Wanderers], R. Roberts [Druids] and Bolton Wanderers], J. Davies [Newton Heath and Druids], Humphrey-Jones, Wrexham], J. Davies [Everton] and Chirk, W. Owen [Chirk] right, G. Owen [Chirk and Newton Heath], W. Lewis [Bangor], J. Doughty [Newton Heath and Druids] first substitute.

During the game, 'keeper A. Pugh of Rhostyllen replaced S. G. Gillam of Wrexham and obviously did well as Wales drew 0-0, the first time ever Wales had prevented the Scots from scoring, the Scots having notched fifty-nine goals in the previous thirteen games between the sides.

SATURDAY 27 APRIL 1889

Ireland 1 (John Lemon) *v.* Wales 3 (Richard Jarrett 3)
At Ballynafeigh Park, Belfast.

Wales: Sam Gillam (Wrexham), William P. Jones (Druids), Di Jones (Bolton Wanderers), Edward P. W. Hughes (Bangor), Tom McCarthy (Wrexham), Patrick Leary (Bangor), Joseph Davies (Everton), Billy Owen (Chirk), George A. Owen (Newton Heath), Richard H. Jarrett (Ruthin), William Lewis (Bangor).
   Referee Thomas R. Park (Scotland).
   Attendance 1,500.

Caps

In 2010 the white cap awarded to Harry Daft in honour of his appearance against Ireland in 1889 was sold at auction for £500.

   Caps were first worn to distinguish players on different sides who in the early days rarely wore distinctive jerseys. They became abandoned when heading became a regular feature of the play. A print of the first international match in 1872 shows both teams wearing caps.

   The first official England caps were awarded in 1886.

Final Table

Scotland	5 points
England	4 points
Wales	3 points
Ireland	0 points

Gazetteer of Players

PRESTON NORTH END

Every player knew what he had to do – to make the ball do the work. As John Goodall once said to me, 'Every man in the team was a master of his craft. What is more every man was a partner. That made our success. We never bothered about who got the goals. They belonged to the side – not the man.'

(*Wickets and Goals – Stories of Play*, J. A. H. Catton in 1926)

There were great forward lines before North End came to the front, but no previous team ever played football with such mathematical precision as North End did. Queen's Park, in the days of Fraser, Anderson, Geordie Ker, G. Angus, J. T. Richmond, and J. L. Kaye, were a most brilliant set, and it is historical that Fraser and Anderson understood what combination meant, but the team as whole did not realise its full possibilities as North End did. I think John Gordon, James Ross, John Goodall, Fred Dewhurst and George Drummond have never been equalled as a forward line. Each man was a star individually; the wing pairs combined perfectly, and John Goodall was the finest pivot that ever lived.

(James W. Crabtree of Burnley, Aston Villa and England)

Goalkeepers
Trainer, James (20)
Trainer was already a Welsh international when he joined Preston from Bolton Wanderers in 1887, where a defeat in his first match was followed by an eight-month unbeaten run. Due to the two-year residential qualifications that applied to professionals, Trainer missed out on an appearance at the 1889 FA Cup final but played the vast majority of the League games in 1888/89, where it would true to say that in a number of games he had little of note to keep him occupied as Preston pushed back their opponents. He later became, for a short spell, a director with the

club but was to die in poverty in 1915. He was capped twenty times for his country.

Mills-Roberts, Dr Robert (2)
Mills-Roberts played just two League matches in 1888/89 but all the FA Cup games in which he kept five clean sheets. An amateur who in his day job as house surgeon at Birmingham General Hospital often had to travel by horse and carriage from his Stroud home to catch a train from Gloucester to wherever Preston were playing. After debuting for Wales against England in February 1885, he went on to make eight appearances for his country. He served with the British Expeditionary Force during the First World War.

Full-backs
Howarth, Bob (18)
Preston-born Howarth formed a formidable full-back partnership with Bob Holmes, both at club and international level. Two years after his debut in 1883 the powerful defender was considered good enough to represent Lancashire in inter-county matches and later played for the North against the South as a prelude to four international appearances. He was to make his final appearance for Preston in March 1899 before retiring to concentrate on his solicitor's practice.

Holmes, Bob (22)
Left-back and the only player to play in every League and FA Cup game in the 1888/89 season. The Preston-born player was capped seven times for his country, including captaining England in the 6-0 defeat of Wales in March 1894. Holmes played a total of 300 League appearances for Preston, scoring just the once in a 1-1 draw against Burnley in October 1895. He served as the president of the Football Players' Union in the mid-1890s as the players sought, unsuccessfully, to increase their wages. Holmes later acted as trainer to Dick, Kerr's Ladies, a team of Preston factory girls who drew large crowds as women's football blossomed from 1917 to 1921.

Whittle, Dick (1/1)
The right-back's only League game saw him score in the 7-0 thrashing of Stoke City.

Half-backs
Graham, Willie (5)
Although he played the first two League games the centre-half was to make only three more appearances. Despite Preston winning all five matches he lost out to the more consistent David Russell and was to leave at the end of the season.

Robertson, Alex 'Sandy' (21/3)
A painter by trade and one of many Scotsmen in the side, Sandy played in all but one of the League matches and scored against Bolton, Derby County and Stoke. However, an injury in the first-round FA Cup match against Bootle saw him miss out on the last League match and the subsequent cup matches in which Preston clinched the Double. He left Preston at the end of the following season after playing only a handful of games. Hard-working at all times, Robertson was also a clever, dainty player who could unlock defences with some wonderful passing. On his retirement from football he moved to South Africa but returned to Europe to fight with the South African contingent on Britain's side during the First World War.

Russell, David (18)
Signed from Scots club Stewart Cunningham, Russell was a strong-tackling defender who scored Preston's winning goal in the semi-final match against West Bromwich Albion. When Preston retained the League title in 1889/90 he played in every League game before a better offer from Nottingham Forest saw him move south. After finishing playing football he later carved out a career on the music-hall stage.

Graham, Johnny (22)
Graham was to miss out on a place in the FA Cup final (after a broken collarbone) but played every League game during a season. A former quarryman Graham, who was as hard as steel and weighed 12 stone 7 pounds, had joined the Lancashire side from Scottish club Annbank during the 1884/85 season. Playing at left-half, the Scottish international was the provider of many fine passes for the lethal combination of Jimmy Ross and John Goodall further up the field. He was also an early master of the art of the long throw being able to hurl the ball into the centre of the pitch from the touchlines. Graham's injury was to see him retire at the end of the season. Outside football Graham was a fine mile and half-mile runner with many prizes to his name.

Forwards

Dewhurst, Fred (16/12)
Inside-left/centre-forward and captain, the master at a Catholic Grammar School, Dewhurst was the first North End player to play representative football when picked to play for Lancashire against London. Scored North End's first League goal in the 5-2 opening day defeat of Burnley and was also first on the score sheet in the 1889 FA Cup final in which Wolves were beaten 3-0, after which he collected the trophy from Major Mandarin. The only amateur in the side, Dewhurst was a rough, no-nonsense player who was a constant danger to opposing 'keepers and not averse to barging

them off the ball. He was good enough to play for his country where he scored in eight of his nine appearances.

Drummond, George (12/1)

Just eighteen years old at the time, Drummond scored three on his debut against Accrington in September 1883. He had travelled south after learning to play football with St Bernard's and it was his value as a versatile player, able to play in virtually every position, that kept him in the side for so many years that in 1900 he was rewarded with a testimonial match that saw the current side play the 'Old Invincibles.' A crowd of 6,000 turned out. A good dribbler he played much of the early part of the 1888/89 season at outside left before settling in at right-half, a position he occupied at the FA Cup final.

Edwards, Jack (4/3)

Edwards scored on his debut against West Bromwich Albion in October and also scored twice in a 4-1 success against Notts County in January, the last of his Preston appearances.

Goodall, Johnny (21/20)

The top scorer in the inaugural Football League season was John Goodall, who in a race to the very end finished with a goal more than his colleague Jimmy Ross. Goodall – known as 'Johnny All Good' – was the side's best player, earning him the honour of being known as the first player to pioneer scientific football. The son of a corporal in the Royal Scottish Fusiliers, Goodall was born in Westminster, London on 19 June 1863, a quirk of fate giving him the right to play internationally for England. After leaving school, Goodall worked as an iron turner and played football whenever possible. He joined Kilmarnock Burns as a fifteen-year-old. A year later he signed for Kilmarnock Athletic and made his senior debut in 1870.

Four years later, in 1884, he was lured south into English football – professionalism was just round the corner and thinly disguised financial arrangements were commonplace, and Goodall joined the Bolton side, Great Lever. Playing his first game for the Lancashire club against Derby County he scored five goals in a 6-0 victory.

In August, Goodall switched his allegiance to Preston North End where he developed a wonderful partnership with Ross. It was during this season that Goodall, who was as quiet off the pitch as he was brilliant on it, first played for England, scoring on his debut against Wales in 5-1 victory. He was to play fourteen times in all, scoring twelve times including two marvellous efforts when England beat Scotland 4-1 in April 1892 – his dad must have been pleased!

At the end of the 1888/89 season Goodall, who stood 5 feet 9 inches tall and weighed eleven stones and nine pounds, had scored fifty goals in only fifty-six first-class appearances for Preston. His speed over the ground, clever footwork, willingness to shoot from any distance and his accuracy in front of goal made him one of the most accurate marksmen the game of football has ever seen.

Not that such success was enough to keep him at Deepdale, as within weeks he signed for Derby County. It appears money was the main reason as along with his brother Archie, who also signed for Derby at the same time, he was given the tenancy of The Plough pub on London Road.

Although Derby won no major trophies while Goodall was there, the side earned a reputation for being the most entertaining in the League, narrowly missing honours on several occasions. Goodall also acted as a figurehead to the young players and in particular to Steve Bloomer.

Gordon, Jack (20/10)

Gordon had debuted in his teens for Preston while working as a joiner before returning to Scotland to play for Port Glasgow Athletic for two years. On his return in 1884, he quickly teamed up with Jimmy Ross down the Preston right and the pair were to prove a lethal combination. Against Hyde United in the 1887/88 season the pair scored thirteen times in a record-breaking 26-0 FA Cup first-round success.

Gordon was lean and sinewy, his long legs taking him past many an opponent before he delivered a perfectly placed and weighted centre. He scored Preston's second goal in the opening day 5-2 win over Burnley and also scored twice in the 3-1 win against Bolton Wanderers in the third League game. In 1891 he was to become Preston's first scorer from the penalty spot and was to make his last of 113 League appearances against Derby County in November 1894, almost thirteen years after making his debut.

Inglis, Jock (1/1)

Inglis scored against Derby in his only League match. Unable to dislodge either Jimmy Ross or Fred Dewhurst, he was to depart the club at the end of the 1889/90 season.

Ross, Jimmy

Edinburgh-born Jimmy Ross was a brilliant inside-forward who, along with his older brother Nick, joined Preston North End in 1883. Developing, in the years before the Football League got started, a good partnership with John Goodall, Ross scored his first goal in the FA Cup in January 1887 when PNE won a highly competitive match in Scotland against one of the game's great teams at the time, Renton.

It was during the following season's competition, however, that Ross, who combined great accurate passing along with a hatful of tricks, put himself into the record books, hitting a then record eight as his side recorded a surely never to be beaten biggest ever win in the world's longest running football competition, Hyde being thrashed 26-0.

In 1888/89 Ross, who was only 5 feet 7 inches tall and weighed just under 11 stone, became the first Preston man to score a League hat-trick and the first in League football to notch four in a match. He finished second to Goodall in the overall scorers' chart and the following season topped it with twenty-two goals. Unlike Goodall he was as lively off the pitch as on it, regularly telling jokes and ribbing his colleagues.

Ross, often called junior to distinguish him from his older brother Nick, was to remain a good scorer of goals over the next eleven seasons, ending up with sixteen League goals in 1891/92 and seventeen in 1893/94, after which he joined Liverpool. Over the following two seasons he scored thirty-seven goals in seventy-three games. Later he enjoyed success at Burnley, scoring twenty-nine times in fifty-one games to assist the Clarets to promotion.

Due to the Scottish selectors' policy of only playing those who resided at home, Ross never represented his country.

Towards the end of his career he joined Manchester City, where he played alongside fellow trade union stalwart Billy Meredith. Ross was one of many top players who, upset at the setting of a maximum wage of £4 a week when he knew he could get £10, helped form the Association Footballers' Union in February 1898. Others who joined included the Villa striker John Devey.

Ross retired from the game at the end of the 1900/01 season and died just a year later aged thirty-six.

Goodall, Archie (2/1)

Irish-born brother of John Archie played just twice, before becoming the first transfer during the season to be approved by the League when he joined Aston Villa. He later joined up with John at the start of the following season when he signed for Derby County where he was to go on and make over 400 appearances at centre-half, two of which were in unsuccessful FA Cup finals in 1898 and 1903.

Thomson, Sam (16/3)

After starting out with Lugar Boswell Thomson, a Scottish international joined Preston from Rangers and in 1888/89 scored crucial goals in the 2-2 away draws at Blackburn and Burnley. A dashing, polished forward Thomson, who scored at the 1889 FA Cup final, later joined Wolves in 1890 before short spells at Everton and Accrington.

ACCRINGTON

Goalkeepers
Horne, Johnny (22)

A fine amateur 'keeper who, despite breaking a rib in the opening fixture, played in every match in 1888/89. However, business commitments reduced his first-team performances to just a single game in 1890/91 and a further three in 1892/93. He also played twice for Blackburn Rovers in the 1889/90 season.

Full-backs

Singleton, Stephen (4)
Singleton was a professional footballer who was released by Accrington at the end of the season.

McLellan, John (19)
A professional player with a fine kick and tackle, McLellan was one of two players to play in all five of Accrington's League seasons, during which he made 101 League appearances without scoring.

Stevenson (22/1)
Stevenson, a professional footballer with Accrington during their first four League seasons, had his best season in 1888/89 in which he played every League match. Scorer of the winning goal against WBA with a 'wicked long shot'.

Half-backs

Chippendale, Peter (6/1)
Played in the first six League games, scoring at Blackburn in the 5-5 draw, before losing his place and after failing to regain it he was not retained at the end of the season.

Haworth, George (21/1)
After signing from Christ Church FC in 1882, Haworth was at Accrington for more than a decade and during which time he made seventy-four League appearances, scoring three times. In 1884/85 Haworth also represented Blackburn Rovers in the FA Cup and was a member of the team that beat Scottish side Queens Park in the final. Captain and defensive leader, he won five England caps in the period 1887–90.

Parkinson, E. (1)
An amateur who played against Bolton Wanderers in March 1889.

Pemberton, Luther (16)
Pemberton, a professional, played thirty-six League games for Accrington over three seasons in which he scored eight goals.

Tattersall, James (17)
After replacing Chippendale, Tattersall established himself at centre-half and went on to make a total of fifty-seven League appearances over the following three seasons without scoring.

Wilkinson, (or Williamson) J. Thomas (4)

A professional player whose four appearances in 1888/89 were added to by a single appearance in each of the next two seasons in which he scored once.

Woods, J. (2)

An amateur player whose two appearances were in drawn matches with Notts County and Aston Villa.

Forwards

Barbour, Billy (19/12)

In September 1888, an angry crowd that wanted Barbour to stay witnessed his departure from Queen of the South Wanderers to Accrington. The Scottish club were suspended for professionalism, Barbour being one of those found to have received free groceries in lieu of pay. Ever present thereafter, he opted to miss the match against Everton in January in order to play for Sunderland Albion in a prestigious friendly against Sunderland. Back the following weekend, Barbour continued to score regularly over the following two seasons before moving to Bury. Turned into a full-back, he nevertheless scored the Shakers' first League goal in 1894.

Brand, R. (17/11)

Brand came south with Barbour from Queen of the South Wanderers. Scored on his debut against Derby and then three weeks later scored a further three against the Rams to become Accrington's first League hat-trick scorer. In January he travelled north to play for Sunderland Albion against Sunderland, and he later joined Albion the following season in which he played just twice for Accrington.

Bonar, James (17)

A professional who played one season for Accrington but failed to score a single goal in seventeen games from inside-right.

Gallacher, P (1/1)

With no player having scored from the inside-right position during the season, Gallacher was given his chance in the last game and opened the scoring in a 2-0 victory over Stoke. A further thirty-eight League appearances were made over the following two seasons in which he scored six goals.

Galbraith, H. (1)

An amateur who played his only League game in the penultimate match of the season.

Holden (6/4)
Holden might have scored Accrington's first League goal in the opening day's fixture against Everton but a lack of records means Holden's first name remains unrecorded and he left the club at the end of the season having scored four times in six League fixtures. He appears to have been an amateur player.

Kirkham, John B. (19/12)
John Kirkham represented Accrington during the five seasons they played in the Football League, and played more games than anyone else (104), also being joint top League scorer with thirty-three.

Lofthouse, Joseph M. (21/2)
Lofthouse is best known for his time at Blackburn Rovers where he twice won FA Cup winner's medals. Was at Thorneyholme Road for two seasons and during which he won one, scoring against Ireland, of his seven England caps. He was later assistant trainer at Everton.

Macbeth, R. (1)
An amateur player who played just the once for Accrington during the period when Brand was with Sunderland Albion.

Robertson, J. (3)
With Bonar having failed to score in twelve League games from inside-right Robertson, an amateur, was given three opportunities to capture a first team place. He did well on his debut, Accrington thrashing Burnley 5-1, but after three games without a goal he was left out of the side and never played again for the club.

Wilkinson, A. (3/1)
Scored in the 2-2 draw away to Burnley and made a further nineteen League appearances over the following two seasons in which he scored ten times. Other professionals registered at Accrington who didn't play during the season were: John Nuttall, William Warsley, Stanton John, Jason W. Hargreaves, James Holding and Robert Clegg – who played just once for Accrington during the 1891/92 season.

ASTON VILLA

Goalkeepers
Warner, James (21)
Supple and shrewd, and agile enough to reach (punch) the most difficult of efforts at goal, Warner played in two FA Cup finals for Villa, both against WBA, gaining a winner's medal in 1887 and a loser's medal in 1892.

Rumours abounded that he sold the latter game, in which he made the last of his 101 appearances for Villa, and as a result he had his pub damaged by irate supporters. He was to die after falling down the stairs at his home in Pittsburgh, USA in November 1943.

Ashmore, Walter (1)
Signed for Aston Villa at the start of the season and played only once before moving on to Aston Unity FC.

Full-backs

Cox, Gersom (22)
One of three Villa players to play in every League game in the first season, Gersom Cox later collected an FA Cup runner's-up medal in 1892. He failed to score for Villa in 102 League and FA Cup appearances.

Coulton, Frank (19)
Played in the first League game against Wolves. An FA Cup winner in 1887, Frank Coulton was a stylish full-back who made sixty League and FA Cup appearances for Villa.

Dawson, Fred (3)
A member of Aston Villa's 1887 FA Cup winning side, Fred Dawson was a tenacious opponent who lined up at left-half in Villa's first League game.

Dixon, Arthur (3/1)
Recruited in August 1888, Arthur Dixon not only scored but was also knocked out on his debut in Villa's first home League game against Stoke. Stayed just one season before moving on to the Victoria Ground.

Half-backs

Yates, Harry (14)
Known because of his 14-stone weight as 'Tubby', Yates was a solid, powerful defender who gained an FA Cup-winner's medal with Villa in 1887 and made twenty-nine League and FA Cup appearances for the club.

Devey, Harry (21)
Harry signed for Villa in August 1887 and was a member of the side that faced Wolves in the opening day's League fixture. A keen, hard tackler, the Birmingham-born player enjoyed bringing the ball forward although his efforts at goal were not successful as he failed to score in eighty-four League and FA Cup appearances. Younger brother of Jack (see below) and Bob who played ten times for Villa from 1892 to 1894.

Burton, John (15)
An FA Cup winner in 1886/87 Burton was a strong, hard-kicking player who played for Aston Villa from April 1885 until an injury forced him to retire in August 1893.

Woollaston, Arthur (4)
Moved to Aston Villa in April 1888, where in addition to four League matches he featured against Witton in the first round of the FA Cup.

Forwards

Brown, Albert (22/7)
Played for a decade for Aston Villa until retiring in July 1894. Comfortable playing at right half, outside-right or inside-right, Albert was the younger brother of Alfred and the two starred in the same forward line during the 1884/85 and 1885/86 seasons. Albert was a member of the 1887 FA Cup winning side and in the 1888/89 season he played in all Villa's League games in which he scored seven times.

Green, Tom (22/14)
Scored Villa's first League goal against Wolves on 8 September 1888. Green, an enthusiastic, hard-working player, had represented WBA at the 1886 FA Cup final before switching to neighbours Villa the following season and playing against his former club at the 1887 FA Cup final where the Throstles lost for a second consecutive year.

Allen, Albert (21/18)
Scorer of Villa's first League hat-trick when Notts County were thrashed 9-1 in September 1888. A good dribbler and fine shot, Allen hit three goals in his only England international appearance against Ireland in 1888. Able to play in a number of forward positions, Albert enjoyed a wonderful understanding with fellow forward Denis Hodgetts.

Garvey, 'Bat' (2)
Recruited from a local junior club in March 1888, Garvey was at inside-left when Villa played their first League game. He was to make only seven first-team appearances before injury forced him to retire at the age of twenty-nine.

Hodgetts, Dennis (17/7)
Born in Birmingham (where he also died), Dennis Hodgetts was a Villa man through and through who served the club superbly both on and off the pitch. Powerful and alert with the ability to use both feet, Hodgetts was also a terrific shot and a superb distributor of the ball. By utilising the outside of

his right foot, he could race down the wing before centring accurately. No wonder he was adored by Villa fans, for whom he scored over 100 goals in all matches. Hodgetts played six internationals for England and won two League championship medals in 1894 and 1896 and two FA Cup winner's medals in 1887 and 1895. Villa's coach in 1899/1900, he was vice president at Villa Park from 1910 until his death in 1945.

Hunter, Archibald (19/6)
One of Aston Villa's early stars who played for the club from 1878 until he suffered a heart attack when playing against Everton on Merseyside on 4 January 1890. Never fully recovering, the player known as 'The Old Warhorse' died four years later at the age of thirty-five. As Villa skipper, Hunter had become the first player to score in every round of the 1886/87 FA Cup, which his side won by beating WBA 2-0 in the final at the Oval. With thirty-three FA Cup goals, he remains Villa's record scorer in the competition. A clever player with a commanding personality, Hunter scored twice when Notts County were thrashed 9-1 early in the 1888/89 season.

Harrison, Tom (1)
A winger who played only once.

Utility
Goodall, Archie (14/7)
Younger brother of the then Preston player John Goodall, Archie played just under a season for Aston Villa, who he joined from Deepdale in October 1888 (thus becoming the first transferred player in League history). Playing at centre-half he scored on his debut against Blackburn Rovers and later his two goals gave his side both points in a 2-1 win at home to Wolves. He left Villa to join up with his brother at Derby County for the start of the following season and when he eventually left there he had played 423 times for the Rams. The son of corporal in the Royal Scottish Fusiliers Archie, after being born there, played eight times for Ireland whereas his brother played on fourteen occasions for his birthplace, England. Both men had strong Scottish accents.

BLACKBURN ROVERS

Goalkeepers
Arthur, John (15)
Herbie Arthur was one of the greatest 'keepers of his generation. Preferring positional play to panache, he played seven times for England and won three FA Cup winners' medals and two Lancashire Cup winners' medals during his nine-season reign as Rovers 'keeper starting in April 1882. Although he began the first Football League season, an injury away to Notts County just before Christmas

saw him miss the majority of the rest of the season. Never fully fit after that, he made a further twenty-five League appearances over the next three seasons but was left out of the Rovers sides for the 1891 and 1892 FA Cup finals.

Suter, Fergus (1)

Suter's single League game, in which he appeared between the posts away to WBA, belies his importance in the development of the game of football, in particular the move away from amateurism and towards professionalism, with Suter's appearance for Darwen alongside his Partick Thistle teammate Jimmy Love during the 1879 FA Cup marking the start of the back-door professionalism that eventually forced the Football Association to change its rules. Suter was a member of the beaten Rovers side at the 1882 FA Cup final but also won the cup three times when Rovers triumphed in 1884, 1885 and 1886. In an era where the Scottish selectors refused to pick players who had moved south he never played for his country.

Holden, William (1)

Born in Darwen in 1860. Rovers borrowed William from Darwen in December 1888 after a goalkeeping crisis arose over Christmas. He was returned to Darwen after playing in a 1-0 defeat at Deepdale.

McOwen, William or Billy (5)

McOwen played fifteen times, fourteen in the League, during his two seasons with Blackburn. He was born in Darwen in 1871. At just under 5 feet 6 inches, he was small for a 'keeper.

Full-backs

Beverley, Jon (8)

A fine full-back who enjoyed three spells with Rovers, playing just a single game in 1879/80 and then returning after a spell with Blackburn Olympic in the summer of 1882. Then after being a member of the 1884 cup-winning side he once again signed for Olympic before finally returning to Rovers for the start of the 1886/87 season. The England international was thirty-one when the 1888/89 season started and although he played six of the first seven games it was no surprise that with just two further appearances he was not retained at the end of the season.

Forbes, John (16)

By deciding to sign soon after the start of the 1888/89 season for Blackburn Rovers from Vale of Leven, the half-back brought to an end his international career at five caps. Having twice lost in Scottish FA Cup finals, Forbes later won the FA Cup twice with Rovers and by the end of his career with the club in 1894 he had made 127 League and FA Cup appearances in which he had scored twice. Forbes was unusual, as he much preferred to pass the ball out of defence rather than kick it long. Later he became a member of the Rovers board and a successful local businessman.

Southworth, James (19)

Brother of Jack, James Southworth played just twenty-seven times for Blackburn Rovers in his three years at the club. Most of these came in his first season in 1888/89 but he was the following season lucky enough to play in the FA Cup final in which Sheffield Wednesday were thrashed 6-1. It proved his final appearance for Rovers.

Half-backs

Douglas, Jimmy (21)

Twenty-eight-year-old Douglas had been one of the Rovers' FA Cup stars in the mid-1880s, helping the side to three consecutive successes in '84, '85 and '86, thus making up for the disappointment of losing to Old Etonians in the 1882 final. Capped for his country before moving south of the border, the Scotsman was a very skilful half-back who played for twelve seasons with Rovers before retiring at the end of the 1891/92 season. Douglas played a combined total of seventy-six League and FA Cup matches in which he scored eight goals.

Almond, William (21/1)

Willie Almond was a local lad who Blackburn signed from Witton at the start of the first League season. He was moved to centre-half when John Forbes arrived from Scotland and missed out on becoming the first Rovers player to play in every League game in a season when he missed the penultimate match. He went on to make a total of sixty-seven League and FA Cup appearances before he departed the club at the end of the 1892/93 season.

Forrest, James (19/1)

One of Blackburn Rovers greatest players, playing in five successful FA Cup finals between 1884 and 1891. He also represented England on eleven occasions and was the first professional to play for his country in a major fixture when he turned out against Scotland in 1886. He was made to wear a different, coarser shirt than his amateur teammates.[7] Debuting on 27 January 1883 for Rovers, he was still playing twelve years later, combining a keen attitude with strong positional sense and an ability to find his teammates with a shrewd, accurate pass. Later became a Blackburn Rovers director.

Barton, Jack (5)

A native of Blackburn, John Barton started out, like many at Rovers, in the ranks of local junior organisation King's Own. Following a spell at local club

Witton alongside Nathan Walton he joined Rovers and made his debut in a
5-1 beating of local rivals Blackburn Olympic in round two of the 1887/88 FA
Cup. It was a competition in which he was to go on and collect two winners'
medals – in 1890 and 1891. Barton played once for England, scoring once in
a 9-1 defeat of Ireland in March 1890. By the time injury brought his career
to a premature end during the 1891/92 season, he had played fifty-three times,
including forty League matches, for Rovers. He died in 1910.

Forwards
Beresford, James (12/4)
Beresford made fourteen League and FA Cup appearances during his
two-year stint with Rovers, debuting against Blackburn Olympic in the
1887/88 FA Cup. He headed Rovers into a 2-1 lead in their first League
game and was a regular in the side up until Christmas. Left out of the side
that made it through to the FA Cup semi-final, he was released at the end
of the season.

In 1883/84, Beresford inadvertently caused Accrington to be expelled
from the FA Cup when he scored two goals in a 5-1 win over Rossendale.
He then returned to Church but was paid a fee to be kept on Accrington's
books. The FA found out and charged Accrington with breaking the rules
and expelled them from that season's FA Cup.

Walton, Nat (20/10)
Nat Walton was an FA Cup winner on three occasions – 1886, 1890
and 1891 – and for many years he and William Townley formed a fine
partnership down the left and the two played in the England side against
Ireland in 1890, Walton's only international match. Later in his career,
Walton converted to goalkeeper, and although he became the Rovers' first
team custodian during the 1892/93 season he departed to Nelson at the
end of the season in a dispute over his contractual terms.

Southworth, Jack (21/17)
John (Jack) Southworth scored Blackburn Rovers first League goal on
15 September 1888. Speedy, unselfish, a good dribbler and deadly in
front of goal, he was a firm fan favourite and it was no surprise when
he earned a call up for England in February 1889, and he scored as his
country beat Wales 4-1. Two further caps followed against Wales in 1891
and Scotland the following year, when he was one of four players born
in Blackburn – the others being Edgar Chadwick, Johnny Holt and West
Bromwich Albion's Reynolds. Southworth scored in both games.

Southworth was one of the Rovers' scorers in the 1890 FA Cup final when
Sheffield Wednesday was thumped 6-1. The following season he was top
scorer in the League and also collected a second FA Cup winner's medal.

Southworth joined Everton for a fee of £400 for the start of the 1893/94 season. Notching twenty-seven goals to again finish as the League's top scorer, he had started the 1894/95 season with nine in nine matches before a serious leg injury forced to him retire prematurely from the game. Jack Southworth was also an accomplished musician and pursued a career as a professional violinist.

Fecitt, Harry (17/12)
Fecitt had two spells with Rovers, of which the 1888/89 was the last and shortest, as despite scoring twelve times in seventeen League games he left to sign for Northwich Victoria at the start of the following season. Earlier he had represented the club from 1883/84 to 1886/87, scoring four times on his debut in an 11-0 thrashing of Rossendale in the FA Cup first round of 1884/85. When Rovers went on to win the competition, Harry Fecitt played in the final against Scottish club Queen's Park and he was also a member of the following season's side that retained the famous trophy.

Townley, William (19/8)
A native of Blackburn, Townley played for Blackburn Olympic before joining Rovers. After starting at centre-forward he was moved to the left wing where he soon blossomed, forming a fine partnership with Nat Walton. He was capped twice by England and won three FA Cup winners' medals. A speedy, tricky winger, he could cross the ball with deadly accuracy. He made 124 League and FA Cup appearances for Blackburn Rovers, of which his best was undoubtedly the 1890 FA Cup final when he became the first man to score a hat-trick. He later became a highly successful coach, with spells in charge at Bayern Munich and with the Dutch National side.

Haresnape, Robert (9/2)
Haresnape played just one season for Blackburn and did much better during it in the FA Cup, where in addition to scoring a hat-trick against Aston Villa in a 8-1 win he scored three more times in three appearances. Later, he played three seasons for Burnley.

Porter, Robert (1)
Porter played in the 5-2 victory at home to Stoke.

Brown, James (4)
Having played with distinction for seven seasons from 1879/80 onwards, James Brown, who as a member of all three sides to win the FA Cup between 1884 and 1886 earned his place in the record books by becoming the only player to score in three consecutive finals, returned to Blackburn Rovers after a two-year non-playing gap for the start of the 1888/89 season. Hopes that his dribbling skills, delicate touch, devastating pace

and eye for a goal (shown at their best with the second goal in the replayed FA Cup final against WBA in 1886) would soon be again back on show were to prove unduly optimistic. In the event, he played only four League games before permanently retiring from the game he had served so well. A solicitor's clerk, he played five times for England, scoring three times.

Whittaker, J. (4)
Whittaker played four of the last six League games of the season and was not retained at the end of the season. His first name is believed to be Bernard.

Duerden, James (2)
Duerden played two games during his only season at Blackburn Rovers, both of which were won against Accrington and Derby County respectively.

Mitchell, W. (1/2)
Mitchell played in the final game of the season, and scored twice. Rovers won 3-0 and Mitchell was never seen again in the side. Has also been listed as 'T.' Mitchell.

Stothert, J. (1/1)
Bohemians player drafted in when Fecitt was unavailable.

BOLTON WANDERERS

Goalkeepers
Harrison, C. E. (19)
Harrison played two seasons at Pikes Lane, making twenty-four appearances in the Bolton goal.

Gillam, S. G. (2)
Gillam conceded five goals in his final appearance as Bolton was beaten 5-2 at home by Preston North End.

Parkinson, J. (2) (1 at full back)
Parkinson played thirty-eight times, the majority in goal, for Bolton over three seasons from 1888/89 to 1890/91. Playing as a forward, he scored his only League goal on the opening day of the 1889/90 season.

Full-backs
Robinson, B. (18)
The full-back made forty-one appearances for Bolton in three seasons of League football.

Mitchell, J. (2)
Mitchell played two games in his only season at Pikes Lane.

Jones, David 'Dai' (12)
Capped fourteen times for Wales, Dai Jones could play in either full-back position where his strong tackling and ability to kick with either foot made him a big favourite at Bolton, where he played for the first ten League seasons in which he made 228 League and twenty-seven FA Cup appearances and scored eight goals. Captain of the Wanderers side that lost out to Notts County in the 1894 FA Cup final, Jones later won a Second Division championship medal with Manchester City, for whom he played 114 times.

Flitcroft, W. (7)
Flitcroft made eight appearances in two seasons at Bolton Wanderers.

Siddons, E. (1) & Mercer, D. (1)
Both men played one game and one season at Bolton.

Half-backs
Roberts, Robert (22/2)
Roberts had played against South Shore in a 5-3 FA Cup first-round victory on 30 October 1886 and was to make eighty-five appearances over the next six seasons.

Weir, David (22/10)
Hampshire-born Weir was ever-present for Bolton in the first season of the Football League, switching from centre-half to forward as the campaign progressed. He scored three times against Accrington on 22 December and thus became the first Bolton player to score a hat-trick in League football. On 1 February 1890 he was to score four times, and his colleague Jim Cassidy five, as Sheffield United were routed 13-0 in an FA Cup tie, a result which is Wanderers' record victory in a major competition. In May 1890, Weir left Bolton to join Ardwick, the predecessor of Manchester City, who were not then in the League. Weir's Bolton performances gained him international recognition and he played against Ireland on 2 March 1889 and a month later against Scotland.

Bullough, P. A. (15/1)
Bullough made a scoring debut against Eagley for Bolton in the FA Cup in the 1884/85 season and was to make fifty-two League and cup appearances for the Wanderers, of which the match against West Brom on 3 November 1890 was the last.

Simmers, W. (2)
Simmers played just twice in a 6-2 victory against Everton and a 4-1 defeat against Burnley.

Scowcroft, J. (9/1)
Scowcroft scored against Blackburn in a 4-4 draw in December.

Dyer, F. (1)
Dyer played in the 5-2 defeat against Preston in November.

Forwards

Davenport, Kenny (22/11)
Kenny Davenport played for Bolton Wanderers for eleven seasons, joining the club from Gilnow Rangers in 1883. Scorer of the first goal in League history when he netted at 3.47 p.m. on 8 September 1888, James Kenyon Davenport was born a stone's throw away from Pikes Lane where he achieved one of the most important feats in the game of football. By the time League football commenced, Davenport was already an England international, the first in Bolton's long history. He played once more, scoring twice in a 9-1 victory against Ireland in Belfast in 1890. Normally an inside-left, Davenport made fifty-six League and twenty-one FA Cup appearances for Wanderers, scoring thirty-six goals.

Milne, Jim (22/6)
Milne played thirty-nine times for Bolton in two seasons of League football and scored nine times, including two against Everton in Bolton's first victory in the League.

Cooper, T. (3/1)
Cooper scored against Burnley in the second match of the season.

Barbour, Alec (14/9)
Barbour's return to the first team at the end of the season helped Wanderers win the final four games of the season to push Bolton away from the re-election zone and into fifth place in the table. Barbour scored seventeen goals in thirty-four League games for Bolton in four seasons of League football. He scored a hat-trick against Accrington in the 1890/91 season.

Brogan, James (22/13)
One of the Wanderers' first professional footballers when he was signed in 1884 from Hearts. Comfortable at either inside- or outside-left, he scored in the opening League game of the season and went on to become Bolton's leading League scorer during a season in which he was ever present. On

leaving the game in 1892, he returned to work in the Scottish shipyards, doing so until he died aged eighty-five in 1951.

Tyrer, Harry (14/2)

Tyrer played just one season of League football with Bolton, but later returned with Darwen, where he made eighty-three senior club appearances between 1895 and 1898.

Owen, G. (7/3)

Owen scored against Accrington, Stoke and Blackburn Rovers.

Turner, James A. (2/1)

Turner scored on his debut in the penultimate match of the season as Wanderers beat Notts County 7-3 at home. He earlier notched a hat-trick as Wanderers reserve side beat West Manchester 9-0 in the FA Cup qualifying round. Turner later became a half-back and after playing in all four matches of the 1893/94 FA Cup he was left out of the side when Bolton faced Notts County in the final, Wanderers going down to a 4-1 defeat. Turner was released at the end of the 1893/94 season after making 108 League and FA Cup appearances. He made one international appearance, scoring against Wales in a 6-0 England victory on 13 March 1893.

McGuinness, H. (1/1)

McGuinness scored in his one League game against Wolves in November 1888.

BURNLEY

Profiles provided by Ray Simpson.

Goalkeepers

Kay, Robert (5)

Goalkeeper Robert Kay first signed for Burnley in the summer of 1884. During his Turf Moor career he appeared only occasionally at first-team level and was not first choice when League football began in September 1888. But after just three matches of that inaugural League campaign he was thrust into the limelight, taking his place between the sticks at West Bromwich. Albion edged home 4-3 and Kay kept his place for the next match, the historic first League match at Turf Moor, Burnley overcoming Bolton 4-1. Robert Kay's fifth and final League appearance for the Turfites was a 1-6 defeat at Notts County, after which he left Turf Moor.

Cox, Walter (13)

Walter Cox was signed by Burnley from Scottish football in November 1888, after the fiasco of the Turfites' 1-7 home defeat by Blackburn, which had featured centre-forward Fred Poland in goal. He immediately impressed on his debut, a 2-0 victory against West Brom, which was Burnley's first clean sheet during that inaugural League season. Cox kept his place for the remainder of the campaign and on into the next season, but in January 1890 he suddenly left Turf Moor. The following month he signed for Everton, appearing in just four senior games, before joining Nottingham Forest. He again featured only briefly for Forest in the Football Alliance during 1890/91.

Smith, William S. (3)

William Smith was Burnley's first-ever goalkeeper in League football, lining up for the Turfites at Deepdale on that historic opening day of the Football League in September 1888. Within two minutes he was picking the ball out of his net as North End scored the first of their five goals, Burnley eventually going down 2-5 to the team destined to win the first League championship. William Smith, an amateur throughout his Turf Moor career, played just seven games spread over the first eight seasons of League football and Burnley won just one of them, the custodian conceding a total of twenty-five goals.

Full-backs

Bury, William Harold (20)

Bury came to Turf Moor from local rivals Padiham in 1887, having built up a reputation as a hard-tackling defender with a number of local clubs. He immediately established a full-back partnership with Sandy Lang, who had also arrived at Turf Moor from Padiham and the two became stalwarts in the Burnley defence. William Bury appeared in twenty of Burnley's twenty-two League games in that historic first season of League football. In the second season, 1889/90, he was ever-present, appearing in every one of Burnley's twenty-two League games. He also scored his only goal at senior level for Burnley during that season, in a 2-1 defeat against Sheffield United in the FA Cup first round at Bramall Lane. He represented Lancashire against East of Scotland and Staffordshire (dates not confirmed).

Hargreaves

A reserve-team player, Hargreaves' only first-team appearance was at left-back in Burnley's 4-3 home victory against Old Westminsters in the FA Cup, 2 February 1889.

Kavanagh

Kavanagh's only appearance at first-team level was at right-back in Burnley's 1-5 defeat at Accrington, 1 December 1888.

Lang, Alexander (Sandy) (21)

Full-back Sandy Lang was Burnley's first captain when League football came to Turf Moor in 1888. He was born at Bridge of Weir, near Paisley, in 1864 and was only twenty when he joined Padiham – then one of Lancashire's leading clubs – in 1884. He was transferred to Burnley in 1885 and was a constant presence during the early years of League football, becoming the first Turf Moor player to complete 100 League appearances in March 1893. One of just two League goals scored by Sandy Lang in his senior career was Burnley's first-ever penalty in November 1891 after the introduction of the spot-kick the previous summer. West Brom were the victims in a 3-2 victory and Joe Reader, later an England international, was the goalkeeper on the receiving end. Lang retired from League football in 1895, joining Nelson, with whom he won a Lancashire League championship medal in 1896. Sandy Lang became a publican in Burnley but died tragically at his home in 1901, aged only thirty-seven.

Half-backs

John (Jack) Abrahams (also spelt Abraham and Abrams) (13/1)

Jack Abrahams arrived at Turf Moor in the summer of 1885, becoming one of Burnley FC's very first professionals. He was a regular in the Burnley defence, usually playing as a wing-half, and along with Danny Friel and Jack Keenan, formed the Turfites' half-back line as League football began in 1888. Abrahams, along with William Bury and William Tait, celebrated Burnley's 4-3 victory at Bolton in September 1888 a little too wildly and all three were suspended for one game by the Burnley Committee for 'imbibing intoxicants too freely'. He scored just one goal in his only League season, hitting the winner in Burnley's single-goal victory against Notts County at Turf Moor at Christmas 1888. He left Turf Moor in the spring of 1889 to play local junior football.

Friel, Daniel (Danny) (22)

Relatively small in stature, but a very talented footballer, Danny Friel was the only ever-present in Burnley's side during the historic first season of League football in 1888/89. By the start of the Football League, Friel had already been at Turf Moor for five years, arriving from Accrington in October 1883, having been tempted to come south from Scotland to further his career. In his early days with Burnley, Friel often played at centre-forward, but such was his versatility that he was equally at home in defence or attack. He was invariably among the first players on Burnley's team sheet week after week, and his overall contribution to the Turf Moor cause should not be underestimated. During 1889/90 Friel was no longer an automatic choice and played his last senior game in November 1889. His record shows just thirty-three senior games for Burnley but his total appearances for the club numbered well over 300 and he is rightly regarded as one of the key figures at Turf Moor in those far-off days.

McFetteridge (also spelt McFettridge and McFetridge), William (16)
Bill McFetteridge was yet another of the rugged Scots who dominated Burnley Football Club in the 1880s and 1890s. He partnered Jack Keenan at half-back for much of his time at Turf Moor and the pair was instrumental in the famous Lancashire Cup win against Blackburn Rovers in 1890. McFetteridge was born in Govan, Glasgow in 1862 and played his early football for the Thornliebank club in the south of the city. He came south to England in 1883 to join Padiham, then a footballing power in Lancashire, before being transferred to Burnley in 1886. He soon established himself as a versatile member of the side, playing both in attack and defence, before making the right half-back position his own. He missed Burnley's first League game in 1888 but continued to perform consistently over the first four seasons of League football, his hard robust style proving very effective in those early days. McFetridge's brother, David, joined Bolton Wanderers from Cowlairs in 1891, and was the Trotters' regular left-winger during the club's successful campaign in 1891/92.

Keenan, Jack (20)
A strong, powerful half-back, Jack Keenan came to Burnley from Clitheroe, his home-town club, in 1884 and quickly established himself in a team consisting almost entirely of Scots. Keenan was a regular in his early days at Turf Moor and his consistency brought him to the fringe of international honours. He was called up to join the England party in March 1888 but was not selected to play against Scotland in Glasgow, watching from the sidelines as England won 5-0. He continued to be a regular choice in the Burnley side during the first years of League football and was outstanding in the famous 2-0 Lancashire Cup final victory against Blackburn Rovers at Accrington in April 1890. Keenan retired from the game in 1893 to work in a local brewery.

Ridsdale, J. (1)
Essentially a reserve-team player, Ridsdale played at right-half, deputising for the suspended Jack Abrahams, in Burnley's 1-4 defeat at Wolves, 22 September 1888. He joined Brierfield in 1889.

Forwards
Brady, Alexander (20/7)
Burnley's leading goalscorer in the first season of League football, 1888/89, was Alex Brady, who was born in Cathcart, Glasgow, arriving at Turf Moor from Partick Thistle in the summer of 1888. Brady scored seven goals in just

twenty matches for the Turfites, mainly playing as a right-winger, before he left to join Sunderland in February 1889. He was transferred to Everton in November 1889, scoring two goals on his debut in an 8-0 victory against Stoke at Anfield. Brady further strengthened an already powerful Everton side, who finished as runners-up to Preston in 1890 before lifting the League Championship Cup themselves in 1891. He was lured back to Glasgow that summer, joining Celtic, and collected a Scottish Cup winner's medal in 1892 as Queens Park were beaten 5-1 at Ibrox. The Celts finished as runners-up to Dumbarton in the Scottish League, although they won both the Glasgow Cup and the Glasgow Charity Cup. He came south again, this time to Sheffield to join the Wednesday as the Yorkshire club began life in the Football League, having been elected to an enlarged First Division. His senior debut in September 1892 was Wednesday's first-ever Football League fixture, a 1-0 win at Notts County. Alec Brady spent the rest of his career in England with Wednesday, who proved to be a redoubtable FA Cup side. After two successive semi-final defeats in 1894 and 1895 they lifted the famous old trophy for the first time in 1896, overcoming Wolves 2-1 at the Crystal Palace.

Brady, W. (9/2)

Inside-forward W. Brady arrived at Turf Moor in December 1888 and immediately won a place in Burnley's senior team for the home fixture with Stoke. Playing at inside-right in place of the injured McKay, Brady scored within fifteen minutes of his debut as the Turfites went on to win 2-1. He kept his place in the team for the rest of the season, scoring twice more, before moving on to Newcastle West End, then playing in the Northern League.

Duckworth, Robert William (1)

Robert Duckworth made just five senior appearances during his time with Burnley, scoring one goal in a 2-2 draw with Accrington in September 1889, his first appearance at Turf Moor. His main Football League experience came in the Second Division with Lincoln City, for whom he was a regular during the Imps' 1894/95 campaign. He later rejoined Burnley but never appeared again at senior level.

Gallocher, Patrick (20/6)

Pat Gallocher has the distinction of scoring Burnley Football Club's first-ever League goal in the Turfites' 2-5 defeat at Preston on the very first day of League football, 8 September 1888. Gallocher left his native Scotland in 1883, aged just nineteen, to join Padiham, then one of Lancashire's leading clubs. After occasionally appearing for Burnley as a guest player, Gallocher moved to Turf Moor in the summer of 1886 and was virtually an automatic choice in the Burnley team for the next three years. A very quick and tricky player with wonderful close ball control, Gallocher, nicknamed 'the

Artful Dodger', played in all but two of Burnley's League matches during that historic inaugural season of 1888/89. He joined Accrington in March 1889, scoring on his debut in the Owd Reds' last match of the season. He spent two full seasons as a regular at Thorneyholme Road, playing in both defence and attack, before leaving to return to his native Scotland in 1892. Pat Gallocher later joined the Army and served his country with distinction in South Africa during the Boer War.

Hibbert, John Salmon (Jack) (1)
A reserve-team player, Jack Hibbert appeared at outside-right in Burnley's 1-6 defeat at Notts County, 27 October 1888.

McCrae, Robert (2)
Bob McCrae joined Burnley in 1884, playing and scoring regularly at senior level in the years leading up to the formation of the Football League. A stonemason by trade, McCrae was also a craftsman with the ball, 'able to manipulate it like few players could and had no superior as a dribbler'. Sadly, by 1888/89 his Burnley career was coming to an end and the first of only two games he played in the Football League was the 1-7 home defeat by Blackburn Rovers in November 1888. He later moved into amateur local football with Union Star.

McKay, William (5/4)
Scotsman William McKay appeared in just five games for Burnley, scoring four goals, including a consolation on his debut, in the Turfites' 1-7 hammering by Blackburn Rovers in November 1888. Just a month later he suffered an injury in Burnley's 1-5 defeat at Accrington, and it was reported that he would be on the sidelines for some weeks. In the event, he never appeared in the senior team again, and by the following season was playing for Newcastle West End, who finished as runners-up in the Northern League.

McMahon, Ross (2)
Centre-forward Ross McMahon was signed by Burnley from Perth junior club Erin Rovers in November 1888 on the same day that goalkeeper Walter Cox arrived from Hibernian. Both players made their debuts immediately in Burnley's 2-0 win against West Brom, the Turfites' first clean sheet of the season. However, McMahon's arrival in English football was a day of mixed fortunes. He was injured after just forty minutes and played no further part in proceedings, leaving Burnley to achieve their victory with only ten men. Three weeks later, McMahon lined up again to lead Burnley's attack in their away clash with Accrington at Thorneyholme Road. Once again he was injured before half-time and had to go off, and once again the Turfites soldiered on for the rest of the game with ten men. No happy

ending this time, however – Accrington easily won the encounter 5-1. In February 1889, Ross McMahon played two more competitive games for Burnley in the FA Cup, managing to complete them both, but didn't score in either. He left Turf Moor at the end of the season.

Mackay (also spelt McKay)

Burnley debut: 8 December 1888 *v*. Stoke (h) Football League, won 2-1. Last game: 2 March 1889 *v*. Derby C (a) Football League, lost 0-1. Confusingly, inside-forward Mackay arrived from Scottish Cup finalists Cambuslang in December 1888, just as his near namesake, William McKay, also an inside-forward, had played what turned out to be his final game for Burnley after an injury.[8] The new Mackay played in all of Burnley's remaining League games that season and scored his first goal in the Turfites' 2-2 draw against Preston in December 1888. He scored the only goal in Burnley's 1-0 victory against Derby at Turf Moor in January 1889, but left the club in the summer of 1889.

Midgley (also spelt Midgeley), Thomas (Tom) (1)

Born in Leeds in 1856, Tom Midgley held teaching posts in Culham, Oxford and Ripon before being appointed as headmaster at Grant's School in Burnley in the late 1870s. While at Carlton Road School (Burnley), as early as 1880 he had children playing Association football. A founder member of Burnley Rovers Rugby Club and its first captain, Midgley was also instrumental in the change to Association football in 1882, again becoming its first captain. Midgley was thirty-two when the Football League was founded in 1888 and at the end of his career he was proud to appear for Burnley in the infant competition. He had travelled to Stoke with the Turf Moor party in October 1888 when William Tait failed to appear and he lined up at inside-right in a 4-3 defeat for the Turfites. It was his only taste of League football. He retired from the teaching profession in 1921, aged sixty-five, and left East Lancashire in 1926 to live out his retirement in Wales. Tom Midgley, one of the father figures of Burnley FC, died in 1957 at the grand old age of 101 years.

Mudie, Leonard (Len) (1)

Mudie played at centre-forward in Burnley's 2-1 victory against Stoke at Turf Moor, 8 December 1888. He left Turf Moor 1889 to join Stoke, and later played for Dundee Wanderers.

Poland, Fred (9)

Fred Poland arrived in Burnley in April 1888 looking for work, having travelled to Lancashire from his home in Scotland. He immediately let it be known around the town that he was a footballer, having played at senior level north of the border, and also that he was both a goalscorer and a goalkeeper. Within two days, Burnley FC heard about him and invited him to play in a friendly match against Newton Heath at Turf Moor. He played at centre-forward and perhaps exceeded expectations somewhat by performing extremely well and scoring two goals in a 7-1 victory. He continued to play well and score goals as the 1887/88 season drew to a close and, needless to say, he was retained by the Turfites ready for the dawn of League football. He began the new season at centre-forward and scored in Burnley's first League fixture at Preston. He then claimed the distinction of scoring the first-ever League goal at Turf Moor, just five minutes after the start of Burnley's 4-1 victory against Bolton on 6 October 1888. 'Poland drew first blood about five minutes from the start, this exploit being received with cheers from the spectators.' (*Burnley Express*)

With five goals in his first eight League games, Poland looked the part, but then it all changed. With the unavailability of both goalkeepers, William Smith and Robert Kay, for the game at home to Blackburn Rovers, the Burnley committee decided to try Poland between the sticks, switching Bill McFetteridge, usually a defender, to centre-forward. Poland performed competently enough but the team as a whole was completely outplayed, going down 1-7. No blame was attached to the emergency custodian, indeed he was praised for his performance, but the fact remains he never played for Burnley again in any position and later emigrated to Australia.

Tait, William (5/5)

William Tait was signed by Burnley during the first week of August 1888 from Newton Heath. He made his League debut at inside-right in Burnley's first-ever Football League match on 8 September 1888, in a 5-2 defeat against Preston at Deepdale. In Burnley's second League match the following week, William wrote his own page of football history when he scored three of Burnley's goals as the Turfites came from 3-0 down to beat Bolton 4-3 at Wanderers' Pikes Lane ground. It was the first-ever hat-trick in League football.

There were then reports of 'certain excesses' by a number of Burnley players following the game at Bolton. A few days later, the Burnley Committee met and William Tait was suspended for a week, along with teammates William Bury and Jack Abrahams (both defenders) for 'imbibing intoxicants too freely'. All three players missed the following game as the Turfites crashed 4-1 at Wolves, and Tait played his next game for Burnley on 29 September at West Brom. He scored the first-ever League goal at West Brom's Stoney Lane ground, their base in those days, and Burnley led 2-0 and 3-2 before going down 4-3 to the Baggies.

He played again (and scored again) in Burnley's next League game, a 4-1 win in the return fixture against Bolton at Turf Moor, the first-ever Football League game to be played at Turf Moor. He played his final League game for Burnley on 13 October at Turf Moor as the Turfites crashed 4-0 to Wolves.

The following Saturday (20 October), he simply didn't turn up for a game at Stoke and Burnley had to play a reserve (Tom Midgley) in his place. The following week there was a comment in the local paper to the effect that 'William Tait had now ceased to be a member of the Burnley team'.

The following season he played in Newton Heath's very first game in the Football Alliance, a 4-1 win against Sunderland Albion on 21 September 1889 at North Road, Monsall. He played in seven Alliance games that season for Newton Heath, scoring once. He later played for West Manchester (Lancashire League) and later Ardwick, the forerunners of Manchester City.

Woods, James (1)
Woods played at inside-left in Burnley's 1-5 defeat at Accrington, 1 December 1888. He left Turf Moor 1889.

Yates, John (Jack) Yates (21/5)
Winger Jack Yates was Burnley Football Club's first-ever international, but before his days at Turf Moor he played a key role in the development of football as the working man's game in the 1880s.

Yates was born in Blackburn in 1861 and became a cotton weaver by trade, playing football with a number of junior clubs in the town. He joined the newly formed Blackburn Olympic in 1880, the working man's answer to the more elitist Blackburn Rovers, quickly becoming one of the new club's stars.

In 1883 Olympic astounded the football world by reaching the FA Cup final. Their opponents at the Kennington Oval were the cup holders, Old Etonians, and Olympic emerged triumphant winning 2-1 after extra time to bring the FA Cup to Lancashire for the first time. After the advent of professionalism in English football in 1885 Blackburn Olympic's fortunes waned as those of Rovers improved and Jack Yates joined Accrington, 'the Owd Reds', in 1886.

In the summer of 1888, with the world of football about to be changed again following the formation of the Football League, Yates moved to Turf Moor as Burnley prepared for the new era to be ushered in. He took his place in Burnley's line-up for the club's first-ever League game at Deepdale in September 1888, and although Preston won the match 5-2, Jack Yates had an excellent game and his fine form continued throughout the season. His consistency was rewarded with selection for the England team to play Ireland at Anfield in March 1889. Once again Jack Yates was on top form, scoring a hat-trick as the Irish were crushed 6-1.

Alas, it was to be his only international appearance and he also lost his automatic place in the Burnley side the following season. He left League football in 1894 and became a publican, for many years running the Brickmakers Arms in Yorkshire Street, close to Turf Moor. He died in 1917, aged fifty-five.

DERBY COUNTY

Goalkeepers

Bestwick, Harold (1)
Having played in the FA Cup in the seasons leading up to the formation of the Football League, the 'keeper played just once thereafter for Derby.

Bromage, Enos (2)
Bromage played in the final two games of the season and was also the man between the Derby sticks when the club suffered their record defeat, beaten 11-2 by Everton in the FA Cup on 18 January 1890.

Marshall, Joseph (16)
Signed from Staveley in 1887, Joe Marshall played in the first League game against Bolton Wanderers on 8 September 1888 and went on to miss just one of the next sixteen games. He moved on to Derby Junction at the end of the season.

Pitman, John (3)
John Reuben Pitman played just three League games for Derby County and his appearance between the posts helped his side capture all six points on offer in his matches.

Full-backs

Ferguson, Archibald (16)
Ferguson signed from Heart of Midlothian as Derby sought to bolster their defence in the run-up to the first season of League football. The side's regular left-back, Archie was a no-nonsense player with the familiar big kick forward of the time.

Latham, Arthur (20)
Signed from Derby Midland by County in 1886, Latham was to be the side's regular full-back in the opening two League seasons. Although he had long since quit playing, in April 1902 he swapped his role as trainer to go between the posts after Derby's 'keeper failed to arrive for the match with Blackburn.

Morley, Haydn (4)
Morley was the first player to be signed by Derby County after the club was formed in 1884, but a player at Notts County at the start of the 1888/89 season. On his return to the Racecourse Ground he joined John Pitman in goal by winning his first three matches, before drawing the fourth to move County off the bottom of the table. The son of William Morley, the man credited with

the practical moves that established Derby County, Haydn Morley later won an FA Cup runners-up medal with Sheffield Wednesday in 1890.

Roulstone, Frank (1)
Roulstone was signed from Sawley Rangers.

Half-backs
Bellhouse, E. W. (2)
Bellhouse played twice, winning one and losing one in January 1889.

Clifton, G. (1)
Clifton played only once, in a 3-2 defeat at home to Bolton Wanderers on Boxing Day 1888.

Harbour (or Hardboard) (1)
Arriving with only ten men at Anfield in October 1888, Derby were forced to borrow a player from the Everton opposition ranks. Harboard never played a first-team game for the Liverpudlians.

Hickinbottom, Ernest (1)
Hickinbottom played in the 3-2 home defeat against Bolton Wanderers on Boxing Day 1888. A local lad, he was rated one of County's most reliable players in the years following their formation and it was while watching the Rams that he died on 2 September 1939.

Hopewell, W. (5)
Fresh from Grimsby Town, Hopewell was introduced to the side after a poor start in which just one game had been won in five League games. His arrival at centre-half failed to revive fortunes and after five losing matches he was back in Cleethorpes before the end of the year.

Monks, Isaac (3)
Monks scored both of Derby's goals in the 2-1 first-round FA Cup success against Staveley the previous season but was at centre-half for the first League games in which his side won one, drew one and lost one.

Roulstone, Walter (21)
Roulstone played for Sawley Rangers before Derby County signed him in 1887 and he was to go on and become the club's first player to complete 100 senior appearances. Twenty-one of these came in the first League season and although the side had finished a miserable tenth he was considered good enough to retain his place the following season when club officials began to import more experienced professionals.

Selvey, Scotch (1)
Like his brother Walter, Selvey made only one senior appearance.

Smith, J. (10)
Smith made a dozen appearances in Derby County's first two League seasons.

Williamson, Albert (19)
Signed from Sawley Rangers at the start of the season, Albert Williamson was a regular at right-half in the first season of League football and later played for Notts County.

Wright, Levi (4/1)
More noted as a cricketer, scoring over 15,000 runs in first-class cricket, Levi Wright played four League games for Derby County in the 1888/89 season and also managed to score against Preston in a 3-2 defeat in September.

Forwards
Bakewell, George (16/8)
A brilliant outside-right who scored twelve goals for Derby County in sxity-four League and FA Cup games, Bakewell had been the second player signed by the club after its formation in 1884, and by taking one of their local rivals, Derby Midland's, best players, they began a pattern that was resented over the years. Bakewell, wafer thin and fast, scored twice on the opening day of the season and towards the end of the season he notched important goals as Derby made a last-gasp (though ultimately unsuccessful) dash to avoid needing to apply for re-election. He later played for Notts County as well as becoming, appropriately enough, a baker.

Chatterton, William (5/1)
One of four Test cricketers to play for Derby County. Played in the first FA Cup match, a 7-0 defeat against Walsall Town in November 1884. Scored against Everton in his second League game but left the club at the end of the season.

Cooper, Lewis (14/7)
Cooper returned from a short spell at Grimsby Town at the start of the season. A scorer for Derby in a 4-1 FA Cup victory against Aston Unity on October 1886, he scored twice on the opening day of the season in a 6-3 victory at Bolton and then towards the end of it he became the first County man to score in four consecutive League matches.

Higgins, Alexander (21/12)
An Ayrshire miner from Kilmarnock, Sandy Higgins signed for Derby at the start of the 1888/89 season and was to go on and finish as top scorer with twelve goals. Four of these came against Aston Villa in March, making him the first Derby player to score a hat-trick for the club. A good dribbler of the ball and a powerful shot, he later signed for Nottingham Forest and appeared in their first League team. In his only international appearance Higgins scored four times against Ireland in March 1885.

Lees, John (5/1)
Another ex-Sawley Rangers player, Lees played intermittently for County in the first two League seasons. Scored in the 4-1 defeat against Wolves.

Needham, Thomas (9/1)
A versatile forward, Needham first scored for Derby in a 6-2 victory against Owlerton on 26 November 1887 and who featured in Derby's first two League campaigns. He scored against Everton in October 1888, a 6-2 defeat that saw County drop to the bottom of the League.

Plackett, Henry (16/2)
Henry Plackett formed the left of Derby's attack with his brother in the first season of League football, at the end of which he moved to Nottingham Forest.

Plackett, Lawrence (22/6)
Lawrence Plackett was to join Nottingham Forest at the end of the 1888/89 season, in which he became the first Derby County player to complete an ever-present season in the Football League. A very fast player, he was twice on the scoresheet in the opening-day 6-3 victory at Bolton. He later played in an England trial match.

Selvey, Walter (1)
Selvey played just one League game for County in between spells at Derby Midland and Derby Junction.

Smart (1)
Smart played in a 4-2 game against Aston Villa on 29 December 1888.

Spilsbury, Benjamin (1/1)
Spilsbury scored the first goal ever recorded by Derby County when the side went down 4-3 against Blackburn Olympic on 27 September 1884. Three times capped for England, he scored five times for his country, including four against Ireland in 1886. While he was certainly playing for Derby at that time,

the record books list him as from Cambridge University, where he was then studying before later moving to Canada as a land agent. He played and scored in his only League game, a 4-2 defeat against Aston Villa over Christmas. He also scored seven goals in eight FA Cup matches for Derby, including the club's first hat-trick in a senior competition, when he assisted the side in a 6-0 defeat of Ecclesfield in the second round of the 1887/88 FA Cup.

EVERTON

Goalkeepers
Smalley, Bob (18)
Smalley was signed from Preston in the summer of 1887 and Everton's 'keeper in the first League game. A well-built, agile 'keeper, he was to retain his place throughout the season and the next before being replaced by Jack Angus.

Joliffe, Charles (4)
Starting in November 1883, Charlie Joliffe played almost 100 times for Everton over the next seven years. Despite losing his place to Bob Smalley the tall, lean 'keeper remained loyal to his home-town club and played on four occasions during the Toffees' inaugural season.

Full-backs
Ross, Nick (19/5)
Having played alongside his brother Jimmy in the Preston North End side beaten in the 1888 FA Cup final by West Bromwich Albion, Nick Ross joined Everton that summer. A brilliant left-back, he was made captain of the side. Although he missed only three games during the inaugural Football League season, and even scored five goals – the first of which was the first League goal by a full-back – Ross again moved on in the summer of 1889. However, his stay at Linfield was to last only a matter of weeks before he once again moved back to Deepdale, where he was to help Preston win the League title for a second time at the end of the 1889/90 season.

Dobson, George (18)
Well built, strong and a good kicker, Dobson had made over 130 appearances for Everton before the Football League action kicked off. Despite a fine season, the man said to be Everton's first professional failed to make it for a second after an injury forced to him retire from the game.

Dick, Alec (9)
Dick made his debut in the opening-day fixture against Accrington but was later suspended for a large part of the season. The first Scottish

professional signed in August 1886 by Everton, Dick was not retained at the end of the first season of League football.

Chadwick, Albert (2/0)
Chadwick made his League debut in a 4-1 defeat at West Bromwich Albion in December 1888. Unrelated to Edgar Chadwick.

Half-backs
Holt, Johnny (17)
Might have made his League debut for Bootle if Everton had been overlooked in favour of their local rivals when the Football League was established. Instead, he moved across Liverpool to join the Blues at the start of the inaugural League season and made his debut in the opening fixture. One of the game's greatest characters at the time, Holt was a non-stop dynamo from his centre-half position whose ability to find his forwards with an accurate pass was an essential part of his play. Ten times capped by England, Holt was to win the League with Everton in 1890/91 and twice finished a FA Cup runner-up with the club. Disliked for his tendency to commit petty and crafty fouls on the blind side of the umpire, Holt was nicknamed the 'Little Everton Devil'.

Weir, Jim (16)
Weir made his debut the previous season in a first-round FA Cup replay against Bolton Wanderers and proved a regular at wing-half in the initial League campaign before signing for Sunderland Albion in October 1889.

Farmer, George (21/1)
Having hit the net regularly for Everton in the previous three seasons, the 1888/89 season proved a more difficult one for Welshman George Farmer in front of goal and he netted only once against Aston Villa in October 1888. He proved much better at setting chances up, creating both his side's goals in the first match against Accrington, and his adept in-swinging corner-kicks proved a constant threat to opposing defences. Capped twice by his country, Farmer was a fine passer of the ball.

Sugg, Frank (9)
Sugg had already played for Bolton Wanderers, Sheffield Wednesday, Derby County and Burnley before signing for Everton at the start of the season. Although he was to play only nine times before moving back to Turf Moor in March 1889, this included appearances in four different positions.

Jones, Robert (1)
Welshman Bob Jones played his only game of the 1888/89 season in the opening-day fixture against Accrington. A burly, reliable reserve, he was

with Everton for over six years before signing for Manchester City. He played once for Wales, against Ireland in 1894.

Kelso, Robert (1)

After signing from Newcastle West End in July 1888, Bob Kelso made his debut against future employers Preston North End in January of the following year. Moving on during the summer, Kelso later returned to Everton in May 1891 after two seasons at Deepdale, and by the time he again moved in 1896, this time to Dundee, he had made 103 appearances and had scored five times. An FA Cup finalist with Everton in 1893, Kelso was a powerful tackler who cleared the ball well.

Forwards

Chadwick, Edgar (22/6)

Everton's only ever-present in the inaugural League season, Edgar Chadwick was one of the best-known players of his generation, combining acumen and accuracy with a wonderful ability to dribble the ball round even the best defenders. He later played every League game in Everton's 1890/91 League championship-winning side. Three times a losing FA Cup finalist (twice with Everton and once with Southampton), Chadwick was capped seven times for England. With over 100 goals for Everton he is one of only eight Blues to reach triple figures for the club.

Davies, Joe (8/2)

Davies was signed from Welsh side Chirk halfway through the season, where the outside-right returned at the end.

Waugh, David (7/2)

Waugh made his Everton debut in the opening League fixture but an injury early in the campaign saw him sidelined before he later returned to occupy the left-wing position. He was not retained for the following season.

Brown, William (6/2)

One of eight players tried by Everton at right-wing during the season. Scored on his League debut against Bolton in November 1888.

Costley, James (6/3)

Costley scored the winner for Blackburn Olympic against Old Etonians in the 1883 FA Cup final. The 1888/89 season was the last of three seasons the outside-left played for Everton. A brilliant dribbler of the ball, the Liverpool-born player scored twice on his League debut for the Toffees at Derby in October 1888 but his failure to hold down a regular place in the side meant the Anfield club did not renew his contract at the end of the season.

McKinnon, Archie (6/4)

Signed from Hibernian at the start of the season, McKinnon made his Blues debut at centre-half in the second League game against Notts County. Five successive appearances at outside-right in October and November saw the Scotsman score four times before he departed the club suddenly and returned to his former club.

Milward, Alf (6/2)

After signing for Everton from Marlow AFC in the summer of 1888, Milward did enough as an eighteen-year-old in his first season to be retained for the next. A marvellous outside-left, he was to go on and make 224 appearances, in which he scored ninety-six goals for the Blues. An ever-present during the 1890/91 League championship season, he was also twice an FA Cup runner-up with Everton and once with Southampton in 1900. Capped four times for England, Milward was a fierce competitor who possessed the ability to deliver the perfect cross-field pass and also shoot from difficult wide angles.

Angus, Jack (5)

Angus was signed as a forward in December 1888, but after failing to impress moved to Sunderland Albion where a conversion to goalkeeper later saw him return to Anfield. He made a further twelve appearances before he was replaced, possibly because of illness, by David Jardine during the 1890/91 championship-winning struggle. Jack Angus died of typhoid on 8 August 1891.

Fleming, George (4/2)

Fleming made history by becoming the first Evertonian to score in League football, but his two goals in the opening day's fixture against Accrington proved to be the only ones he scored. The utility forward failed to hold down a regular place in the side and was released at the end of the season after having made a total of eighty-six appearances for Everton and scoring forty-seven times.

Briscoe, William (3)

Having hit twenty-five goals in sixty-six pre-League appearances for Everton, Billy Briscoe failed to establish himself in the League side and was released at the end of the season.

Lewis, William (3)

Bangor's first professional footballer signed for Everton in August 1888 in anticipation of making it big in the Football League. The centre-forward played in the Blues' first League match but after just three appearances he returned to Bangor and helped the club win the Welsh Cup for the first time. He later played twenty-seven times for Wales (a then record) in which he scored twelve times.

Coyne, J. (2/1)
Coyne played for Gainsborough Trinity before joining Everton where he scored the winning goal on his debut against Burnley in November.

Davie, George (2)
Signed to strengthen Everton's attack, Davie debuted against Burnley in a 3-2 win in November 1888 but after just one more League appearance he moved to Sunderland the following summer. He later made sixty-two senior appearances for Arsenal.

The following made their only Everton appearance during the 1888/89 season:

Keys, J.
Keys was deputised for Bill Lewis at Aston Villa.

Morris, R.
Morris played at Stoke in December 1888.

Parkinson, Henry
Parkinson was deputised for George Farmer against Accrington in December 1888.

Pollock
Pollock was deputised for Jimmy Holt in a 6-2 defeat at Bolton in September 1888.

Roberts
Roberts was deputised for Jimmy Holt at home to Wolves in February 1889.

Stephenson, George
The right-half played at Wolves in January 1889.

Warmby, Harry
Warmby was reserve to Jimmy Holt, who made his only Everton appearance when he played against Aston Villa in September 1888.

Wilson, Walter
Reserve left-back Wilson made his only appearance for Everton when he took Nick Ross's position on the last day of the inaugural season in a match that saw the Blues beat Blackburn Rovers 3-1.

Higgins, Mike

Higgins' only League game against Aston Villa in September 1888 was his last of 178 appearances for Higgins' home-town club. He debuted against Darwen in October 1880 and although he generally played at half-back, his reliability, love of football and consistency meant he also served the Toffees in a further seven positions. A Liverpool Cup winner on three occasions.

NOTTS COUNTY

Goalkeepers

Holland, John (9 (8 in goal))

Holland played for County in the two seasons prior to the start of League football. His final appearance for the club came as outside-left at Wolverhampton Wanderers in February 1889.

Owen, Hugh (1)

In a solitary League appearance at the start of his short time at Trent Bridge, Owen conceded seven goals as Preston North End moved through the 1888/89 season unbeaten.

Sherwin, Mordecai (1)

'Mordy' Sherwin was a big favourite with Magpies fans during his seven years between the posts from September 1883 onwards, especially when he performed a cartwheel after every County goal! As he was 17 stone and just 5 feet 9 inches tall, this must have been no mean effort. Nimble, agile and reliable, the 'keeper played only one League game in 1888/89. In his summer role as wicketkeeper for Nottinghamshire County Cricket Club, he took 611 catches and made 225 stumpings, good enough to earn him three Test matches for England and a tour of Australia in 1886/87.

Widdowson, Tom (12)

Widdowson made the 'keeper's position his own after joining County from Forest midway through the inaugural Football League season.

Full-backs

Clements, John (12)

Clements joined County just after the season started from local club St Saviour's. Debuted in the 6-1 slaughter of Burnley, he went on to make a further eleven League appearances by the end of the season. Having made only two further League appearances, he joined Newton Heath in 1892/93.

Cursham, Harry (8 (of which 3 were at centre-forward)/2)
Younger brother of Arthur, another firm favourite with early County fans, Cursham joined Notts aged eighteen in 1877 and was still good enough to be playing in the first team a decade later, although five of his matches in the 1888/89 season were at full-back rather than his usual inside-left position. When he did play upfront, he scored twice in consecutive weekends as, for the only time in the season, County won back-to-back matches with victories against WBA and Wolves. Harry Cursham was very much a product of his generation, being a brilliant dribbler who in 1904 was quoted as bemoaning how 'individual play was being sacrificed in the cry of combination [team play]'. Capped eight times for England Cursham, who scored fifty-three goals in fifty-three League and FA Cup appearances for the Magpies, would be a candidate for a place in any all-time Notts County XI. Cursham currently holds the record for the most FA Cup goals, with forty-eight in the competition proper and one goal in a fourth qualifying-round match.

Guttridge, Frank (17)
Guttridge played in the first League match and, after signing for Nottingham Forest the following season, he later returned to County for a brief spell in 1894. He was a fine cricketer who umpired at the highest level.

McLean, Tom (12)
A strong defender with a powerful clearing kick, Tom McLean enjoyed two spells with Notts County. The first, between 1888 and 1892, included twelve appearances in the first League season, and returned after a season at Derby County in 1892/93, only for a knee injury to bring his playing career to an end. He was desperately unlucky to suffer an injury late in the 1890/91 season that kept him out of that season's FA Cup final in which Notts County lost 3-1 to Blackburn Rovers. He later became assistant trainer, serving County in the role from 1908 to 1929.

Morley, Haydn (2)
Son of William Morley, the man credited with the practical moves that established Derby County in 1884. Signed in March 1886, Haydn Morley played just two League games during his time at Trent Bridge before moving to Derby later in the season. Quick, with a good kick, his tactical awareness was later of benefit to Sheffield Wednesday where he was a member of the side that made it through to the 1890 FA Cup final.

Snook, Herbert (1)
Snook was with Notts County for just under a year after signing in January 1888, playing his only League game against Aston Villa in December.

Later, as a businessman, sportsman and Liberal politician, he occupied a prominent position in Nottingham for many years.

Half-backs

Brown, George (19/1)

Signed from Forest, Brown stayed one season in which he was a regular in the County side and then moved back to Forest. He scored against Blackburn Rovers in a 5-2 defeat in December.

Dobson, Charles (1)

Signed in 1880, Charles Dobson played his only League game of a nine-year career with the Magpies against Aston Villa in December 1888. Younger brother of another fine County player, right-back Alf, he played once for England against Ireland in Belfast in March 1886, with the away side winning 6-1.

Emmitt, Herbert (4)

Emmitt debuted for the Magpies in what was then their record victory, 11-1 against Wednesday Strollers in the FA Cup in 1881. The 1888/89 season was to be his last at Trent Bridge and his final match was not a particularly auspicious occasion, with Notts going down 7-3 to Bolton Wanderers.

Shelton, Alf (21)

Shelton joined County after Notts Rangers folded during the summer of 1888. He then went on to make over 200 League and FA Cup appearances including the 1891 and 1894 finals, collecting a runner's-up and winner's medal respectively. Hard-working and difficult to beat, Alf Shelton was considered good enough to be selected six times for England. He turned down the chance of higher wages to play for newly formed Liverpool in 1892 and later served as a County director for ten years till 1910.

Shelton, Charlie (15/1)

A robust half-back with an infectious never-say-die attitude, Charlie Shelton was one of three famous Nottingham brothers, because in addition to Alf, his older brother (see above), Harry played for Forest in the 1870s.

Warburton, Benjamin (2)

Warburton signed at the start of the season and played in the first League game for County at Everton. Only one further appearance followed before he left the country to work for the (British) Government in South Africa.

Forwards

Allin, Tom (6/2)

Allin was one of a number of players who were given a chance at centre-forward for Notts County. He did well in his first match, scoring twice against FA Cup holders WBA, but failed to find the net in a further five games and was released at the end of the season.

Bailey, L. F. (1/1)
Bailey played once, and scored once, but Notts lost 5-3 to Derby County at a match played at the Castle Ground.

Brown, John (1)
Brown has the unfortunate record of playing only one League game, being on the wrong end of the Magpies' equal record defeat when Aston Villa thrashed them 9-1. He had done better in the previous four seasons, and in October 1887 he twice scored four goals in matches against Leek and, ironically in light of what was to happen the following season, Aston Villa respectively.

Cooke, Tom (1)
Cooke was one of six new men in the Notts side when they faced Aston Villa at home in December 1888.

Daft, Harry (19/8)
One of County's all-time greats, Daft made his debut against Rotherham Town in a 15-0 victory in the FA Cup first round on 24 October 1885. Almost nine years later, he played his full part in the club's finest ninety minutes when the Magpies beat Bolton Wanderers 4-1 in the 1894 FA Cup final, consolation for defeat to Blackburn Rovers in the 1891 final in which Daft also played. A former Corinthian, Daft was capped five times for England. Daft was a speedy winger who not only centred superbly but had a wonderful eye for a goal. He made a total of 173 League and FA Cup appearances for County in which he scored eighty-one goals. A first class cricketer, Daft also played 190 Nottinghamshire matches.

Galbraith (1)
Despite dense fog for the match at Blackburn, the correspondent for the *Nottingham Daily Express* had apparently seen enough to be confident to declare that Galbraith, newly arrived from Dundee, 'will probably not be heard of again'. He wasn't!

Gunn, Bill (1)
Gunn was one of the giants of the early years of organised football. Before the rules of the game made it compulsory in 1882 to use two hands, Bill Gunn was one of the first great throw-in artists who played for Notts County from 1882 to 1890. As a tall winger standing 6 feet 2 inches tall, and weighing 14 stone, his great strides and power, allied to an ability to

dribble with the ball, often took him past his opposing full-back. The great writer J. A. H. Catton compared him to a 'big stag', and was surprised he only played twice for his country, offering the opinion that it may have been because of 'rather individual style'.

Gunn also played 363 first-class cricket matches for Nottinghamshire and eleven tests for England. It was said of him that he only needed three strides between the wickets. He was also a successful businessman; in 1885 he set up Gunn & Moore with Thomas James Moore. To this day, under the ownership of the Unicorn Group, the company still manufactures cricket bats and clothing. Gunn carried his love of County with him by later funding many key purchases, including that of James Cantrell in July 1904 and then record signing Billy Matthews from Aston Villa in October 1903. He later acted as president of the club in the 1920s.

Harker, Edward (2)
After playing in the first League fixture against Everton, Edward Harker played just once more during the 1888/89 League season and was to leave the club in November 1889, bringing to an end a seven-year association with County in which he also made twelve FA Cup appearances, scoring twice.

Hodder, William (20/3)
Hodder missed only two games during the League season and also scored a crucial goal in the 2-1 success against WBA in January. However, with County finishing eleventh and forced to seek re-election, at the end of the season his services were not retained and he moved to Forest.

Jackson, Harry (5/3)
With over 100 goals in not many more matches, Harry Jackson was prolific in the four seasons prior to League football. Nineteen came from just twenty-one FA Cup appearances but the 1888/89 season was a much more difficult affair and despite three goals in three end-of-season matches, Jackson found himself being allowed to move on to Forest.

Jardine, Robert (18/9)
Playing at outside-left, Bobby Jardine achieved the remarkable feat of scoring five goals as Burnley were hammered 6-1 on 27 October 1888. It meant he had scored seven times in the first seven matches, and two games later he scored another important goal as County drew 3-3 with Accrington. In 1889, Jardine was moved to play at inside-right and failed to score in eight matches as County struggled. The Scotsman, the first from that country to be employed professionally by a Nottingham club, was not retained at the end of his only season at County.

May, Edward (11/3)

Ted May joined County from Burslem Port Vale halfway through the inaugural Football League season. He scored twice in the 3-0 home defeat of Wolves in January and was considered good enough for County selectors to retain him for the following season. He ended up making thirty-eight League and FA Cup appearances for the club in which he scored nine goals.

May, William (4)

May played alongside his twin brother Ted against Blackburn Rovers and Derby County, but with only four appearances and no goals, Bill May moved to Notts Rangers when the season ended.

Moore, Albert (10/3)

The end of the 1888/89 season was to bring Albert Moore's six-year spell with Notts County to an end, though not before he had scored the club's first League goal on 15 September 1888. In addition to his three League goals Moore also scored six times in seventeen FA Cup appearances, including a hat-trick against Lincoln Ramblers in October 1887.

Shaw, Alf (2)

Shaw was an inside-forward who played League football with County, Nottingham Forest and later Loughborough Town.

Wardle, Edwin (2)

Wardle was one of a number of County players who were at the club for the first League season only. He played in the first and last games of the season but failed to score.

Weightman, Fred (1/1)

Weightman played and scored in his only League game against Aston Villa in December 1888.

Stoke FC

'It was in 1888/89 that Stoke began to follow the prevailing fashion of engaging Scotchmen.' (*The Sporting Chronicle – the Rise of the Leaguers*)

Goalkeepers

Merritt, Wilf (1)

Signed at the start of the season from Leek as understudy to Billy Rowley, Merritt was to make just five appearances over three seasons before returning to his previous club.

Rowley, Billy (21)

The former postman was in his second spell at Stoke when the 1888/89 season kicked off. He had stayed for less than a year in 1883/84 when he played as a centre-forward but on his return from Port Vale in August 1886 had switched from scoring to saving goals. He is described by Tony Matthews in *The Who's Who of Stoke City* as 'a fine, fearless 'keeper with an enormous kick. He handled the ball, and was never afraid to go in where it hurts [when the legs and boots were flying]. Consequently, he suffered a lot of injuries – even breaking his breast bone during the 1890/91 season – and although he remained as a player with the Potters until his retirement in 1897 he made less than 150 first-team appearances.'

Rowley played twice for England. Both games were against Ireland and in the second in 1892 his full-back colleagues Tommy Clare and Arthur Underwood joined him in the side. In 1895 Rowley became secretary-manager at Stoke, a post he held for almost three years.

Full-backs

Clare, Tommy (21)

Believed to be Stoke's first full-time professional, Clare was captain of the side at the start of the inaugural Football League season. Four times capped by England, he played for the Potters for well over a decade to tot up 251 first-team appearances in which he scored six goals. According to Matthews Clare, 'An inspirational player, he was a splendid header of the ball, was quick off the mark, strong and purposeful in the tackle and ever-reliable, always working for the team.' He later emigrated to Canada where he died in 1929.

Underwood, Alf (22)

A local lad who had signed for Stoke in the summer of 1887, Underwood went on to make 131 first-team appearances before a knee injury brought his career to an end six years later at the age of twenty-four. Underwood, who gained two caps for his country, formed a formidable partnership with Tommy Clare, both players standing 6 feet tall and weighing over 13 stone. He was described by Matthews as 'a prodigious kicker and reliable to a degree, but who occasionally tackled far too rashly'.

Harry Montford

Montford joined from local club Newtown in 1888 and made just one League appearance. He later went on to play for Stoke Town.

Half-backs

Gee, Fred (1)

Gee was signed at the start of the season but had to wait until the final match before making his debut, deputising for Ed Smith. A busy player, he left Stoke at the end of the following season after having made twenty-one appearances and scoring five goals.

Ramsey, Bob (21)
Signed from Port Vale in the summer, Ramsey lined up at right-half in the first game against West Bromwich Albion. Although he failed to score during his twenty-one appearances in the season and at the time had only one FA Cup goal to his career with Stoke, that didn't stop him becoming the club's first League hat-trick scorer in their 7-1 home win over Accrington on 1 March 1890. After making forty-seven appearances, in which he played in every outfield position, Ramsey finished his career back at Port Vale.

Shutt, George (21/1)
Capable of playing in all three half-back positions, Shutt was one of only two players (Smith being the other) who featured in Stoke's first FA Cup tie in November 1883 and the first League game against WBA. He was a regular in the side for almost nine years until his departure to Hanley Town at the end of the inaugural Football League season.

An intelligent, sure-footed player, Shutt represented his country in March 1886, playing superbly in a 6-1 win against Ireland. It was Shutt's goal against Aston Villa in November 1888 that earned Stoke their first League draw.

Smith, Eli (21)
Know as 'Father' to his teammates because of his work as a vicar in the local church, Eli Smith was signed from local side Tunstall in 1883. Tough-tackling, he was among the first group of players to sign professional forms at the Victoria Ground.

Forwards
Baker, Charles (1)
After signing from Stafford Rangers towards the end of the 1888/89 season, the inside-forward made his Stoke debut in the final game of the season. Baker signed for Wolves in August 1891 but returned to the Victoria Ground in January 1893 and by the time he again moved on in the summer of twenty-eight appearances in which he had scored thirteen goals.

Barr, Bob (3)
After signing in the summer from Hurlford, Bob Barr failed to impress and left to play for Abercorn at the season's end.

Edge, Alf (19/3)
Edge became one of Stoke's first professionals when he signed in the summer of 1884. Capable of playing in any of the forward line positions,

Alf Edge was quick over short distances, had plenty of skill and worked tirelessly for his team. He holds the record for the most goals in an FA Cup tie for Stoke, having hit five in a 10-1 thrashing of Caernarfon Wanderers in October 1886. Edge helped Stoke to a win in the Football Alliance Championship, which set them up for immediate re-election back to the Football League following their replacement by Sunderland at the end of the 1889/90 season.

Dempsey, Alf (1)

In a League match between Preston and Stoke in 1888, two Stoke players didn't arrive at the ground and Dempsey, along with Bill Smalley, was borrowed from the home side. They didn't help Stoke, though, as North End ran out 7-0 winners.

Hendry, Billy (2)

Hendry played for West Bromwich Albion against Stoke on the opening day of the season before joining the Potters in March 1889. He stayed until January the following year when he moved to Preston North End. A whole-hearted player with good aerial abilities, he later played for Sheffield United, Dundee, Bury, Brighton United and Shrewsbury Town. As captain of Sheffield United it was said that Hendy's advice helped nurture the talents of Ernest Needham, one of the Blades' greatest players and an England international.

Hutchinson, Billy (1)

Hutchinson was signed from local side Fenton Red Star in 1888, but after just one League game and failing to impress Stoke manager Harry Lockett he moved to Long Eaton Rangers.

McSkimming, Bob (22/6)

McSkimming played for Kilmarnock and Hurlford before trying his luck with Stoke at the start of the Football League. His six goals in twenty-two League appearances made him Stoke's first top scorer in a League season, but in the summer of 1889 he joined Port Vale.

Milarvie, Bob (15/5)

Milarvie moved south from Hibernian to sign for Stoke only weeks after the Football League season had started. A useful left-winger, he again moved on to join Port Vale at the end of the season. He later played for Derby County and the Newton Heath and Ardwick, where he lost out on a first-team place to Billy Meredith.

Moore, Tom (1)
Moore was at Stoke for just over four months, arriving and returning to Arbroath after playing only once.

Lawton, George (13/1)
An orthodox right-winger, George Lawton scored against Burnley in a 4-3 game but left before the 1888/89 season ended to play for Altrincham.

Sayer, Jimmy (7)
Known as 'the greyhound' because of his blistering pace over 30–40 yards, Sayer was signed from Yorkshire side Sheffield FC, the world's oldest club. Captain once for England, he was a competitive outside-right who later returned to play for his home-town club Mexborough Town.

Slater, George (2/1)
An inside-forward signed by Stoke from Hanley United at the start of the season, Slater later emigrated to the USA where he lived out the rest of his life.

Smalley, Bill (1)
In a League match between Preston and Stoke in 1888, two Stoke players didn't arrive at the ground and Smalley, along with Alf Dempsey, was borrowed from the home side. Stoke lost 7-0.

Staton, Frank (4/2)
Staton was signed from local side Goldenhill Wanderers in September 1887. He played in Stoke's first four competitive League matches and scored two goals, the first of which is credited as Stoke's first League goal. He moved to Stafford Road, Wolverhampton, at the end of 1888/89.

Wainwright, Tom (1)
Wainwright played just a single League game before signing for Stoke Priory.

Jimmy Sloane (11/1)
Signed at the start of the season from Rangers, Sloane scored on his debut against Burnley in October 1888. After failing to repeat the feat in the ten games that followed, he re-signed for Rangers in January 1889.

Tunnicliffe, Billy (9/4)
Tunnicliffe was signed from local side Hanley Town at the start of the season, and after playing in the first game against WBA he then netted twice a fortnight later in a 3-0 home win over Notts County, the Potters' first victory in League football. He was signed for Middlewich at the end of the season.

WEST BROMWICH ALBION

Pen pictures written by Tony Matthews.

Goalkeeper

Roberts, Bob (22)

Roberts was Albion's first international, capped by England against Scotland in March 1887, the first of three outings for his country. A giant of a man, who wore a size 13 boot, he made eighty-four senior appearances for Albion in two spells with the club (1879/90 and 1891/92), gaining two FA Cup runners-up medals in 1886 and 1887, followed by a winner's medal in 1888. He was an ever-present in Albion's first League season. He was born in West Bromwich in 1859 and died in Byker, Newcastle, in 1929.

Full-backs

Horton, Jack (19)

A rock-solid defender who spent seventeen years with Albion as right-back, from 1882 to 1899. During this time he made 152 senior appearances, gaining an FA Cup runner's-up medal in 1895. He was born in West Bromwich in 1866 and died in the town in 1947. Brother of Ezra (below).

Walker, Luther (12)

A tidy player, equally adept with his head and feet, Walker could kick a ball an almighty distance. Sadly, injuries and poor health restricted him to just nineteen senior appearances for Albion in nine years between 1883 and 1892. He was born in West Bromwich in 1860 and died in the town in January 1903.

Green, Harry (9)

Green spent ten years with Albion, 1881–91, during which time he made sixty-five senior appearances, gaining an FA Cup winner's medal in 1888, having collected runners-up prizes in the two previous finals. Sure-footed and strong, he was also born and died in West Bromwich, in 1860 and 1900 respectively.

Ramsey, Bob (1)

Bob Ramsey's son, Sir Alexander, became Lord Mayor of West Bromwich in 1931 and held office for four years. Bob himself was a reserve right-back with Albion for two seasons (1888–90) making just one League appearance versus Stoke in December 1888. He went on to play for Kidderminster Harriers and was also coach at Middlesbrough (1900–02). He was born in Hereford in 1867 and died in the North East of England.

Half-backs

Horton, Ezra (8)

Known as 'Ironsides', he was as tough as they come, never flinched, was always aggressive in his approach and very sporting. Another West Bromwich-born player (1866), he made eighty-three appearances for the club between 1882 and 1891, playing in successive FA Cup finals of 1886, '87 and '88, gaining a winner's medal in the latter. He skippered the team at times and played in each of Albion's first thirty-six FA Cup games (from 1883). In fact, he starred in Albion's first FA Cup tie and the club's first-ever League game. He died in West Bromwich in 1939.

Perry, Charlie (20)

A cool and efficient defender, Perry served Albion for twelve years as centre-half (1884–96) and then as a director for six (1896–1902). He won three England caps, played in four international trials, appeared twice for the Football League and in all made 219 first-class appearances for the Baggies (sixteen goals scored). He lined up in four FA Cup finals – 1886, 1887, 1888 and 1892 – gaining winner's medals in the last two. Born in West Bromwich in 1866, Charlie died in the same town in 1927. His brothers Tom and Walter also played for Albion's League side.

Timmins, George (22)

Known as 'Darkie', Timmins amassed a total of sixty-one appearances for the club in twelve years as left-half (1879–91), gaining two FA Cup runners-up medals (1886 and 1887) and one winner's medal (1888). Skilful and determined, he could also play inside-left. He, too, was born in West Bromwich in 1858 and died there in 1926.

Milard, Albert (1)

Milard made five appearances in Albion's defence between 1888 and 1892 when he moved to Halesowen. Born in West Bromwich in 1868, he went on to become a school caretaker in the town where he died in 1930.

Oliver, Harry (1)

Oliver made only one League appearance for Albion (*v.* Burnley in November 1888). He spent six months with the club after joining from Small Heath (Birmingham) where he returned in January 1889. He was born and died in Birmingham, in 1863 and 1935 respectively.

Forwards

Bassett, Billy (21/11)

Regarded as the finest right-winger of his day, outside-right Billy Bassett charged down the flank like a whippet before sending over his centre, whether high or low. He was clever on the ball, possessed a powerful right-foot shot and served the club for a grand total of fifty-one years: thirteen as a player (1886–99), six as a coach (1899–1905), three as a director (1905–08) and twenty-nine as chairman (1908 until his death in West Bromwich in 1937).

He scored seventy-seven goals in 311 first-class matches, played in the 1888 and 1892 FA Cup-winning teams and in the losing side of 1895; he was capped sixteen times by England (eight coming in successive games) and he was at his very best in the 1893 match when, with Scotland winning 2-1, Bassett played brilliantly to create golden opportunities for Edgar Chadwick and Fred Spiksley to lead England to a 5-2 victory. Bassett also represented the Football League on three occasions, an England XI once, and starred in six international trials. From 1930–37 he was a member of the Football League Management Committee, was on the England selection panel in 1936/37 and was also a Justice of the Peace. He was born in West Bromwich in 1869.

Hendry, Billy (16/3)
Born in Dundee, Scotland, in 1864, Billy had speed, headwork and wholehearted endeavour. He spent the season of 1888/89 with Albion as centre-forward, during which time he scored four goals in eighteen appearances before transferring to Kidderminster Harriers, later assisting Stoke, Preston, Sheffield United, Dundee, Bury, Brighton United, Watford and Shrewsbury Town. He died from a heart attack in Shrewsbury in 1901.

Woodhall, George (10/3)
Woodhall was the perfect partner to Bassett on Albion's right wing. Nicknamed 'Spry' he was all vim and vigour, could shoot with both feet and often popped up inside the 'half-circle' when least expected. He scored twenty goals in seventy-four first-class appearances for Albion between 1883 and 1892, gaining an FA Cup winner's medal in 1888 (when he scored in the final *v.* Preston) after collecting loser's medals in the previous two finals. He won two England caps and was the first Black Country-born player to score in a full international (against Scotland in 1888). He left Albion for neighbours Wolves and, after four seasons in non-League football, retired in 1898. He died in West Bromwich in 1924, four days after his sixty-first birthday.

Bayliss, 'Jem' (22/2)
Tipton-born 'Jem' Bayliss was twenty-one when he joined Albion in 1884, playing as wing-half or centre-forward. He remained with the club as a player until retiring in 1892, having been appointed a director in 1891 – a position he held until 1905 when he became a life member of the club until his death in West Bromwich in 1933. A resolute and confident footballer, a real gentleman both on and off the pitch, he scored thirty-six goals in ninety-five senior appearances for Albion, playing in two losing FA Cup

finals (1886 and 1887) and gaining a winner's medal in 1888. He was also capped by England in 1891 and six years later read his own obituary in a newspaper while on holiday in Gibraltar. He returned home to the Black Country to tell everyone he was 'fighting fit' and lived on until his death in West Bromwich in 1933.

Pearson, Tom (22/12)

Inside-left Tom Pearson was the club's first true goalscorer, claiming eighty-eight goals in 171 first-team appearances for the club between 1886 and his retirement with a serious leg injury in 1894. Born in West Bromwich in 1866, he had endurance, willpower, a strong shot and distinctive short gait. He was alert and precise in front of goal and played in three successive FA Cup finals of 1886, '87 and '88, gaining a winner's medal in the third. Tom died in West Bromwich in 1918.

Wilson, Joe (20/4)

The only Birmingham-born player in Albion's ranks, Wilson was a smart, unobtrusive outside-left with good pace who served Albion from 1887 to 1890 when he moved to Kidderminster Harriers. He scored twenty goals in fifty-three senior games for the club and helped Albion win the FA Cup in 1888. He had the pleasure of scoring Albion's first-ever League goal, in their opening-day 2-0 victory at Stoke. Wilson, who went on to become a League linesman and then referee, was a goldsmith by profession. He died in Birmingham in 1952, aged ninety-one.

Walter Perry (9/4)

Inside-forward Walter Perry, brother of Charlie, was born in West Bromwich in 1868 and scored seven goals in fifteen League and cup games for the club in two spells between 1886 and 1900. He also played for Wolves and Burton Swifts and was Albion's reserve-team manager in 1906/07, before becoming a linesman. He died in West Bromwich in 1928.

Crabtree (1)

Reserve forward Fred Crabtree made his one and only appearance for Albion on the last day of the season, celebrating the occasion with the game's only goal. He was born in West Bromwich in 1865 and, after leaving Albion in 1889, he moved to London where he became a referee as well as a cricket coach. He died in 1939.

Shaw, Charlie (1/1)

An outside-left, Shaw scored on his Albion debut (and only game for the club) in a 4-3 home League win over Burnley in September 1888. Born in Willenhall in 1862, he had spells with Wolves and Walsall Swifts before joining Albion and later returned to the Saddlers. He represented both the Staffs FA and Birmingham FA. He died in Wolverhampton in 1931, having worked as a licensee in the town for many years.

Haynes, George (5)
Haynes spent five years as a reserve inside-forward with Albion, from 1887–92. He scored once in ten appearances during that time. He was born in West Bromwich in 1865 and died in the same town in 1937.

WOLVERHAMPTON WANDERERS

Goalkeepers
Baynton, Jack (18)
Baynton, who could also play in defence, missed four League games in 1888/89. One of the club's founder members in 1877, he spent twelve years with Wolves (up to 1889), during which time he played in twenty-eight first-class matches. Born in Wolverhampton in 1859, he was initially a pupil-teacher at St Luke's school, Blakenhall, and later a master at All Saints school, Hockley, Birmingham. He played in the losing FA Cup final of 1889 (*v.* PNE) and later became a senior referee. Baynton died in 1932.

Rose, William Crispin (4)
Rose was, in his day, the best goalkeeper in England. Born in London in 1861, he had a varied career that took him from Small Heath (Birmingham) to Swifts (London), PNE (1885/86), Stoke (1886–89), Wolves (1889–94), Loughborough Town and Wolves again (1895/96). He also represented Wiltshire, Staffordshire and London, gained four England caps, and made a total of 155 senior appearances for Wolves, gaining an FA Cup winner's medal in 1893. Instrumental in the formation of the Player's Union (now the PFA), Wood became a licensee and shopkeeper in Birmingham where he died in 1937 – 2 miles from Blues' St Andrew's.

Full-backs
Baugh, Dick (22)
Baugh was an ever-present in 1888/89. A teak-tough full-back, he scored once in 227 appearances for Wolves, whom he served for ten years, from 1886 to 1896 when he joined Walsall. Born in Wolverhampton in 1864 and a pupil at St Luke's school, Blakenhall, he played for Rose Villa, Wolverhampton Rangers and Stafford Road FC before joining Wolves. He won two England caps and appeared in three FA Cup finals, gaining a winner's medal in 1893. Baugh's son, also named Dicky, played for Wolves, WBA, Exeter City and Kidderminster Harriers. Baugh senior died in 1929.

Mason, Charlie (20)

Mason was a superb full-back, competent, keen and competitive, who missed two games out of twenty-two in the first season of League football. Born in Wolverhampton in 1863, he played for Wolves from 1877 (founder member) until 1892, making 108 senior appearances and scoring two goals. He was the first Wolves player to win a full cap – for England *v.* Ireland in 1887 – and later added two more to his tally. In 1888, he guested for West Brom Albion (the FA Cup winners) in the Championship of the World game against Renton, the Scottish Cup winners. Mason died in Wolverhampton in 1941.

Half-backs

Allen, Harry (22)

A formidable defender, Allen scored thirteen goals in 152 appearances for Wolves between 1886 and 1894, when he retired to become a licensee. Born in Walsall in 1866, he played for the Town Swifts before joining Wolves. Capped by England on five occasions, he played in two FA Cup finals, scoring the winner (*v.* Everton) in his second of 1893. He was one of only two ever-presents in Wolves' League side in 1888/89. Allen died in Walsall in 1895, aged only twenty-nine.

Fletcher, Albert (16/1)

Fletcher was a terrific wing-half, strong and efficient, who was described as being a 'man mountain'. He joined Wolves in 1886 and remained with the club until 1891, when he was forced to retire after breaking his leg *v.* Aston Villa earlier that year. He scored twice in seventy-six appearances for Wolves, playing in the 1889 FA Cup final. He also won two England caps. He had two stints as assistant trainer at Milineux (1891–96 and 1896–1915). Born in Wolverhampton in 1876, Fletcher died in the same town in 1940.

Lowder, Arthur (18/1)

Lowder was another local player, born in Wolverhampton in 1863. A founder member of the club in 1877, he remained with Wolves until 1891 when he too retired through injury. Standing at just 5 feet 5 inches tall, he was a left-half with a strong tackle. Lowder played in Wolves' first-ever FA Cup tie and first-ever League game. He was capped once by England and also played in the 1889 FA Cup final defeat by PNE. He died in Taunton in 1926.

Benton, Jack (1)

Benton, born in Wolverhampton in 1865, was a burly reserve wing-half who also played for Stafford Royal, Willenhall and Blakenhall among others. He made just one League appearance in 1888/89.

Cannon, Alec (7)

Cannon was a reliable wing-half who made fifteen appearances for Wolves during his two years with the club (1887–89). Born in Cannock in 1865, he joined Kidderminster Harriers (from Wolves).

Dudley, Bob (1)

Dudley was a strong, well-built left-half whose only appearance for the club was against Notts County in the last League game of the 1888/89 season, when he deputised for Lowder ahead of the FA Cup final. He was born in Audley, Staffs, in 1864.

Forwards

Brodie, Jack 13/10

Brodie, a buddy of Jack Baynton's, was a first-rate centre-forward who bagged ten goals in thirteen League games in 1888/89. He was a Wolves player from 1877 to 1891, during which time he scored forty-four goals in sixty-five League and FA Cup games, skippering the team in the 1889 final defeat by PNE. Born in Wightwick near Wolverhampton in 1862, Brodie was capped three times by England and had the pleasure of scoring Wolves' first-ever competitive goal, in an FA Cup tie against Long Eaton Rangers in 1883. He became a director of Wolves after retiring. He died in 1925.

Cooper, Jeremiah (7/6)

Cooper was a strong-running inside-forward who joined Wolves in August 1888 but was forced to retire with a serious ankle injury in May 1891, after scoring six goals in twenty-six games for the club. Cooper was born in Heath Town, Wolverhampton, in 1865.

Hunter, Tom (20)

Hunter made twenty appearances as a utility forward for Wolves in 1888/89. He served the club for three years from 1886 to 1889, scoring thirteen goals in thirty-five appearances, five coming in a 14-0 FA Cup win over Crosswell's Brewery in November 1886. He joined Kidderminster Olympic as player-manager on leaving Wolves, and later became chairman of Kidderminster Harriers. Born in Walsall in 1863, he died at his home in Kidderminster during the great flu epidemic of 1918.

Knight, Tom (17/5)

Knight was a play-anywhere forward who had a good strike record with Wolves – seventeen goals in thirty-three appearances made between 1886 and 1890, when he retired through injury. Born in Wolverhampton in 1864, Knight played for Willenhall Pickwick before moving to Wolves.

Wood, Harry (17/12)

Wood was an England international inside- or outside-left who scored 126 goals in 289 League and FA Cup appearances for Wolves, whom he served in two spells, the first from June 1885 to July 1891, and his second from December 1891 to June 1898. He initially played for Walsall Town Swifts and then Kidderminster Harriers. In between his two spells with Wolves, he returned to Walsall, and in 1898 moved to Southampton, later playing for and acting as trainer of Portsmouth before becoming a licensee near Fratton Park. Born in Walsall in 1868, Wood won three England caps (1890–96), appeared in three FA Cup finals for Wolves (winning in 1893), and two for Southampton (losing them both). He scored sixty-two goals in 158 games for Saints, who he also helped win four Southern League championships. He was eighty-three when he died in Portsmouth in 1951.

Wykes, David (18/1)

Wykes was an eager inside- or centre-forward who scored sixty-nine goals in 179 appearances for Wolves between 1888 and 1895. Born in Walsall in 1867, he played for Bloxwich Strollers, Wednesbury Town and Walsall before joining Wolves. Sadly, his life ended due to typhoid fever and pneumonia, at the early age of twenty-eight, just twenty-four hours after playing for Wolves against Stoke in a First Division game in October 1895.

Anderson, Nick (2)

Anderson, born in Wolverhampton in 1865, spent just one season (1888/89) with Wolves, making two appearances at centre-forward.

Tomkyes, Tommy (1)

Tom spent two seasons with Wolves, during which time he was first reserve to centre-forward Jack Brodie. He made just one senior appearance (*v.* Notts County in January 1889) and on leaving the club signed for Stafford Road. He was born in Halesowen in 1867.

White, Walter (4/2)

White scored twice in Wolves' first-ever League victory (4-1) against Burnley at home in September 1888. Born in Halesowen in 1864, he played for Coombs Wood before spending two seasons with Wolves (1888–90, two goals in four games overall) after which he joined Cradley St Luke's.

Footnotes

1   'Liverpool, in those early days, was well detached from the football hot-bed of East Lancashire, but was the largest town in terms of population, in the Northern group. Why Mr McGregor invited Everton and not Bootle is now lost in the mists of time, the most likely explanation being, is that the Anfield ground was reserved for the sole purpose of association football. Bootle, like many other teams at the time shared their ground with the local Cricket Club.' (Onslow, Tony, *Everton FC: The Men from the Hill Country*)

2   Allen's three goals make him Villa's first League hat-trick scorer and the 9-1 defeat remains County's record defeat, equal with matches against Blackburn Rovers in 1889 and Portsmouth in 1927.

3   *Cricket and Football Field* attributed the first goal to Friel.

4   This report did not name the scorers, but they are recorded as being Hunter and Brodie for Wolves, and Pearson for Albion.

5   It could have been that the ball had come off a defender first, as in 1888 an attacking player would be placed on-side if the ball came to him off an opponent. At the same time, a 'goal' was more likely to be disallowed if a forward, standing behind the defenders, obstructed the view of the 'keeper. It goes without saying that the offside rule was just as contentious in the first season of League football as it is today.

6   The term Lacemen for Notts County was derived from industrial Nottingham's association with the hosiery trade and its stocking machine, from which developed the lace machine.

7   Forrest had played three times before, but this was first occasion
     when he declared himself a professional. In some books it is argued
     that his shirt was the result of the Scots objecting, professionalism
     not being legalised there until 1893.

8   Original research had William McKay and Mackay as the same player,
     further confusion caused by variation in spelling in newspaper reports.
     Subsequent research revealed that these were two different players.

Acknowledgements & Bibliography

The author would like to thank the following people for their help with this book:

Jim Fox
Robert Boyling
Tony Matthews
Roger Booth
David Wood
Peter Holme
Ray Simpson
Ruth Jones

The following works have been helpful references in the research for this book:

Arnold, Peter And Christopher Davis, *The Hamlyn Book of World Soccer* (1973)
Catton, J. A. H., *The Story of Association Football* (Reprint, 1926)
Dykes, Garth, *Meadow Lane Men: The Complete Who's Who of Notts County* (2005)
Francis, Charles, *History of Blackburn Rovers FC, 1875–1925* (2005)
Goodall, John, *Association Football* (1898)
Hayes, Dean, *Who's Who of Preston North End* (2006)
Hunter, Archibald, *Triumphs of the Football Field* (1890)
Inglis, Simon, *League Football And The Men Who Made It, 1888–1988* (1988)
Jackman, Mike, *Blackburn Rovers: The Complete Record* (2009)
Marland, Simon, *Bolton Wanderers: The Complete Record* (2011)
Matthews, Tony, *Who's Who of Aston Villa* (1989)
Matthews, Tony, *Who's Who of Everton* (2004)
Matthews, Tony, *Who's Who of Stoke City* (2005)
Matthews, Tony, *Wolverhampton Wanderers: The Complete Record* (2012)
Mortimer, Gerald, *Who's Who Of Derby County* (2006)
Onslow, Tony, *Everton FC: The Men From The Hill Country* (2002)
Purnell's *Encyclopedia of Association Football* (1972)
Wall, Sir Frederick, *50 Years Of Football 1884–1934* (2005)